I welcome this comprehensive collection of essays, which will help and inspire institutions in the Arab world to adopt newer pedagogies and to give open and distance learning its rightful place in the region's higher education systems. For too long the development of this region has been held back by very directive teaching methods favouring rote learning. This book will promote positive change.

Sir John Daniel
OC

Learning technologies are emerging at a fast pace. However, there is a massive gap between the potential and actual realization of these technologies. A balanced mixture of learning technologies and pedagogy is needed to fill it. Passion and practice are very important in applying this mixture, and this book is a contribution to bridging the gap between learning technologies and pedagogy.

Abdullah Almegren
General Manager, National Center for e-Learning and Distance Learning
Ministry of Education
Saudi Arabia

The editors have brought together an outstanding group of researchers to examine how innovation in education is unfolding in this region and how it will impact education, particularly by an efficient use of technology. Readers will find in this book a quite comprehensive and fascinating tour of emerging trends and promising initiatives that are already contributing to reshaping education in the Gulf. As such, it is a must-read for understanding how the countries in the region promote the transformation of their education systems, both at school and university levels, and the role that teacher capacities have to play. It is not only a book about technology but also about evolving pedagogies in the Gulf.

Francesc Pedró
Chief, Education Policy ED/EPLS/EDP
UNESCO Education

This book is a timely and important contribution to transform education and training in the Arab Gulf countries. As these countries evolve and continue to develop at a fast rate, they need to educate and train their citizens to meet their human resources needs. The use of innovative pedagogies and emerging technologies can provide meaningful high-quality and effective education and training.

Badrul Khan
Founder
McWeadon Education

Transforming Education in the Gulf Region

Countries in the Arab Gulf are currently experiencing some of the fastest rates of growth and progress in the world. *Transforming Education in the Gulf Region* argues that education systems in these countries need to use innovative pedagogies and best practices in teaching and learning to educate all citizens so that they obtain the knowledge and skills to be productive members of society. This book will contribute to the transformation of education in the Gulf countries by suggesting best practices, research outcomes and case studies from experts in the Gulf region.

It has become increasingly evident in recent years that Gulf countries need to use emerging learning technologies to cater for the needs of learners and to provide maximum flexibility in learning. There is also a growing practical need to use electronic technologies, since learning materials are more widely available in electronic formats than in paper-based formats. This book focuses on the role of emerging technologies and innovative pedagogies in transforming education in six Gulf countries in the region (Saudi Arabia, United Arab Emirates, Kuwait, Qatar, Oman and Bahrain). With contributions from experts around the world, this book argues that the time is right for Arab Gulf countries to make the transition to electronic learning and that they need to implement the outcomes of research and adopt best practices to transform and revolutionize education to prepare learners in the Gulf region for the twenty-first century.

Transforming Education in the Gulf Region should be of interest to academics and students in the areas of higher education, learning technologies, education policy and education reform. It should also be of interest to educators, researchers and policy makers in the Gulf region.

Khalid Alshahrani has a PhD in e-learning from Monash University and MA in TESOL Studies from the University of Queensland, Australia. As an Assistant Professor, he has taught undergraduate and postgraduate courses – including at the Saudi Naval Academy and Hamdan Bin Mohamed Smart University (HBMSU) in the Gulf region – related to e-learning and language teaching since 2003, both face-to-face and online. He is currently leading the National Academic Talent Development Program (NATDP) at the King Abdullah University of Science and Technology (KAUST) in Saudi Arabia. His current research interest lies in the new and emerging technologies and how it plays out with the existing practices and norms of teaching and learning. Dr Alshahrani has published a number of book chapters and articles and actively participates in local and international conferences.

Mohamed Ally is Professor in the Centre for Distance Education and Researcher in the Technology Enhanced Knowledge Research Institute (TEKRI) at Athabasca University, Canada. He was Director of the Centre of Distance Education and Director of the School of Computing and Information Systems at Athabasca University, Canada. Dr Ally obtained his PhD from the University of Alberta, Canada. His current areas of research include mobile learning, e-learning, distance education, problem-based learning and use of emerging learning technologies in education and training.

Routledge Research in Education

For a complete list of titles in this series, please visit www.routledge.com.

163 **Technology-Enhanced Language Learning for Specialized Domains**
Practical applications and mobility
Edited by Elena Martín Monje, Izaskun Elorza and Blanca García Riaza

164 **American Indian Workforce Education**
Trends and Issues
Edited by Carsten Schmidtke

165 **African American English and the Achievement Gap**
The Role of Dialectal Code-switching
By Holly K. Craig

166 **Intersections of Formal and Informal Science**
Edited by Lucy Avraamidou & Wolff-Michael Roth

167 **Women Education Scholars and their Children's Schooling**
Edited by Kimberly A. Scott and Allison Henward

168 **The Improvised Curriculum**
Negotiating Risky Literacies in Cautious Schools
By Michael Corbett, Ann Vibert, Mary Green with Jennifer Rowe

169 **Empowering Black Youth of Promise**
Education and Socialization in the Village-minded Black Church
By Sandra L. Barnes and Anne Streaty Wimberly

170 **The Charter School Solution**
Distinguishing Fact from Rhetoric
Edited by Tara L. Affolter and Jamel K. Donnor

171 **Transforming Education in the Gulf Region**
Emerging learning technologies and innovative pedagogy for the 21st century
Edited by Khalid Alshahrani and Mohamed Ally

172 **UNESCO Without Borders**
Educational campaigns for international understanding
Edited by Aigul Kulnazarova and Christian Ydesen

173 **Research for Educational Change**
Transforming researchers' insights into improvement in mathematics teaching and learning
Edited by Jill Adler and Anna Sfard

Transforming Education in the Gulf Region
Emerging learning technologies and innovative pedagogy for the 21st century

Edited by Khalid Alshahrani and Mohamed Ally

LONDON AND NEW YORK

First published 2017
by Routledge
2 Park Square, Milton Park, Abingdon, Oxon OX14 4RN

and by Routledge
711 Third Avenue, New York, NY 10017

Routledge is an imprint of the Taylor & Francis Group, an informa business

© 2017 selection and editorial matter, K. Alshahrani & M. Ally; individual chapters, the contributors

The right of the editor to be identified as the author of the editorial material, and of the authors for their individual chapters, has been asserted in accordance with sections 77 and 78 of the Copyright, Designs and Patents Act 1988.

All rights reserved. No part of this book may be reprinted or reproduced or utilised in any form or by any electronic, mechanical, or other means, now known or hereafter invented, including photocopying and recording, or in any information storage or retrieval system, without permission in writing from the publishers.

Trademark notice: Product or corporate names may be trademarks or registered trademarks, and are used only for identification and explanation without intent to infringe.

British Library Cataloguing in Publication Data
A catalogue record for this book is available from the British Library

Library of Congress Cataloging in Publication Data
Names: Alshahrani, Khalid, editor. | Ally, Mohamed, editor.
Title: Transforming education in the Gulf region : emerging learning technologies and innovative pedagogy for the 21st century / edited by Khalid Alshahrani and Mohamed Ally.
Description: New York : Routledge, 2016. | Series: Routledge research in education ; 171 | Includes bibliographical references.
Identifiers: LCCN 2016002228| ISBN 9781138657007 (hardback : alk. paper) |
ISBN 9781315621586 (ebook)
Subjects: LCSH: Educational change--Persian Gulf States. | Educational
technology--Persian Gulf States. | Education, Higher--Persian Gulf States. | Education and state--Persian Gulf States.
Classification: LCC LA1431.2 .T73 2016 | DDC 370.9536--dc23
LC record available at http://lccn.loc.gov/2016002228

ISBN: 978-1-138-65700-7 (hbk)
ISBN: 978-1-315-62158-6 (ebk)

Typeset in Galliard
by Saxon Graphics Ltd, Derby

Contents

List of contributors	xi
Foreword	xix
Preface	xxiii
Acknowledgements	xxvii

PART I
Theoretical perspectives   1

1   Adapting technology-enhanced learning to students'
    culture: faculty perspectives   3
    RASHA AL OKAILY

2   Situated learning, pedagogic models and structured
    tasks in blended course delivery   17
    DAVID PRESCOTT

3   Technology-enhanced language instruction: are we in
    the loop?   36
    SALEH AL-SHEHRI

4   Blended learning: a promising learning and teaching
    approach for higher education institutions in the Arab
    States of the Gulf – a proposed open system model   52
    HEND MAHMOUD MERZA

5   A conceptual model for the effective integration of
    technology in Saudi higher education systems   67
    ABDULRAHMAN M. AL-ZAHRANI

PART II
Practical applications 81

6 Mobile learning in Gulf Cooperation Council countries: theory and practice 83
HESSAH ALSHAYA AND AFNAN A. OYAID

7 PresentationTube: a network for producing and sharing online video lectures at Sultan Qaboos University 98
ALAA SADIK

8 Initiatives to innovate education to prepare Qatar for the future 110
MOHAMED ALLY, MARTHA ROBINSON AND MOHAMMED SAMAKA

9 Use of social media in technology-enhanced learning 126
ALI S. AL MUSAWI

10 Student-centred learning analytics dashboards to empower students to take responsibility for their learning 139
NAIF R. ALJOHANI, HUGH C. DAVIS, MOHAMED ALLY AND SYED ASIM JALAL

11 Flipped classroom as a form of blended learning 150
AZIZAH AL ROWAIS

12 Managing the change during e-learning integration in higher education: a case study from Saudi Arabia 167
KHALID ALSHAHRANI AND LEN CAIRNS

13 MOOC in the Arab world: a case study 178
KHALID ALSHAHRANI AND MOHAMED ALLY

14 Smart classrooms in the context of technology-enhanced learning (TEL) environments: a holistic approach 188
SALAH AL-SHARHAN

PART III
The future   **215**

15 Towards teaching and learning mathematics using mobile technology   **217**
FATIMA M. AZMI AND AQIL M. AZMI

16 The future of mobile learning and implications for education and training   **224**
DAVID PARSONS

Epilogue: looking to the future   237
Glossary   239
Index   242

List of contributors

Naif R. Aljohani is Assistant Professor at the Faculty of Computing and Information Technology in King Abdul Aziz University, Jeddah, Saudi Arabia. He holds a PhD in Computer Science from the University of Southampton, UK. He received a bachelor's degree in Computer Education from King Abdul Aziz University, 2005. In 2009, he received a master's degree in Computer Networks from La Trobe University, Australia. His research interests are in the areas of mobile and ubiquitous computing, mobile and ubiquitous learning, learning and knowledge analytic, semantic web, data mining, Web Science, technology enhanced learning and human computer interaction.

Mohamed Ally is Professor in the Centre for Distance Education and Researcher in the Technology Enhanced Knowledge Research Institute (TEKRI) at Athabasca University, Canada. He was Director of the Centre of Distance Education and Director of the School of Computing and Information Systems at Athabasca University, Canada. He obtained his PhD from the University of Alberta, Canada. His current areas of research include mobile learning, e-learning, distance education, problem-based learning and use of emerging learning technologies in education and training. He was recently involved in the delivery of a MOOC. Dr Ally is Past-President of the International Federation of Training and Development Organizations (IFTDO) and is one of the founding Directors of the International Association of Mobile Learning (IamLearn). He recently edited seven books on the use of emerging technologies in education. His book *Mobile Learning: Transforming the Delivery of Education and Training* won the Charles A. Wedemeyer Award for significant contribution to distance education.

Ali S. Al Musawi obtained his PhD on Learning Resources and Technology Centres in 1995 from the University of Southampton, UK. He works for the Sultan Qaboos University, Sultanate of Oman, since 1985. At present, he is an Associate Professor at the Instructional and Learning Technologies Department at the College of Education. He has published several journal research articles, chapters in reviewed books, and papers; and contributed in many conferences, symposia, and workshops. He conducted and compiled several national, regional, and Arab studies and reports. He wrote a book on cooperative learning in 1992, contributed in writing another in 2003 and an educational lexicon in 2014; and published a book on learning resources and technology centers in 2004. He also translated, with others, two books on e-learning strategies and instructional multimedia to Arabic in 2005 and 2010. Dr Ali has several activities in fields of instructional skills development, study skills, instructional design, and web-based design; his interests include Arabic poetry; he published two anthologies in addition to other hand-written ones.

Rasha Al Okaily is a lecturer who has been teaching at tertiary level at a number of universities in the United Arab Emirates and Jordan. She holds a master's degree in Applied Linguistics and Translation and is currently a PhD student in e-Research and Technology Enhanced Education, Lancaster University, UK. Her current research interests lie in designing technology enhanced learning experiences and activities through focusing on pedagogy as an underlying principle. She is also a member of the International Association for Mobile Learning (IAmLearn) and has published papers in the area of mobile learning, Bring Your Own Device (BYOD), eLearning, and technology integration in language learning.

Azizah Al Rowais is an Assistant Professor of Curriculum and Instruction at Prince Sattam bin Abdul-Aziz University, Saudi Arabia. She previously served as Vice-Dean of Preparatory Year Program Deanship at the university. She is a certified trainer who has a membership at Canada Global Consulting and Training Centre. A researcher who published different research articles in Education.

Khalid Alshahrani has a PhD in e-learning from Monash University, and MA in TESOL Studies from the University of Queensland, Australia. As an Assistant Professor, he has taught undergraduate and postgraduate courses – including at the Saudi Naval Academy and Hamdan Bin Mohamed Smart University (HBMSU) in the Gulf region – related to e-learning and language teaching since 2003, both face-to face and online. He is currently leading the National Academic Talent Development Program (NATDP) at the King Abdullah University of Science and Technology (KAUST) in Saudi Arabia. His current research interest lies in the new and emerging technologies and how it plays out with the existing practices and norms of teaching and learning. Dr Alshahrani has published a number of book chapters and articles and actively participating in local and international conferences.

Salah Al-Sharhan is the Vice President for Academic Affairs at the Gulf University for Science and Technology (GUST), Kuwait, and an Associate Professor in Computer Science Department. He earned his PhD in Systems Design Engineering with an emphasis on Computational Intelligence from the University of Waterloo, Canada, in 2002. Dr Al-Sharhan's research interests span different areas such as intelligent systems, data clustering and classifications using soft computing algorithms, and the application of computational intelligence techniques to a variety of real life problems. In addition, Dr Al-Sharhan developed several e-learning and e-health models and participated in developing strategic plans for different sectors in Kuwait such as the e-learning strategy for the Ministry of Education. He was the Program Manager of the e-learning project (which consisted of 10 different projects) which is a splendid national project, introduced eLearning to all the schools of the State of Kuwait. Furthermore, Dr Al-Sharhan's has an intensive teaching experience in the field of the Computer Science/Engineering, MIS, and Intelligence System areas. He taught in several institutions such as GUST, Kuwait University and University of Waterloo on undergraduate and graduate levels. Dr Al-Sharhan's experience spans a wide range of areas by his distinguished courses in IT/Engineering training programs, e-learning: strategy development, implementation and teacher readiness, project management, soft skills training, electronic management, PMO – Program Management Office, enterprise architecture and IT governance and quality assurance: software engineering/SQA. Dr Al-Sharhan served as a member, program chair, track chair and organizer in many regional and international scientific conferences and associations related to education, e-learning, e-services, e-systems, innovations in information technology, in the Middle East and internationally.

Hessah AlShaya is an Associate Professor of Educational Technology at Princess Nourah Bint Abdul Rahman University, Riyadh, Saudi Arabia. She holds a PhD in Education Technology and has published several papers on the subject. Dr AlShaya is interested in e-learning in general, and in mobile learning specifically. She served as the Director of e-learning and Distance Education at Princess Nourah Bint Abdul Rahman University and is currently the head of the department of Educational Technology. She has published two books: one about the use of technology in education for students with special needs, and the other one on the fundamentals and applications of Educational Technology.

Saleh Al-Shehri is an Assistant Professor of Mobile Learning and TESOL at College of Education, King Khalid University, Saudi Arabia. Behaviour of students playing with the social media and mobile phones, and their affordances for language learning, are the core interests for his research and academic career. Other research interests include design-based research and connectivism. Saleh is currently focusing on prospects of mobile learning in Saudi Arabia and the Arab world, and the effect of mobile social media on EFL students.

Abdulrahman M. Al-Zahrani is Assistant Professor of Educational Technology in the Department of Educational Technology, Faculty of Education at the University of Jeddah, Jeddah, Saudi Arabia. His primary research interests include e-learning, flipped classroom, virtual reality, distance learning, instructional design, digital citizenship, professional development, and technology integration in higher education. He has several published research papers in local and international journals. Also, he has delivered many oral presentations at international educational conferences, and conducted several training sessions including faculty development, flipped classroom, digital citizenship, and instructional design strategies. Dr Al-Zahrani received a master's degree in Educational Technology from King Saud University, Riyadh, Saudi Arabia and a PhD in Educational Technology from La Trobe University, Melbourne, Australia.

Aqil M. Azmi is an Associate Professor at the Department of Computer Science, King Saud University, Riyadh, Saudi Arabia since 1999. He received his BSE in ECE (Electrical & Computer Engineering) from the University of Michigan, Ann Arbor, Michigan, and MSc in EE and PhD in Computer Science from the University of Colorado, Boulder, Colorado. He taught graduate and undergraduate courses and is currently supervising several MSc and PhD students. His current research interests include application of computers in religious studies, Arabic natural language processing, bioinformatics, and algorithms in general. He has many publications with over 15 papers in ISI journals.

Fatima M. Azmi is an Associate Professor who has joined Zayed University-Department of Mathematics and Statistics in 2013. For a period of 14 years prior to this, she taught both graduate and undergraduate Mathematics courses in King Saud University, Riyadh, Saudi Arabia. She has also supervised master students and conducted research in pure Math area. She has many articles published in different ISI journals. She has also trained and prepared gifted high school students selected from all over Saudi Arabia for the Math Olympiad competition. She obtained her PhD in Mathematics from the University of Colorado, Boulder, Colorado. Her interest are in equivariant cyclic homology and cohomology theories, equivariant Chern–Connes characters associated to the Dirac operator on spin manifolds, K-homology, C^*-algebras, Fréchet algebras and univalent functions. Her current interest lies in the use of mobile technology and its applications to enhance students learning of Mathematics. Her published articles can be obtained from Google scholar or Academia.

Len Cairns retired from his full time position as Associate Dean (Engagement and International) in the Faculty of Education at Monash University, Australia at the end of 2013. He continues to research, write and work as a Visiting Professor at Middlesex University, UK and occasional Visiting Scholar at New York University, New York. Also he has recently worked for the University of Tasmania, Australia. Len's recent publications have been in the area of online learning, workplace learning and on competence and capability in vocational and professional education.

Hugh C. Davis is Professor of Learning Technologies in the Web and Internet Science Research Group (WAIS) at the University of Southampton, UK. He is also one of the University Directors of Education and he is the Director of the Institute for Learning Innovation and Development (ILIaD). Hugh has been involved in hypertext research since the late 1980s starting with an interest in the applications of hypertext for learning, going through open hypertext systems and then to architectures for adaptation and personalisation. He has extensive publications in these fields, and experience of starting a spin-off company with a hypertext product. His current research interests are all concerned with how technologies can change our perception and experience of learning (which is a branch of Web Science), and include personal learning environments (PLEs), educational repositories (EdShare), educational analytics and semantic applications in education.

Syed Asim Jalal is working as an Assistant Professor at the University of Peshawar, Pakistan. He received his PhD in Computer Science from the University of Southampton, where he was part of the Web and Internet Science (WAIS) research group in the School of Electronics and Computer Science. He received his master's degree in Computer Software Engineering from the National University of Science and Technology (NUST), Pakistan and received his BS Computer Science degree from the University of Peshawar, Pakistan. His research interests include mobile human computer interaction, mobile learning, technology enhanced learning and linked data.

Hend Mahmoud Merza received a doctorate in Educational Administration in 2004 from King Saud University, Riyadh, Saudi Arabia. She has 30 years of experience in public and higher education in Saudi Arabia. She has published 6 papers and books, and she has designed and delivered more than 10 training programs for the community service and development. Her fields of interest are quality assurance, training, and blended learning. She is currently working as Quality Assurance and Accreditation Manager at Saudi Arabia Branch of the Arab Open University.

Afnan A. Oyaid is an Associate Professor of Educational Technology at Princess Nourah University, Riyadh, Saudi Arabia. She graduated in 2004 from the University of the West of England, UK, with a BA (Hons) in Modern Languages and Information Systems, and in 2005 gained an MSc in Educational Technology from Bristol University, UK. In 2009 she was awarded a PhD in Educational Technology by Exeter University, UK. Dr Oyaid has published several papers in her field of specialty and is particularly interested in e-learning, mobile learning, the educational applications of social media and the use of educational technology for people with special needs. She has published a book on the latter subject, with another in press.

David Parsons is National Postgraduate Director for The Mind Lab by Unitec, providing postgraduate qualifications for teachers in digital and collaborative learning throughout New Zealand. He is the founding editor-in-chief of the *International Journal of Mobile and Blended Learning (IJMBL)*, the official journal of the International Association for Mobile Learning, and has edited several books in this field of research, including *Innovative Mobile Learning: Techniques and Technologies* (Information Science Reference, 2009.) His work

xvi *List of contributors*

has been published in a range of journals, including *Computers & Education, IEEE Software and Transactions on Learning Technologies*, and he has presented at many major conferences including mLearn, IADIS Mobile Learning and the IEEE International Conference on Advanced Learning Technologies. He is a member of the International Association for Mobile Learning, a committee member of the Australia New Zealand Mobile Learning group (ANZMLearn) and a professional member of the British Computer Society.

David Prescott works at the American University of Sharjah where he supervises and examines MA TESOL students' theses and teaches Leadership and Management in the MA program. At the undergraduate level he has taught courses concerned with effective educational use of digital resources and he developed the Professional Communication course which all engineering undergraduates are required to study in their junior (third) year. He holds a PhD in Education (Curtin University, Western Australia), a diploma in Second Language Teaching (Massey University, New Zealand). In 1990, he was elected a Fellow of The Royal Society of Arts, Manufactures and Commerce for services to teacher training for the Federal Government funded Australian Adult Migrant Education Service (AMES). He is the lead editor of English in *Southeast Asia: Varieties, Literacies and Literatures, Resolving Classroom Management and School Leadership Issues in ELT: Action Research Reports from the United Arab Emirates* and co-editor of *Agendas for 21st Century Engineers*, all published by Cambridge Scholars Publishing, Newcastle upon Tyne, UK.

Martha Robinson received her Master of Distance Education degree from Athabasca University, Canada, and her Bachelor of Education in Secondary School Education from the University of Alberta, Canada. She has over 25 year's experience as a teacher and trainer, curriculum developer, resource developer and evaluator, and instructional designer for individualized learning and distance learning. She has published articles on e-learning and mobile learning adoption and research in Qatar, mobile learning for English language training and workplace training, and industry/academia collaboration in mobile learning implementation and research. She received Best Paper recognition for her work entitled *Transition to e-learning in a Gulf Arab country*. Her research interests focus on the needs of learners and include cultural impact on e-learning and mobile learning, mobile learning for workplace training and support, and mobile learning for development.

Alaa Sadik is Associate Professor of Educational Technology and currently works at the Department of Instructional and Learning Technology, College of Education, Sultan Qaboos University, Sultanate of Oman. He received his PhD degree in Educational Technology from the University of Hull, UK, in 2003. He worked at the Arab Open University, Oman, South Valley University, Egypt, and Partners for Competitive Egypt project, funded by the USAID, Egypt. He has more than 10 years of experience in teaching and research in the fields of e-learning, distance education, and multimedia. He published many papers in refereed journals and international conferences within the last ten years. He received the World Summit Award 2013 and Khalifa Award 2014 for his contributions to the use of technology in teaching and learning. He is interested in the integration of computer software and web applications into the curriculum in developing nations.

Mohammed Samaka is an Associate Professor of Computer Science in the Department of Computer Science and Engineering (CSE), College of Engineering at Qatar University, Qatar. He obtained his PhD and master's degree from Loughborough University, UK and a post graduate diploma in Computing from Dundee University, UK. He obtained his bachelor of Mathematics from Baghdad University, Iraq. His current areas of research include wireless software architecture and technology, mobile applications and services, networking, e-learning, and computing curricula development.

Foreword

In few countries in the world, if any, has the pace of change in education been as fast or the hopes regarding the outcome of further change been as high as in the Arab Gulf countries represented in this book. It is an old cliché that foreign travel broadens the mind, but nevertheless I found this to be so true when I came, late in my career, to be introduced to distance education in the Arabian Gulf. Perhaps the evolution of distance education in the Americas and Europe that I have been part of for half a century was not quite as ponderous and incremental as it looked when viewed from Riyadh or Bahrain, but certainly the visitor there is struck by an extraordinary and perhaps surprising degree of enthusiasm for innovation in education in those and other Gulf cities, surprising perhaps because it has not been as widely reported as are developments in many other regions. That being so, I was delighted to have the chance to preview this new book, a valuable contribution to putting at least some of the story of research and development of contemporary distance education in the Gulf into the international literature.

Three aspects of modern Arab society appear to converge to make this enthusiasm for distance education so intense and so relevant to the region's current social, economic and cultural development. First is the most obviously relevant, which is the wide availability among this comparatively affluent population of computer, internet and mobile communication technologies and the software that goes with them. The most recent data at the time of writing (2015) indicate that a remarkable 96 per cent of the Bahraini population and 93 percent in the UAE have internet access (up from 71 per cent in both countries just three years previously), with over 18 million people online in the Kingdom of Saudi Arabia, including over 5 million subscribers to Facebook (www.internetworldstats.com/stats5.htm#me).

Closely related as a second factor that is driving academics and others to explore new ways of thinking about education, and specifically searching for new and better ways of teaching, is the significance of these nations' demography and their populations' age distribution, with a large and increasing number in what has often been called the 'net generation'. Universally, it is probably the case that the most enthusiastic users of new communications technologies are the under-25 year olds, and these in, for example, the Kingdom of Saudi Arabia constitute roughly half the population.[1]

Other related demographic incentives and pressures driving the need for fresh thinking about education include the management of changing expectations about women's roles in society as well as providing for the needs of guest workers.

Third, for those who have responsibility for developing economic policy as well as specifically educational policy, the challenge has been recognized for several years across all countries: it is to give high priority to an evolution from reliance on extraction industries towards industries and services that draw more heavily on intellectual capital. Doubtless there are still some university administrators, professors and educational policy makers in the Gulf countries – as in every country – who have not yet fully appreciated that twenty-first-century economies based on knowledge industries cannot be developed solely in a framework of traditional twentieth-century structures, with teachers and students herded into classrooms on fixed brick-and-mortar campuses. The generation of academics and administrators who have grown into adulthood in the age of social networking are generally well aware that the classroom itself has changed from a place for information dissemination to a venue for interaction with content through media and creation of knowledge through interaction with fellow learners under the leadership of enquiring scholars. And perhaps more importantly there is general recognition that knowledge that is not continuously updated very quickly becomes outdated, so that learning and teaching for a twenty-first-century knowledge economy must continue through the life-span. There can be no other solution to the need for continuous learning than distance education, and thus we see in the Gulf region, as in the rest of the world, an explosion of interest, activity and experimentation in developing methods for teaching a multitude of students who no longer cross the threshold of a physical campus – that is, pure distance education. Surely in the century-long history of distance education there has never been a time when social and economic need has met with the technological facility as well as advanced insights into the true character of what it means to learn as in the environment in which programmes may be developed and delivered at the present time. Such a view is, if true, universally true, and is true no less in the Arab Gulf nations than elsewhere in the world. I trust the evidence of the chapters in this book will go some way to support this view.

Although I have to resist the temptation to address the merits of each of these chapters, I hope I might be forgiven for selecting and pointing out just a few of the key words that caught my eye as I looked over the various titles and headings, for even in those few words we can capture a sense of the directions being taken by some of the region's leading educationists in their pursuit of innovation and swift evolution, to which I have referred. I was delighted to see, for example, that the book gives prominence to chapters that introduce issues of theory as well as application. The theory-based discussions cover quite a wide range of topics, but what is especially encouraging is to see many chapters in which readers are asked to postpone for a short time thinking about specific technologies and applications and to think first about the framework or model in which the application is to occur (the term 'model' used specifically in half the chapters in Part I). I was most pleased to see that in both the editors' introductory chapter, as elsewhere, readers are brought face to face with the invitation to consider 'pedagogy'. Too often in articles and chapters about distance education and its in-class application in blended learning attention becomes fixated on very short-term questions about what particular technological application is most successful, there-and-then. This is very understandable in the heat of pressure to have today's class of students achieve their best, but in the long run it is at least as important for teachers and researchers to study in depth the pedagogical foundations of their practice. Perhaps for some an immersion in educational philosophy, the psychology of learning and curriculum theory is too much (although personally I do not think it should be), but at least everyone who attempts to provide teaching to students in another place and/or another time should inform themselves about the research findings and perhaps the reported biographies and personal experiences of their predecessors who approached very similar questions, albeit when the technologies available to them were far simpler (and more demanding).

Two other features stand out for me in the pages that follow. First, I was also pleased to see good visibility given to questions about how faculty have responded to the changes that are inevitable as their institutions move to evolve a new paradigm of education. The kinds of changes that are necessary in teaching that fully employ communications technologies, especially outside the classroom, requires change in the professor's self-concept, his or her role within the university, indeed in society itself, and this is a phenomenon that has to be more understood before it can be better managed. It requires a recognition that change for both faculty and students, if it is to be really significant, means far, *far* more than simply changing one technology for another, but as new pedagogy evolves to make full use of the technology so does the total culture in which the actors participate.

Managing culture change is the second major issue I see in many chapters in the book, and, as every thoughtful person is well aware, in the Arab Gulf countries, change in culture is a very sensitive process, and one that deserves to be more fully analysed, discussed and researched as a basis for handling it carefully and successfully. Dealing with such change is another thread throughout the book (which includes one chapter that carries a specific invitation to consider 'managing the change') that one hopes will help start conversations on this vitally important topic.

I conclude, therefore, that in the book in front of you, you, the reader, can hope to find a beautiful snapshot illustrating the dynamism and activity of a cross section of the academics throughout the Arab Gulf states who are addressing their attention to the application and the potential application of today's communication technologies, both within the classroom and in extending the classroom through distance learning. You will also find threads that raise important issues for closer examination and further discussion regarding the theory, the models and the rationale for this activity as well as specific applications. Finally, you will also find questions raised – not all answered of course, but also worthy of further research – regarding the broader social, cultural and economic effects of this changing educational world. It should make fascinating reading, and perhaps inspire some readers to join the leaders who have written here and participate also in study of this new world of distance education.

Michael Grahame Moore
Distinguished Professor Emeritus
College of Education
The Pennsylvania State University
Founder and editor, *The American Journal of Distance Education*

Note

1 Caryle Murphy, Saudi Arabia's Youth and the Kingdom's Future. Middle East Program Occasional Paper Winter 2011. Woodrow Wilson International Center for Scholars' Environmental Change and Security Program.

Preface

The Arab Gulf countries are currently developing at a fast pace, requiring flexible and efficient education systems to educate and train citizens to contribute to their development. At the same time, the Gulf countries have a large percentage of young citizens who are very comfortable using information and communication technologies. Hence there has to be a paradigm shift in education in the Gulf countries to educate the present and new generations of learners. The current education paradigm was developed before the innovative technologies that are being used today were invented, before the internet, before the information age. Therefore, Gulf countries have to transform the education system using emerging learning technologies and innovative pedagogy in order to educate their citizens to contribute to society and to meet their developing needs. As research and best practices on the use of emerging learning technologies and pedagogy evolve, there is a need to implement the outcomes of research and best practice to transform and revolutionize education and prepare learners in Gulf region for the twenty-first century.

This book, by presenting theoretical perspectives on the use of emerging technologies and innovative pedagogies in education and presenting case studies' best practices that educators can implement, is a contribution to the transformation of education in the Gulf countries. It also looks to the future of technology to enable educators to prepare to use emerging technologies in the education system. The following pages will add value to teachers and professors who, to meet the needs of learners, want to implement emerging technologies and innovative pedagogy in their delivery. In addition, researchers can use this book to find out what research has been conducted, and what should be in the future. Administrators and managers of education systems can also benefit, since its chapters covers the implementation of emerging learning technologies and planning for the future.

Transforming Education in the Gulf Region falls into three parts. The first two concern theoretical perspectives and practical applications; the final part looks to the future of emerging technologies and innovation pedagogies. The first five chapters, comprising Part I, provide background information and consider the theory behind the use of emerging technologies and innovation pedagogies in education. The nine chapters in the practical applications section give examples of how emerging technologies and innovation pedagogies are used in the Gulf countries. The final three chapters, Part III, outline how education will be transformed using emerging technologies and innovation pedagogies.

Chapter 1 examines how faculty members adapt their use of technology-enhanced learning (TEL) activities to students' cultural norms in a private university in the United Arab Emirates (UAE). Some constraints were highlighted by participants, along with suggestions on how to adapt technology integration to ensure the cultural acceptability of TEL activities. Chapter 2 reports on aspects of a case study of a blended course delivery in the American University of Sharjah in UAE, particularly with respect to situated learning, pedagogic models and task structure. This chapter concludes with comments about course participant attainment and the importance of 'rich', structured tasks that involve problem-based learning and offer students opportunities for creative and critical thinking, essential behaviours for transitioning from the academy to the workplace. Chapter 3 reviews some of the previous approaches and studies that have evaluated the potential of technology for language instruction. It also evaluates technology-mediated language learning at a tertiary institution in Saudi Arabia, and whether students and teachers benefited from the implementation of technology tools.

In Chapter 4, Merza proposes an Open System Model of Blended Learning, which comprises five elements: inputs, process, outputs, feedback and external environment. The author proposes that the model be implemented at higher education institutions across Gulf Cooperation Council (GCC) nations to speed up the process of providing local markets with highly skilled workers and responding to the increasing demand among workers in these countries for flexible higher education programmes. Chapter 5 discusses levels of adoption of technology in higher education through three main perspectives: the practitioner, the pedagogical and the administrative. The author argues that the effective integration of technology in developing countries, which are highly influenced by social, religious and traditional educational structures, occurs in the intersection between these three perspectives.

Chapter 6 explores the concepts, benefits, implementation and issues that surround mobile learning in GCC countries. The focus of the chapter is on the ways in which mobile learning is advancing in GCC countries, and the challenges and expectations involved in the development of mobile learning. Chapter 7 introduces a video presentation recording application and online video sharing platform, PresentationTube network, which has been developed by the author. The chapter describes the technology and methodology used in the development and evaluation of this network. Quantitative and qualitative techniques were implemented to collect data and report on the usability of the network and effectiveness of video presentations. Chapter 8 explores a wide range of initiatives to innovate education in Qatar, based on its 2030 National Vision. It describes the use of innovative learning technologies in Qatar to prepare workers and students to achieve the nation's strategic goals.

Chapter 9 discusses students' use of social media in educational environments in the GCC countries. It explores research in this area by analysing results from previous studies on the patterns of students' use of social media in learning and exchange of information. Chapter 10 explores the use of student-centred learning analytics dashboards and discusses the significance of directing the analytical results of such dashboards to students, rather than focusing on teachers and managers only. The authors argue that results of these reports are likely to empower students to take responsibility for their own learning. Chapter 11 discusses the use of flipped classroom as a form of blended learning and describes concerns that have been raised and best practices centred around the flipped classroom in the GCC region. Chapter 12 sheds some light on the challenge of managing change during e-learning integration. It examines the role of leadership in the change process surrounding the implementation of e-learning at one Saudi Arabian university. The authors raise questions about the current and future role of e-learning deanships in Saudi universities.

Chapter 13 introduces and explores the first MOOC initiative in the Arab world – *Rwaq*, the first platform to deliver Arabic MOOC to Arabic-speaking learners through Arabic-speaking lecturers. Chapter 14 introduces a comprehensive model of smart classrooms as a part of an approach to implement an efficient Technology Enhanced Learning (TEL) environment. The proposed model is based on an integrated framework to implement a holistic TEL approach that enables educators to design efficient teaching–learning to overcome these challenges. In addition, a new integrated competency level is presented to ensure teacher–instructor readiness in a new TEL environment.

The final three chapters look to the future use of emerging technologies and innovative pedagogy. Chapter 15 highlights the importance that both teachers and students have regular access to technologies that support and advance mathematical sense making, reasoning, problem solving and communication. The authors' reason that educational researchers ought to pay more attention to the technology-related teaching practices of mathematicians to better understand and enhance innovations in mathematics teaching at all levels. Chapter 16 is structured primarily as a series of 'top fives' under different headings, intended to highlight some of the concerns regarding m-learning, both now and in the future. It should be noted that these concerns are legitimate in the context of GCC. These cover m-learning myths and misunderstandings, m-learning innovations, and both the potentials and risks for m-learning in the future. Together, these various perspectives on m-learning seek to provide an inclusive view of what m-learning means today, recognition of the best achievements of m-learning so far and an agenda for the future that will, we hope, assist us in gaining the maximum benefits from m-learning while minimizing the potential negative effects of technological, social and pedagogical change. The final chapter addresses some of the challenges of innovation in education in the GCC region.

Mohamed Ally, PhD
Khalid Alshahrani, PhD

Acknowledgements

We would like to thank the following reviewers:

Kevin Schoepp, Hend Al-Khalifa, Nathaniel Ostashewski, Hind Alotaibi, Nagwa Abou El-Naga, Hanny Alshazly, Jerry Pon, Troy Priest, Muhammad Sabri Sahrir, Emre Sezgin, Helmi Norman, Rasha Al Okaily, Shelagh McGrath.

We also would like to thank Heidi Lee, Thomas Storr, Dave Wright and Emma Hinde of Routledge who worked with us to publish this book.

Part I
Theoretical perspectives

1 Adapting technology-enhanced learning to students' culture
Faculty perspectives

Rasha Al Okaily

Introduction and context

The United Arab Emirates (UAE) is a cosmopolitan country with a large number of higher education (HE) institutes, both local and international. Universities in the UAE are shaped by cultural complexities in various ways (Findlow, 2006). Government universities accept UAE nationals only, while private universities accept students from the UAE and other nations. This means that each university has its own cultural mix. Faculty in both types of universities, however, are mainly expatriates from around the world. When it comes to English language teaching, the majority of faculty are Westerners or Western educated. The term 'Westerners' in the UAE is often used to refer to American, British, Canadian, Australian and European people in general, whether they are natives of these countries or educated in them, and 'Large-scale importation of Western-trained language teachers to teach in a non-Western educational context poses challenges because teachers and students tend to operate from within their own distinct social, cultural and educational paradigm' (Diallo, 2014, p. 1).

This study focuses on faculty perceptions in a private university where the majority of students are UAE and Saudi nationals. In this university, men and women study on separate campuses, one for women and one for men. Hence, the prevailing student culture is the Arab, Islamic, conservative. The university policy is rooted in Arabic and Islamic tradition, and the rules, regulations and policies stipulate that all behaviours, activities, dress codes and so on should conform to this culture. This determines instructors' choice of pedagogy, resources, learning activities, assignment types, classroom activities and ways of interaction. This study explores how the use of technology-enhanced learning (TEL) activities and assignments is affected by such conformity to students' cultural norms and university policy.

Problem statement

With the integration of technology into teaching and learning, it has been generally noticed that there is unease among some female students with regard to assignments that incorporate online activities, particularly recording speech and publishing to an online forum. This prompted an earlier study (Al Okaily, unpublished) in which the findings showed that some students tended to resist online speaking activities for three main reasons: motivational, technical and cultural. This led to the recommendation of further research into the cultural norms that affect technology integration in teaching and learning and the choice of TEL activities that are acceptable in order to avoid any unnecessary cultural tensions.

This paper investigates the effect of the prevailing cultural norms on TEL with the purpose of contributing to the body of literature that informs expatriate faculty on what TEL practices may or may not be acceptable within the cultural practices of a private university in the UAE.

Culture, globalization and TEL

Studies conducted in some HE institutes in the UAE take a geo-ethnic stance, where language, religion and tradition are seen to shape cultural norms. Findlow (2001) points to the two most apparent characteristics of culture being the Arabic language and the Islamic religion, and Rapanta (2014) uses spirituality as one of the traits through which she analyses cultural practices of students in a government HE institute.

Official documents of the university where this study was conducted also state that the university's mission and vision are deeply rooted in Arab Islamic culture. However, important ecological factors, such as the fast-paced economic growth and the changing demographics through importation of foreign work force, have been described as affecting national identity and causing 'cultural fragility' (Hopkyns, 2014, p.3), 'cultural tsunami' (Hatherley-Green, 2014, p.2) or 'global–local values conflict' (Findlow, 2001, p.1), leading to challenges in the educational context (Diallo, 2014). To face these challenges, the government is taking various measures to strengthen the national identity and heritage of the UAE (Hopkyns, 2014). This, in turn, led some HE institutions to orient Western faculty about the differences between Western and Middle Eastern cultures in an attempt to avoid what they term cultural pit-falls (Rapanta, 2014).

There are some other factors that play an important role here. English has become a lingua franca in the UAE to facilitate communication between UAE inhabitants, both locals and expatriates (Randal and Samimi, 2010), and is the medium of instruction in most HE college majors. Add to this a persistent call by policy makers for increased technology integration in education in both government and private universities. If we place these factors against the background of the fast economic growth of the UAE, the result is then a society that is being affected by globalization to a high degree. Spring (2008) explains that the two driving forces of globalization are economy and technology. He also refers to, and endorses, Tollefson and Tsui's (2007) view that technology and English are mediation tools for globalization.

Putting all the above factors together (Figure 1.1), we have a culture that is under two opposing forces. The first is globalization, and the second is government policies to reinforce national identity, heritage and the Arabic language. The push and pull of these forces is resulting in a culture that is constantly changing and in

Technology-enhanced learning 5

Figure 1.1 Factors affecting culture in the UAE.

need of continuous reassessment to determine the boundaries between the acceptable and the unacceptable.

On the other hand, both institutional policies and cultural norms affect TEL pedagogies and choices. Goodfellow and Lamy (2009) explain that neither online learning technologies nor the pedagogies related to them are culturally neutral and refer to Hannon and D'Netto's (2005) assertion that institutional needs, structures and strategies play a role in forming the learning experiences of online learning technologies. Dunbar (1991) asserts that technologies carry the characteristics of the countries that developed them, which may cause a cultural mismatch when used with other groups of people with different cultural norms. Al Hunayyan and Al-Sharhan (2009, p. 2) explain this by pointing out that 'Arab countries have some rich cultures and religious beliefs, which may be violated seriously in the light of the current trends in virtual learning.'. Akinyemi (2003) points to the importance of taking socio-cultural factors into consideration when introducing new technologies and reiterates the possibility of cultural mismatch when incorporating virtual learning. I would like to stress here that, since culture is seen to be dynamic and changing through the effects of globalization, the above cited literature on the culture–technology fit belongs to the time in which the research was conducted and can serve as a pointer to the need for further research into cross-cultural pedagogy to ensure that 'quality education is delivered in a culturally accessible form' (Prowse, 2014, p. 1).

Research questions

How do the prevailing cultural norms affect technology integration in a private university in the UAE?

1 How do faculty members perceive and assess students' culture?
2 How do the students' cultural norms affect faculty's choice of TEL activities and assignments?

Methodology and method

This study is qualitative research concerned mainly with faculty perspectives on how prevailing cultural norms influence their technology integration practices. The research paradigm adopted is constructivist (Mackenzie and Knipe, 2006), with hermeneutic phenomenology that aims to give rich descriptions of the experiences of participants (Smith, 1997) in order to 'get beneath the subjective experience and find the genuine objective nature of things as realised by an individual' (Kafle, 2013, p. 186). Creswell (2009) notes that phenomenology is both a philosophy and a method because it aims at understanding lived human experiences as described by participants. The notion that the researcher needs to bracket his or her own experience (Creswell, 2009) is challenged here. Being a faculty member in the same university and experiencing the same phenomenon makes the researcher's views relevant to the study. Flood (2010) proposes the notion of co-constituality, which is the process of meaning making based on a blend of the participants' as well as the researcher's views. Therefore, the researcher's views on technology integration in this particular teaching context are shaped by the same prevailing cultural norms.

Data collection and participants

Although a number of data collection methods are possible, conducting interviews are typically associated with phenomenological studies (Kinnunen and Simon, 2012), hence this was the chosen method of data collection. Semi-structured interviews were conducted with five faculty members who are known within the university for their integration of technology in teaching (a purposive sample). They are either Westerners or Western educated, and comprise one female and four male instructors with experience in the university ranging from two to nine years. The demographic data of the participants are presented in Table 1.1. The researcher tried to prompt participants to give their views and interpretations on

Table 1.1 Participants' demographic data

	Origin	Gender	# years in the University	Teaching context
Participant 1	Egypt (Western educated)	Female	9	Female classes – Male classes
Participant 2	Syria (Western educated)	Male	5	Female classes – Male classes
Participant 3	Canadian	Male	9	Female classes – Male classes
Participant 4	American	Male	2	Female classes – Male classes
Participant 5	British	Male	9	Female classes

areas identified by the researcher as possible cultural pitfalls. Meaning making in this case does not only depend on the participants' experience, but on the researcher's experience of the same phenomenon in the same learning context.

Procedure

The purpose of the interview was explained to the participants and the anonymity of their responses was also assured. Participants consented to audio recording of their interviews. Each interview started with a general plan only (Flood, 2010) and questions were broadly stated to allow the participants to give as rich descriptions as possible. Sub-questions were added – in the form of probes and prompts – when needed and for the purposes of prompting participants to elaborate or clarify. The critical incident analysis technique (Tripp, 1993) was employed to elicit detailed examples from participants. Tripp (1993), as cited in Hamlin (2004), defines this technique as 'interpretations to the significance of an event' (p. 171).

Participants were invited to talk about their perspectives on technology integration and culture and to reflect on the link between them. First, they were asked how they integrate technology and what TEL activities or assignments they use with their students. Then they were asked to describe the students' cultural norms. Later, participants were asked if such norms affected their choice of TEL activities in any way.

The sub-topics ranged between what technologies the interviewees were reluctant to use for cultural reasons, and which TEL activities they had used but later decided not to use again, for similar reasons.

Validity and reliability

There are limited ways to validate qualitative research other than respondent validation (Cohen, Manion and Morrison, 2009). After transcribing the audio-recorded interviews, the script was then shown to the participants for validation. Participants kept their transcripts overnight. They had enough time to read them carefully and decide once more if they were willing to share their views for the purpose of this study. They were reassured regarding the anonymity of their responses, and they confirmed that the transcripts were a true account of the interview.

Subjectivity may still be an issue here, since the selection and interpretation of data can be influenced by the researcher's own views being immersed in the same context as the respondents'. Cohen et al. (2009) explain this:

> there is a risk that, since data and interpretation are unavoidably combined (the double hermeneutic), the subjective views of the researcher might lead to him or her being overselective, unrepresentative and unfair to the situation in hand in the choice of data and the interpretation placed on them.
> (p. 540)

Therefore, avoidance of being overselective is attempted here, as is representation of all relevant views. The comments that were not directly related to the research questions, such as conversational digressions, were the only ones not included in the findings.

Data analysis

Flood (2010) refers to a number of psychologists, such as van Kaam (1966), Giorgi (1970) and Colaizzi (1978), who have suggested frameworks to interpret interviews in phenomenological studies as a measure to increase rigour. This study adopts Giorgi's (1975) four-stage model for interpreting interviews (Figure 1.2).

Findings

In terms of technology integration, participants mentioned a number of TEL activities that they use with their students. They have mainly adopted a strategy of caution and trial and error to determine what works best. Some examples include (but are not exclusive to) the use of the learning management system (LMS) Blackboard, discussion forums, Quizlet (an online forum for creating quizzes), Edmodo (LMS), online videos, audio/video recording and sharing, various English as a Second Language (ESL) websites, WebQuests, web searches and so on.

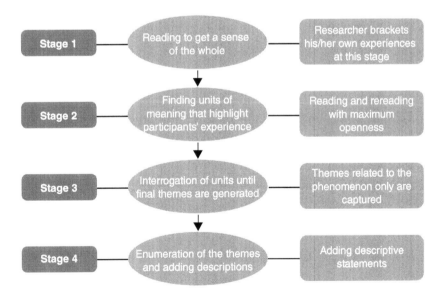

Figure 1.2 Giorgi's four-stage model for interpreting interviews.

Participants' perception and assessment of students' culture
The prevailing culture

All participants described the prevailing culture in relatively similar ways – as conservative Islamic. They mentioned that there is a 'common heritage' and referred to a shared tradition that is 'deeply rooted in religious beliefs'. This is seen to be governing students' behaviours and preferences to a large degree as well as governing instructors' behaviours and choices, as will be shown later.

Having said this, a participant also acknowledged that within this conservative culture there is much variation between students' cultural identities. 'You can't say there's a prevailing culture. There are prevailing expectations of the culture about certain things. How people meet those expectations varies from family to family.'

This idea of 'how people meet cultural expectations' echoes Gutierrez and Rogoff's (2003) idea of describing cultures through people's activities and degree of engagement in cultural practices. One way instructors do this is by assessing degrees of conservativeness by the way in which students, particularly females, dress. A participant described, at length, how he takes clues from students' dress code, differentiating between students who wear the traditional Emirati dress with a black veil (*shayla*) and the full cover of the hair (*hijab*) or the full cover of hair and face (*niqab*). He explained that his choice of pedagogy and type of technology to use in class is governed by conclusions made upon observing students' dress code and how students interact with each other:

> So that has governed my thinking in how conservative group of students is. I notice how many are uncovered and how many covered … I'm happy to see the students who are uncovered being friendly with somebody even wearing the *niqab*. I like to see how they get on together. This is part of observing how I deal with them.

It is quite clear here that the participant links dress code to the degree of engagement in cultural practices and uses the interaction, or degree of friendliness, between students with different degrees of cultural commitment to determine his approach and choice of pedagogical tools.

Dress code came up in another instructor's response as an indicator of how students tend to blend in with the group. The participant explained how in other societies there is a great value placed on individualism, whereas in his particular environs students attempt to be part of the group, blend in, and not 'stand out' in many aspects, one of which is dress code: 'Those who attempt to stand out are … looked at negatively. Like when someone dresses differently.'

The instructor went on to describe how students try not to differ from the norms in order not to be seen as different from the group. This may reflect the Hofstedean dimension of 'collectivism' that Hofstede (1986) explains as placing high value on commitment to the in-group and to tradition. However, the same participant said earlier that meeting cultural expectations varies from family to family, showing that the degree of collectivism can vary. In fact, Triandis (1994) emphasizes this point by adding that all people carry both individualist and collectivist tendencies. Students here (i.e. in this university) may show different degrees of collectivism, but not necessarily show the same degree elsewhere in their lives. It depends on the degree of each individual's involvement in cultural practices.

Culture is changing

Instructors pointed out the fact that culture is changing. They expressed their surprise when students acted in a less conservative manner than one would expect of them. For example, one instructor who thought that there was an 'unwritten law' prohibiting the use of social media expressed his surprise when some of his female students asked him if they could be friends with him on Facebook, Twitter and Instagram. Another instructor described how boundaries are shifting and how he expected them to continue to shift away from conservatism:

> It will be interesting to see what happens with particularly the use of social media. That's what I'm keeping my eye on. This place is relatively conservative, but it is way less conservative than when I first started in here nine years ago. Totally different!

This change in culture could well be a manifestation of the effect of globalization, as established earlier in the paper, and how this is changing people's attitudes.

Effect of students' cultural norms on faculty's choice of TEL activities and assignments

Participants are particularly cautious with activities that may require exposure to the outside world, or where interaction is more public than private, as in social media. Other language-learning activities that involve use of Internet websites, online activities or videos are also deemed not controlled enough for use in the classroom.

Refraining from using social media

All participants expressed their reluctance to use social media with their students, despite any possible educational value in doing so (Blankenship, 2011; Moran, Seaman and Tinti-Kane, 2011).

> There's all kinds of stuff that you can do on Facebook to run a course ... There are female teachers who use WhatsApp with their female students by creating a group and the message can reach the whole class in an instant ... But I'm not going to do that, because it's not culturally appropriate.

Upon further probing, four of the five participants indicated that using social media with students may be culturally inappropriate. Male instructors particularly pointed to the fact that they did not want direct contact with female students because it would be culturally unacceptable. 'It's almost an unwritten law [prohibiting the use of social media]. Especially if the teacher is a male and the students are females,' one commented, and another 'Most of them [female students] don't feel comfortable communicating with their teachers on social media.' Some male instructors said they would not mind using social media with male students. However, none of them indicated that they actually tried it: 'As a male teacher, if I were teaching male students, then maybe it's okay. I don't know. I would have to decide that at the time. A female teacher can do social media, maybe.'

Gender seems to have an effect here. The issue is more prominent when the instructor's gender is different from the students'.

Use of online activities

In general, much care is seen to be required when choosing any teaching resources. These need to be culturally, politically, religiously and ethnically appropriate, with special emphasis on religious conservativeness. The same applies to online internet resources.

In this regard, the participants expressed the following precautions.

Going on the web with your students

Examples of what might go wrong are many. A participant pointed out that he never goes on the web in class because there is not enough control over what might come up. Another instructor mentioned an incident in his class when he wanted to search for something and clicked on one of Google's suggested search terms. The search resulted in some inappropriate links that embarrassed him in front of his students. He explained that it was 'nothing serious, but I felt embarrassed at that time. And I realised that I had clicked something without noticing what it was.'

Another instructor mentioned that he feels 'bothered' by the ads that pop up on the ESL websites to which he refers students because:

> They're inappropriate. I do not know if the students notice them. Perhaps they don't, but I still have to be aware. Things like that would not bother me if I was in another environment [but] I have to be very culturally aware when I'm using technology in this environment.

The participants' remarks show their awareness of the socio-cultural factor to which Akinyemi (2003) refers. Participants feel uncertain of whether this can be considered a 'violation' of culture or religious beliefs, as Al-Hunayyan and Al-Sharhan (2009) point out.

12 Rasha Al Okaily

Playing online videos from YouTube

Videos have always been a useful instructional tool. However, even when the instructor screens a chosen video for appropriateness, playing it online was seen by instructors to be risky. They mentioned a number of things that might go wrong. One instructor explained why.

> At the end of the video there is a list of suggested videos, or there could be something at the bottom, or worse is the comments. If you scroll down, you may find swearing and all kinds of bad language, which is a fact of life, and the students realise that it's a fact of life too, but context is very important. There's a certain learning context here. I think we're required not to put those things on display. So when we can avoid them, we do. These are cultural considerations.

Although this 'cultural consideration' might not be exclusive to Arab, Islamic culture, it certainly is a characteristic of it. Therefore, this participant sees it as important.

Another instructor pointed to the fact that internet speed is sometimes not reliable. He mentioned a recent incident that caused discomfort for him and possibly for his students as he was playing a video for them.

> Yesterday, the YouTube video froze ... it happened when the guy [a swimmer] was getting out of the water. You look at the students and you think 'Are they bothered?' And you don't know because I'm bothered, working in this environment. I'm rushing ... to distract the students from the frozen picture of the half-naked man just because [the clip] stopped with him getting out of the water.

It is quite clear here that, for this instructor, this incident caused a considerable degree of discomfort. A different instructor explained that now he tends to show documentaries about nature, or outdoor activities like skydiving. Obviously, here, cultural conflict was dealt with through adaptation or modification of choices rather than elimination of technology use. Other faculty members have, unfortunately, solved this problem of culture–technology fit by avoiding TEL activities altogether.

Requiring students to record a video or audio of themselves as part of a project

Some assignments require students to create a video where they demonstrate their learning of a new language skill. This can be somewhat problematic in the present cultural context. Female students, who are assumed by society to be more conservative, are usually expected to resist such assignments even if they do not appear in the video and only their voice is recorded. One instructor expressed his reservations: 'I teach girls and that [assignments that involve creating a video] would be culturally inappropriate. It is difficult to tell them record a video and bring it to me.'

I would like to stress here that this is an expectation instructors have of students. There are cases (in the same teaching context) where female students agreed to do online video-recorded speaking assignments and did so successfully (Al Okaily, 2013), but a few of them showed discomfort (Al Okaily, in press).

Interestingly, a female instructor mentioned an incident with male students who refused to do a similar assignment – they had to listen to and summarize a podcast, then record a video of themselves presenting this summary. She said:

> I asked them to upload their videos on YouTube and send me the link. A lot of the male students resisted doing it. Those who did the assignment sent the video to me and refused to share it or upload it to YouTube. They said that it might go viral, especially among group members, so they didn't want to do it, especially because they were talking in English. They didn't feel comfortable exposing themselves to others.

In both examples, gender issue surfaces again.

Remarks and implications

What can be understood from this study is that in a conservative type of culture like the one described here technology integration in teaching and learning can be inhibited. However, some faculty managed to find ways around limitations through adapting their practices to be more considerate to the prevailing cultural norms. It would be highly beneficial if such adaptations are shared, to encourage other faculty to integrate technology in teaching in contexts similar to those of this university.

Another remark is that in the critical incidents that instructors described we can notice that culture–technology clashes happened when the instructor was of a different gender from students. Examples included male instructors who refrained from using social media with female students, or male students who refused to do an assignment where they were required to share video projects on YouTube, given to them by a female teacher, even with private settings. Male instructors who teach female students seem to be more embarrassed when culturally sensitive incidents happen.

No generalization is attempted here due to the limited number of participants. Instead, this phenomenological study aims to draw a picture of the reality from participants' experiences rather than make generalizations or assumptions.

Limitations and recommendations for further research

This study was conducted on the women's campus and the participants were all based in the women's campus too. However, all instructors occasionally go to teach in the men's campus. Additional participants from the men's campus could have informed this study to help paint a more comprehensive picture of the situation.

This study mainly deals with instructors' perspectives. To get a better assessment of the situation, students' perspectives could also be investigated in order to see if the two perspectives match and what implications this might have. A further limitation to the study was the fact that, of the five instructor participants, there was only one who was female. Thus, it could be argued that the participant sample was not balanced in terms of gender.

References

Akinyemi, A. (2003). Web-based learning and cultural interference: perspectives of Arab students. In A. Rossett (ed.), *Proceedings of World Conference on E-Learning in Corporate, Government, Healthcare, and Higher Education* (pp. 1858–1862). Chesapeake VA: AACE. Retrieved from www.editlib.org/p/12239

Al-Hunaiyyan, A. and Al-Sharhan, S. (2009). The design of multimedia blended e-learning systems: cultural considerations. In *Signals, Circuits and Systems (SCS), 2009 3rd International Conference* (pp. 1–5). IEEE. Retrieved from http://ieeexplore.ieee.org/xpls/abs_all.jsp?arnumber=5412342

Al Okaily, R. (unpublished paper). Online speaking practice: benefits and barriers. In A. Pallas and M. Ally (eds), *The international handbook of mobile-assisted language learning*.

Al Okaily, R. (2013). Mobile learning and BYOD: implementations in an intensive English program. *Learning and Teaching in Higher Education: Gulf Perspectives* 10(2). Retrieved from http://lthe.zu.ac.ae/index.php/lthehome/article/view/141

Blankenship, M. (2011). How social media can and should impact higher education. *Education Digest* 76(7), 39–42. Retrieved from https://www.wdhstore.com/hispanic/data/pdf/nov29-howsocial.pdf

Cohen, L., Manion, L. and Morrison, K. (2011). *Research Methods in Education* (7th ed.). London: Routledge.

Colaizzi, P.F. (1978). Psychological research as the phenomenologist views it. In R.S. Vale and M. King (eds), *Existential phenomenological alternatives for psychology* (pp. 48–71). New York: Oxford University Press.

Creswell, J.W. (2009). *Research Design: Qualitative, Quantitative, and Mixed Methods Approaches* (3rd ed.). Thousand Oaks CA: Sage.

Diallo, I. (2014). Emirati students encounter Western teachers: tensions and identity resistance. *Learning and Teaching in Higher Education: Gulf Perspectives* 11(2). Retrieved from http://lthe.zu.ac.ae/index.php/lthehome/article/view/158

Dunbar, R. (1991). Adapting distance education for Indonesians: problems with learner heteronomy and a strong oral tradition. *Distance Education* 12(2), 163–174. Doi:10.1080/0158791910120203

Findlow, S. (2001). Global and local tensions in an Arab Gulf state: conflicting values in UAE higher education. Presented at Travelling Policy/Local Spaces: Globalisation, Identities and Education Policy in Europe, United Kingdom.

Findlow, S. (2006). Higher education and linguistic dualism in the Arab Gulf. *British Journal of Sociology of Education* 27(1), 19–36. Doi:10.1080/01425690500376754

Flood, A. (2010). Understanding phenomenology: Anne Flood looks at the theory and methods involved in phenomenological research. *Nurse Researcher* 17(2), 7–15. Retrieved from http://rcnpublishing.com/doi/full/10.7748/nr2010.01. 17.2.7.c7457

Giorgi, A. (1975). An application of phenomenological method in psychology. In A. Giorgi, C. Fischer and E. Murray (eds), *Duquesne studies in phenomenological psychology* (vol. 1, pp. 23–85). Pittsburgh PA: Duquesne University Press.

Goodfellow, R. and Lamy, M.-N. (2009). Introduction: a frame for the discussion of learning cultures. In R. Goodfellow and M.-N. Lamy (eds), *Learning cultures in online education* (pp. 1–14). London: Continuum. Retrieved from http://oro.open.ac.uk/13012/

Gutierrez, K.D. and Rogoff, B. (2003). Cultural ways of learning: individual traits or repertoires of practice. *Educational Researcher* 32(5), 19–25. Doi:10.3102/0013189X032005019

Hamlin, K.D. (2004). Beginning in journey: supporting reflection in early field experiences. *Reflective Practice* 5(2), 167–179. Doi:10.1080/14623940410001690956

Hannon, J. and D'Netto, B. (n.d.). Cultural perspective in online learning. Presented at the Conference of the Open and Distance Learning Association of Australia (ODLAA), Adelaide, South Australia.

Hatherley-Greene, P. (2014). The border crossing index: implications for higher education teachers in the UAE. *Learning and Teaching in Higher Education: Gulf Perspectives* 11(2). Retrieved from http://lthe.zu.ac.ae/index.php/lthehome/article/view/133

Hofstede, G. (1986). Cultural differences in teaching and learning. *International Journal of Intercultural Relations* 10(3), 301–320. Retrieved from www.sciencedirect.com/science/article/pii/0147176786900155

Hopkyns, S. (2014). The effects of global English on culture and identity in the UAE: a double-edged sword. *Learning and Teaching in Higher Education: Gulf Perspectives* 11(2). Retrieved from http://lthe.zu.ac.ae

Kafle, N.P. (2013). Hermeneutic phenomenological research method simplified. *Bodhi: An Interdisciplinary Journal* 5(1), 181–200. Retrieved from www.nepjol.info/index.php/BOHDI/article/view/8053

Kinnunen, P. and Simon, B. (2012). Phenomenography and grounded theory as research methods in computing education research field. *Computer Science Education* 22(2), 199–218. doi:10.1080/08993408.2012.692928

Mackenzie, N. and Knipe, S. (2006). Research dilemmas: paradigms, methods and methodology. *Issues in Educational Research* 16(2), 193–205. Retrieved from www.iier.org.au/iier16/mackenzie.html

Moran, M., Seaman, J. and Tinti-Kane, H. (2011). Teaching, learning, and sharing: how today's higher education faculty use social media. Pearson Learning Solutions. Retrieved from http://iopscience.iop.org/1538-3881/120/3/1579

Prowse, J.K. (2014). Cross-cultural comparison: piloting an analytical framework. *Learning and Teaching in Higher Education: Gulf Perspectives* 11(2). Retrieved from http://lthe.zu.ac.ae/index.php/lthehome/article/view/159

Randall, M. and Samimi, M.A. (2010). The status of English in Dubai. *English Today* 26(1), 43. Doi:10.1017/S0266078409990617

Rapanta, C. (2014). 'Insha' Allah I'll do my homework': adapting to Arab undergraduates at an English-speaking university in Dubai. *Learning and Teaching* in *Higher Education: Gulf Perspectives* 11(2). Retrieved from http://lthe.zu.ac. ae/index.php/lthehome/article/view/177

Smith, S.J. (1997). The phenomenology of educating physically. In D. Vandenburg (ed.), *Phenomenology and educational discourse* (pp. 119–144). Durban: Heinemann.

Spring, J. (2008). Research on globalization and education. *Review of Educational Research* 78(2), 330–363. Doi:10.3102/0034654308317846

Tollefson, J.W. and Tsui, A.B.M. (2003). *Medium of instruction policies: Which agenda? Whose agenda?* New York and Oxford: Routledge.

Triandis, H.C. (1994). Theoretical and methodological approaches to the study of collectivism and individualism. In U. Kim, H.C. Triandis,C. Kagitcibasi, S.-C. Choi and G. Yoon (eds), *Individualism and collectivism: theory, methods and applications* (pp. 41–51). London: SAGE.

Tripp, D. (1993). *Critical incidents in teaching: developing professional judgement.* London: Routledge.

van Kaam, A. (1966). *Existential foundations of psychology.* Pittsburgh PA: Duquesne University Press.

2 Situated learning, pedagogic models and structured tasks in blended course delivery

David Prescott

Introduction

The information in this chapter is derived from a case study investigation of a humanities and social sciences elective course offered at the American University of Sharjah (AUS) in the United Arab Emirates (UAE). In the semester in question, twenty-six students studied the course, predominantly seniors (only three were junior-year students), and nine students were in their final semester. Three different AUS colleges were represented in this student cohort, with a gender ratio of fifteen female to eleven male students. In keeping with the American model of higher education, students at AUS need to complete humanities and social sciences requirements as components of their undergraduate study.

EDU307 Teaching and Learning in Electronic Environments is a blended course that addresses in particular the AUS General Education Program Goals:

- develop the skills and abilities to thoughtfully seek information, critically analyse sources and clearly formulate complex ideas
- investigate how digital technology can facilitate inquiry and the advancement of knowledge (AUS, 2013–2014)

These goals are apposite for tertiary students at the threshold between the academy and the professional and commercial world they will inhabit in their work careers.

In this chapter, the significance of these goals will be discussed in relation to situated learning, pedagogic models and structured tasks, which were integrated to promote the intellectual growth of the students. Comment will be included concerning the students' personal dynamics that aided and impeded this growth and also concerning the significance of the three factors in fostering student attainment of Bloom's higher-order cognitive skills of application, analysis, synthesis and evaluation, which underpin the liberal arts ethos of the American University of Sharjah.

Case study

Case study method frames the information presented and discussed in the remainder of the chapter, considering the blended course as a 'bounded system' (Stake, 2008, pp. 119–120). The examination of the factors, situated learning, pedagogic models and structured tasks relates particularly to the AUS General Education Program Goal 'investigate how digital technology can facilitate inquiry and the advancement of knowledge' and builds on a previous descriptive case study conducted when the course was introduced in the Fall semester 2011. The objective of the previous case study was to:

> examine the learning approach followed during the course and to trace the student reflection on the course content and practice by giving value to their reflections. The overall pedagogic intention is to strengthen the course through dialogue and collaboration between student and professor.
> (Prescott, 2013, p. 21)

In the Spring semester of 2014 the course comprised a class of twenty-six students from three colleges at AUS, with fifteen female and eleven male students. The students were a mixture of juniors (three students) and seniors (the remainder) with nine in their final semester. Six students were from the College of Arts and Sciences and four were studying Literature and Language, with one student studying Mathematics and the sixth student Environmental Science. Eighteen students were from the College of Engineering, and two were from the School of Business Management, studying Business Administration. Apart from the pragmatic reason of degree structure, students choosing EDU307 were interested in the course objectives as they relate to workplace needs following graduation. The elective status of such courses results in student cohorts who are atypical, for which a case study is an appropriate approach. Furthermore, as Burns points out, 'case study is the preferred method when "how", "why" or "what" questions are being asked' (Burns, 1990, p. 313). The study seeks to understand more about 'context and process', a strength of the case study method (Flyvberg, 2011, p. 314).

The descriptive case study that yielded the information discussed in the remainder of the chapter seeks to address the question: What evidence can be identified to indicate that the students attained the course objectives?

The course objectives specified at Appendix A

The significance of the factors, situated learning, pedagogic models and structured tasks will be discussed for the opportunities they provided for intellectual growth of the students. There will also be comment about the personal dynamics that aided and impeded this growth and for the significance of the factors in fostering student attainment of Bloom's liberal arts-underpinning higher-order cognitive skills of application, analysis, synthesis and evaluation.

In order to contextualize subsequent discussion, the course of study will be explained in the following section.

The course of study

All courses at AUS are accredited by the Commission for Academic Accreditation of the Ministry of Higher Education and Scientific Research in the UAE as well as by the Commission on Higher Education of the Middle States Association of Colleges and Schools (MSCHE), Philadelphia, USA.

The course adopts an orthodox blended-learning approach integrating different learning environments (Graham, 2005). Face-to-face methods are combined with online, computer-mediated procedures, creating an integrated approach for both professor and learners. The educational philosophy that informs the course draws strongly on constructivism and social interaction. Students studying the course are expected to be actively involved through a mix of individual, pair and teamwork activities involving projects, exploratory investigations, workshops and seminars as well as more standard academic tasks such as reports and critical reviews. In this approach there is a strong concern to assist students in developing their understanding of learning theories and related teaching approaches so as to be able to react intelligently to the vast array of available digital information, whatever their field of study.

This concern relates closely to the Information Literacy Competency Standards for higher education endorsed by the US Association of College and Research Libraries (ACRL) and to the development of life-long learning, which the ACRL sees as central to the mission of higher education institutions. Development of students' intellectual abilities of reasoning, critical thinking and understanding how to learn provides a basis for continued growth beyond the classroom. Practice with self-directed investigations relating to internships, first professional positions and responsibilities in all arenas of life is considered a key outcome for college students by regional and discipline-based accreditation associations such as the MSCHE.

To address these matters, students worked in key areas germane to information literacy and experiential learning: website elements, digital social environments (blogs, social media), materials (writing, presentation and review) and collaborative online exchange. In this blend of different learning environments face-to-face classroom methods were combined with online, computer-mediated procedures, creating an integrated approach for both professor and learners. Much of the course was conducted through electronic modes such as Blackboard (course management software called iLearn at AUS), student blog communities, an AUS LibGuide (software from Springshare [2014], which links course materials, library web pages and course management system resources with remote server hosting), websites and other online teaching resources in order to demonstrate and build knowledge about digital teaching and learning. Face-to-face learning was nonetheless an important aspect of the course, both in the regular classes and also in the collaborative learning and practical tasks, which were significant elements of the course requirements. The approach sits well with findings from an extensive investigation conducted by Paechter and Maier (2010), which noted that students 'preferred face-to-face learning for communication purposes in which a shared understanding has to be derived or in which interpersonal relations are to be established' (p. 292), while online learning was favoured for skills development in self-regulated learning.

Finally, the course was conducted in a manner that sought to develop a community of practice by strong emphasis on professionalism and ethics. These are the fundamental tools for enabling lifelong learning, according to the OECD (2004). Such learning principles align with the AUS General Education Program Goals: Goal E, 'reflect on the consequences of individual and collective human action', Goal H, 'develop the skills and abilities to thoughtfully seek information, critically analyze sources and clearly formulate complex ideas' and Goal I, 'investigate how digital technology can facilitate inquiry and the advancement of knowledge' (AUS Undergraduate Catalog, 2014–2015). The approach contrasts with the transmission model of education still prevalent in the Middle East North Africa (MENA) region (Diligent, 2011). In the next section, the significance of situated learning will be discussed.

Situated learning

This approach is based on the view that that learning is not simply the transmission of abstract and decontextualized knowledge from one person to another, or to others. Rather, learning is embedded in social co-participation; it is a 'sociocultural phenomenon rather than the action of an individual acquiring general information from a decontextualized body of knowledge' (Kirshner and Whitson, 1997). Situated learning was first proposed by Lave and Wenger (1991) as a model of learning in what they described as a community of practice. Wenger (2007) later described these communities as being:

> formed by people who engage in a process of collective learning ... a group of engineers working on similar problems, a clique of pupils defining their identity in the school ... In a nutshell: Communities of practice are groups of people who share a concern or a passion for something they do and learn how to do it better as they interact regularly.

Three elements distinguish a community of practice from other groups. First, a community of practice has an *identity* marked by a shared domain of interest, which distinguishes its members. Second, *the community* members engage in joint activities and discussions; they assist one another and share information. These relationships facilitate learning from each other. Over time, a community of practice develops a shared range of resources and experiences, *which they can utilize to address problems*. This is the shared practice.

There is ample evidence that teaching and learning about skills in meaningful contexts reinforces the significance of the skills by demonstrating their appropriate uses in authentic communication situations (Amare and Brammer, 2005;

Predmore, 2005; Yang, 2010; Kreber and Klampfleitner, 2013). Early work by Paris and Winograd (1990) showed that transferring responsibility for monitoring learning to students through development of problem-solving strategies improves their learning because of an increased awareness of their thinking in applying these strategies. Improved levels of motivation and positive self-perception may also result and the social exchange environment of a developing community of practice recalls aspects of Vygotsky's (1978) theory of socially mediated learning. This collaborative, learner-centred approach, where students are actively engaged in the discovery and construction of their own knowledge and meaning through attempting solutions to real problems from their surrounding environment, reflects Choo (2007), who aptly states 'There is an increasing need to train students to solve real-world problems so that they can handle complex problems in their workplace' (p. 187).

Students in EDU307 worked in three blog communities, which also became their communities of practice. Structured tasks, described later in the chapter, engaged students in discovery and construction of knowledge and meaning through solving real problems in their communities. Situated learning supported the pedagogic models and structured tasks that, combined, shaped the work students undertook in this course.

In the following section the influence of the three pedagogic models that enabled the students to build communities of practice will be discussed.

Three pedagogic models

1. Bartlett-Bragg's five-stage educational blogging model

Bartlett-Bragg (2003) describes options for integrating blogging into teaching, presents guidelines for the use of blogs and discusses theory that supports the use she describes. The significant part of her work is concerned with presenting a pedagogic strategy that can be used to enhance reflective learning by using blogs. Her five-stage model (shown in Figure 2.1) moves from recording personal feelings to evaluation and writing for a more general audience to personal reflections on learning to developing a voice or style and the reporting of classroom events to reflecting on knowledge learned and providing guidance for other readers.

The three blog communities in EDU307 were especially useful for collaborative student engagement in many of their tasks and in particular for their work on critique of significant professional and academic literature. For this academic task they used a five-point critique structure (Prescott, 2007) and initially worked in groups of three to write critiques and peer review colleagues' work from their own blog community, then for a second critique from another blog community. The next stage was to repeat the process of writing critiques and reviewing

Establishment ➔ Introspection ➔ Reflective monologues ➔ Reflective dialogue ➔ Knowledge artefact

Figure 2.1 Bartlett-Bragg's five-stage model of blog community development.

22 David Prescott

colleagues' work, but this time writing in pairs reviewing an assigned critique and a critique of choice. Finally, they critiqued individually the Manuela Paechter and Brigitte Maier article 'Online or face-to-face? Students' experiences and preferences in e-learning', as this article has a high degree of relevance to the work with which the students were engaged. This work is explained in more detail in the section concerning structured tasks. A list of articles students critiqued is at Appendix B.

2. Ruben Puentedura's SAMR model

Students used the four-stage SAMR model (SAMR and Bloom's Taxonomy, 2014) to guide practical aspects of their work. The model provides an excellent framework for self-directed investigations and projects and provides support for students transitioning from the comfortable world of the tertiary institution and its support systems to the world of work. In EDU307 students were introduced to the model with nearly two thirds of the course completed and with the important challenge of a practical project imminent. An adaptation of the SAMR model incorporating elements students in EDU307 engaged with is in Figure 2.2.

This work relates to Bloom's Taxonomy, an alignment on which Puentedura has elaborated in a number of documents including SAMR and Bloom's Taxonomy (2014). Tasks at the substitution stage of the model are equivalent to recall tasks. As the complexity of tasks increases through augmentation and modification and finally to redefinition, so too the cognitive engagement becomes more complex, requiring behaviours ranging from understanding through application, analysis and evaluation to creation.

At the redefinition level students were challenged to synthesize understandings from professional literature critique on the one hand and an authentic case study

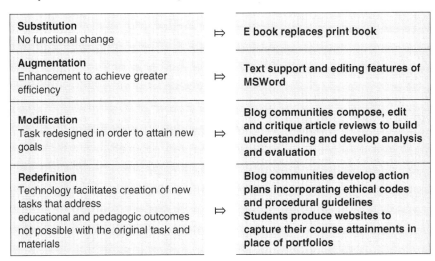

Substitution No functional change	⇒	E book replaces print book
Augmentation Enhancement to achieve greater efficiency	⇒	Text support and editing features of MSWord
Modification Task redesigned in order to attain new goals	⇒	Blog communities compose, edit and critique article reviews to build understanding and develop analysis and evaluation
Redefinition Technology facilitates creation of new tasks that address educational and pedagogic outcomes not possible with the original task and materials	⇒	Blog communities develop action plans incorporating ethical codes and procedural guidelines Students produce websites to capture their course attainments in place of portfolios

Figure 2.2 SAMR model adapted to coursework.

Pedagogic models and structured tasks 23

(Higgins, 1998) on the other to draft, discuss and finalize action plans to guide their practical work. Furthermore, they were expected to develop, design and maintain websites that stored and displayed their coursework following principles of effective web design, which they studied during the course.

3. Blended learning five interactions model

Clearly, engagement with situated learning and collaboration through engagement in structured tasks requires students to become closely engaged in their own learning. This means it is necessary to shift to a paradigm of learning that allows students to explore and engage in multiple levels of learning. This type of student engagement can be achieved with a mix of the interactions in the blended learning model shown in Figure 2.3.

This model supports students' undertaking real-world activities to consolidate understanding and develop the authentic skills they will be able to use as they advance into their academic and real-world future. Such attainments are in keeping with societal expectations. During his visit to the UAE in 2014, Andreas Schleicher, one of the architects of the Organization for Economic Co-operation and Development's (OECD) Pisa Examination and its special adviser on education policy, pointed out that 'skills are highly predictive of your future success' (Skills are more important than formal qualifications, 2014). The data presented by Mr Schleicher showed there is a high demand for problem solvers, effective communicators and creative thinkers. Students must be able to go beyond learning content, as 'the knowledge economy does not pay for what you know, but for what you can do with what you know'.

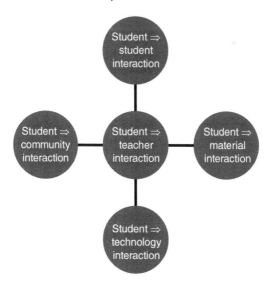

Figure 2.3 Five interactions of a robust blended learning model (adapted from Teach Thought, 2015).

In the section that follows student engagement with structured tasks will be briefly discussed.

Structured tasks

Over 100 years ago W. T. Harris warned of the restricting influence of the classroom: 'The habit of teaching with too much thoroughness and too-long continued drill ... often leaves the pupil fixed in lower stages of growth and unable to exercise the higher functions of thought' (Harris, 1898, p. 7, cited in Mann, 1979, p. 349) With Harris's warning in mind, tasks in EDU307 drew on the Opening Minds project of the United Kingdom Royal Society of Arts (RSA Opening Minds), which focuses on equipping students for a life beyond education in the technological and global contexts of society, as an exemplar. The project emphasizes learning, citizenship, relating to people, managing situations and managing information. The Royal Society of Arts has challenged the traditional view that these issues develop naturally in the classroom and argued has that these are competencies that should be taught. The philosophy at the core of the Opening Minds project rests on an attitude as to how teaching and learning are organized and to the purpose of education that is very different from a traditional approach. This project, with its emphasis on sharing objectives with students and learning to use digital technology for developing discerning information handling and effective communication and problem-solving skills, provided an appropriate foundation for rich tasks in EDU307.

The concept of rich tasks is characterized:

> What is *not* meant is a common usage; that is a technology or media rich task. A rich learning task is one that involves learners in higher order cognitive skills such as those in Bloom's Taxonomy; that is application, analysis, synthesis and evaluation. In undertaking such tasks learners are involved in solving problems, identifying hidden meanings and patterns, relating knowledge from several areas, drawing conclusions, assessing the value of ideas and theories, verifying the value of evidence and comparing and discriminating between ideas.
> (Prescott, 2004, p. 135)

The influence of pedagogic models and situated learning is clearly seen by a brief examination of the rich, structured tasks students worked with in EDU307. For instance, work at the knowledge artefact stage of the Bartlett-Bragg five-stage model of blog community development culminated in three significant products. First, the students each wrote individual article critiques, which were then shared among community members. Second, they developed blog community action plans to foster effective and principled interactions within these communities. Third, they developed of a set of website evaluation criteria for the appraisal of peers' websites.

Pedagogic models and structured tasks 25

The journal article critique work (Figure 2.4) illustrates how a pedagogic model, structured tasks and situated learning can be integrated to provide a learning pathway to advance students' intellectual growth. The elements of this pathway are comprised of, first, the five-point article critique, which provides students with an effective tool for critiquing academic and (in their careers) professional literature. The structured article critique task that 'shadows' the three advanced stages of Bartlett-Bragg's five-stage model of blog community development (reflective monologue, reflective dialogue and knowledge artefact) supports the students through familiarization with the article critique, engaging outside a familiar community and finally producing individual knowledge artefacts.

Five point article critique (Prescott, 2007)

Context and credentials	What is the context of the article; what is it concerned with; who are the authors; what are their credentials and authority?
Concern/focus	What is the main concern; what is the focus of the article?
Evidence	What evidence or data is presented; by what method(s) [tables, figures, statistics, discussion and so forth]?
Methodology	What methods were used to obtain the data?
Findings	What are the main findings, conclusions or arguments?

Structured article critique task

Reflective monologue	Critique article in groups of 3 drawn from students' own blog communities and peer review another group's critique from same community
Reflective monologue	Critique article in groups of 3 drawn from students' own blog communities and peer review another group's critique from different community
Reflective dialogue	Critique article in pairs from students' own blog communities and peer review another group's critique (self-choice)
Reflective dialogue	Critique article in pairs from students' own blog communities and peer review another group's critique (assigned)
Knowledge artefact	Individual critique of Online or face-to-face? Students' experiences and preferences in e-learning Manuela Paechter and Brigitte Maier. This study involved a sample of 2000+ students of both genders, studying in 29 Austrian universities. The article was highly germane to EDU307 students in that it reported students' preferences for online communication when information is disseminated in contrast to their preference for face-to-face interaction when they have to establish a joint solution or social relations with other course participants. In other words it was an endorsement of the teaching approach taken with students in EDU307.

Figure 2.4 Integration of pedagogic model, structured tasks and situated learning.

26 *David Prescott*

The final two stages of the critique task dealt with situated learning in that they required students to engage with academic and professional literature and to 'thoughtfully seek information, critically analyse sources and clearly formulate complex ideas' in preparation for these obligations in their professional careers or in further post graduate academic study.

Other integrated structured tasks involved development of personal websites, which became the artefact of record of each student's engagement with the course content. These websites allowed for the consolidation and application of a range of investigative work, which included investigating exemplar and defective websites, identifying factors that determine effective website design, reading professional literature and examining existing website evaluation models. This work resulted in the development of individual websites and the design, trial and implementation of a website evaluation instrument (Appendix C).

At the redefinition level of the SAMR model the following teamwork was significant. First, students worked on the development of guidelines for effective teamwork. These guidelines grew out of the investigation of an authentic case study of the North Sea Piper Alpha oil rig disaster (Higgins, 1998), a case study that illustrates the seriousness of basic communication failures, failure to plan ahead and inadequate emergency decision-making procedures. Students developed guidelines within their blog communities to highlight the importance of communication, documentation, analysis, risk reduction monitoring and review. They then carried these understandings to their practical project teams to inform and support the practical projects they undertook, listed at Appendix D. Furthermore, student teams developed instructional materials such as a set of visuals for the teaching of elementary mathematics, (virtual) bridge design software for engineering freshmen, and a brainstorming and mind-mapping mobile phone app. The salient aspects of these knowledge artefacts are that they build on relationships between people and enable students to connect prior knowledge with authentic, contextual learning. In these situations, students' roles change from passive observers to active participants, allowing the learning to occur through collaboration and 'sharing of purposeful, patterned activity' (Lave and Wenger, 1991, p. 40).

This chapter will conclude with comment about the students' attainment and the personal dynamics that aided or impeded growth and attainment.

Attainment

AUS students are required to evaluate their courses of study near the conclusion of each semester. In these university-wide evaluations they respond to two sets of questions, course related and instructor related. Respondents specify their level of agreement or disagreement on a five-point agree–disagree scale for a series of statements in question sets. Students are able to add reflective comments after each question set in order to clarify or to amplify their ratings. The EDU307 evaluations in Spring 2014 compared favourably with overall Department of English faculty and overall AUS faculty for both course- and instructor-related questions.

Apart from these course evaluations, student attainment can be measured by student performance in the assessment tasks. In this course, the average 84.90 and standard deviation of 5.05 compared favourably with an earlier delivery of the course in 2013 – average 88.78 with standard deviation of 3.05, revealing a greater spread of results in the course under discussion. In the practical assignment (17.51 against 16.49), the materials assignment (13.50 against 13.65) and the website assignment (17.57 against 18.38), results again revealed a close similarity, with standard deviations being higher (and results more spread) in the latest course offering, that under discussion in this chapter.

More useful were the personal reflections that students produced once the course was completed and they had been able to consider what they had experienced, what they had carried over from the course, and its relevance to their subsequent study or work. Evaluation after a course has been completed and time has passed rarely happens (Taylor, 1996); it is much more common for evaluation to occur at, or even before, the completion of a course, as in the case of the university evaluations already commented on.

The post-course reflection about collaborative learning concentrated on three key issues:

- joint intellectual efforts by students as opposed to joint intellectual efforts by students and the professor;
- student groups working together to search for understanding;
- solutions to create an artefact or product of learning.

The student responses [R = 21/N = 26] were analysed using Srivastava's Iterative Analysis framework (what the data reveal, what the researcher wants to know, what interaction exists between these two elements) (Srivastava and Hopwood, 2009).

In terms of students' joint intellectual efforts, the use of blogging, both within students' 'home' communities and with members of other blog communities, was endorsed as a means of facilitating these efforts. The approach allowed power to move 'from the teacher to students ... who were allowed to express their ideas and opinions while also receiving the guidance and feedback of the professor' if required. The work benefitted in particular the practical project, where work needed to be divided up 'for effective completion of the project'.

In terms of student groups working together to search for understanding, students identified this as a characteristic of working together on an assignment with the focus moved away from the professor and power and responsibility residing with the students. Discussion of ideas, listening to other points of view and comparing answers to create a cohesive response were considered important because 'in many instances students present unique ideas that give new insight to their peers'. It was agreed that this process results in authority that is with the 'whole community of students'.

In terms of solutions to create an artefact or product of learning, the student responses showed the value placed on reflection upon their own learning process and how this enabled a more appropriate response to the needs of the target learner group (materials assignment), client (practical project) and viewer (website assignment). The point was also made by many students that reflection on and integration of personal learning experiences eventually allows for the creation of a solution unique to a particular group working together on a project. In these responses it can be noted that students articulate a high level of attainment in terms of the course objectives.

Conclusion

Integration of situated learning, pedagogic models and structured tasks offers much that is beneficial and relevant to university students transitioning from the academy to the workplace. The effective use of digital resources and provision of opportunities for students to be active participants in building their knowledge and developing their skills is beneficial if the engagement with technology is strongly underpinned by sound educational procedure. The case study reported in this chapter has identified three practices that contribute to attainment of Bloom's higher-order cognitive skills; application, analysis, synthesis and evaluation.

First, engaging students in 'rich', structured tasks that involve problem-based learning and offer opportunities for creative and critical thinking is important. Open-ended tasks that offer possibilities for student ownership and self-direction but which require personal management and communication are important elements to aid individual development. Second, pedagogic models that aim to facilitate enquiry and the advancement of knowledge are integral to 'rich' tasks. Finally, situated learning can engage students in active, socially oriented learning and provide opportunities for the integration of new knowledge into existing understandings. This can encourage capacity building for enabling lifelong learning as defined by the OECD (2004).

In this study it is clear that a majority of students were able to make substantial attainment of the course objectives, as evidenced by their overall results, their performance on individual tasks, their evaluations of the course and their reflective comments on the three issues discussed earlier. Further endorsement is clear in this student comment: 'It is a very, very interesting course and opened broader perspectives for us in terms of utilizing technologies into constructive learning and teaching.'

However, one of the challenges of this teaching and learning approach is the strong commitment expected from students. Robertson, Fluck and Webb (2004) have noted that passive learners will not have the capacity to meet the learning challenges fundamental to the work reported in this case study. The final word rests with the student for whom the course remained a mystery: 'The course is very, very, very vague. I felt I was a lab rat.'

References

Amare, N. and Brammer, C. (2005). Perceptions of memo quality: a case study of engineering practitioners, professors, and students. *Journal of Technical Writing and Communication* 35(2), 179–190.

American Library Association (2012). Information literacy competency standards for higher education. Retrieved from www.ala.org/acrl/standards/informationliteracy competency

American University of Sharjah, Undergraduate Catalog (2014–2015). Retrieved from www.aus.edu/info/200144/information_and_support/343/university_cat alogs/1

Bartlett-Bragg, A. (2003). Blogging to learn. Retrieved from http://knowledgetree. flexiblelearning.net.au/edition04/pdf/Blogging_to_Learn.pdf

Burns, R.B. (1990). *Introduction to research methods*. Melbourne: Longman.

Choo, C. B. (2007). Activity-based approach to authentic learning in a vocational institute. *Educational Media International* 44(3), 185–205.

Diligent, L. (2011). Teaching conditions faced by teachers in the rural Middle East and North Africa [web log post, 22 November]. Retrieved from https://expattutor.wordpress.com/tag/teaching-conditions-in-public-schools-in-north-africa/

Flyvbjerg, B. (2011). Case study. In N.K. Denzin and Y.S. Lincoln (eds), *The Sage Handbook of Qualitative Research* (pp. 301–316). Thousand Oaks CA: Sage.

Graham, C.R. (2005). Blended learning systems: definition, current trends and future directions. In C.J. Bonk and C.R. Graham (eds), *Handbook of blended learning: global perspectives, local designs* (pp. 3–21). San Francisco: Pfeiffer.

Harris, W.T. (1898). Psychological foundations of education. Cited in L. Mann (1979). *On the Trail of Process*. New York: Grune & Stratton.

Higgins, B. (1998). *Spiral to Disaster*. BBC, UK.

Kirschner, D. and Whitson, J. (eds) (1997). *Situated cognition: social, semiotic and psychological perspectives*. Mahwah NJ: Lawrence Erlbaum Associates.

Kreber, C. and Klampfleitner, M. (2013). Lecturers' and students' conceptions of authenticity in teaching and actual teacher actions and attributes students perceive as helpful. *Higher Education* 66(4), 463–487.

Lave, J. and Wenger, E. (1991). *Situated Learning*. New York: Cambridge.

OECD (2004). Policy brief: lifelong learning. Retrieved from www.oecd.org/dataoecd/17/11/29478789.pdf

Paechter, M. and Maier, B. (2010). Online or face-to-face? Students' experiences and preferences in e-learning. *Internet and Higher Education* 13(4), 292–297.

Paris, S.G. and Winograd, P. (1990). How meta-cognition can promote academic learning and instruction. In B.F. Jones and L. Idol (eds), *Dimensions of thinking and cognitive instruction*. Mahwah NJ: Lawrence Erlbaum Associates.

Predmore, S.R. (2005). Putting it into context. *Techniques* 80, 22–25.

Prescott, D. (2004). Opening minds and rich learning: learning, information and communications technology. In A. Hashimi and N. Hassan (eds), *English in Southeast Asia: prospects, perspectives and possibilities* (pp. 123–140). Kuala Lumpur: University of Malaya Press.

Prescott, D. (2007). Article review for undergraduate science students. *Malaysian Journal of ELT Research* 3. Retrieved from www.melta.org.my/modules/tinycontent/Dos/majer_article_2007_prescott.pdf

Prescott, D. (2013). One of those give-and-take kinds of courses. *English Australia Journal* 28(2), 21–37.
Robertson, M., Fluck, A. and Webb, I. (2004). Children, on-line learning and authentic teaching skills in primary education. Retrieved from www.educ.utas.edu.au/users/ilwebb/Research
RSA Opening Minds (n.d.). Retrieved from www.rsaopeningminds.org.uk/about-rsa-openingminds/
SAMR and Bloom's Taxonomy: assembling the puzzle (2014). Retrieved from https://www.graphite.org/blog/samr-and-blooms-taxonomy-assembling-the-puzzle
The National (2014), 'Skills are more important than formal qualifications, UAE educators told', 6 January. Retrieved from www.thenational.ae/uae/education/skills-are-more-important-than-formal-qualifications-uae-educators-told
Springshare, Inc. (2014). Retrieved from www.springshare.com/
Srivastava, P. and Hopwood, N. (2009). A practical iterative framework for qualitative data analysis. *International Journal of Qualitative Methods* 8(1), 76–84.
Stake, R.E. (2008). Qualitative case studies. In N.K. Denzin and Y.S. Lincoln (eds), *Strategies of qualitative inquiry*, 3rd ed. (pp. 119–150). Thousand Oaks CA: Sage.
Taylor, R. (1996). Training cultures and teaching cultures. IATEFL Research SIG Newsletter, pp. 121–127.
The 5 interactions of a robust blended learning model (n.d.). Retrieved from www.teachthought.com/wp-content/uploads/2013/04/5-interactions-of-a-blended-learning-model.jpg
Wenger, E. (2007). Communities of practice: a brief introduction. Retrieved from http://wenger-trayner.com/introduction-to-communities-of-practice/
Yang, X. (2010). How to achieve authentic context in classroom oral English teaching. *Journal of Language Teaching and Research* 1(3), 339–342.

Appendix A Course objectives

- identify and apply the basic elements common to various approaches for website evaluation;
- explain and illustrate, by example, the ethical and social implications of teaching and learning in an electronic environment (a Content Management System [CMS] or a Virtual Learning Environment [VLE]);
- demonstrate by example the ethical and social implications of teaching and learning in a digital social environment (forums, shared whiteboards, e-portfolios, weblogs and wikis);
- demonstrate the ability to use digital technology to enhance analysis, description and presentation;
- construct and maintain a website that summarizes knowledge acquired on the course, embodies elements conducive to teaching and learning, and demonstrates positive, beneficial collaborative online learning behaviours

Appendix B Articles critiqued

Brooks, C.D. (2011). Space matters: the impact of formal learning environments on student learning. *British Journal of Educational Technology* 42(5), 719–726.

Chambers, A. and Bax, S. (2006). Making CALL work: towards normalization. *System* 34, 465–479.

Chen, X.-B. (2013). Tablets for informal language learning: student usage and attitudes. *Language Learning and Technology* 17(1), 20–36.

Hamat, A. and Embi, M.A. (2005). The application of learning theories to the design of course management systems. *International Journal of Pedagogies and Learning* 1(2), 57–64.

Hungerford-Kresser, H., Wiggins, J. and Amaro-Jiménez, C. (2011). Learning from our mistakes: what matters when incorporating blogging in the content area literacy classroom. *Journal of Adolescent and Adult Literacy* 55(4), 326–335.

Kear, K. et al. (2010). From forums to wikis: perspectives on tools for collaboration. *The Internet and Higher Education* 13(4), 218–225.

Li, Q. (2007). Student and teacher views about technology: a tale of two cities? *Journal of Research on Technology in Education* 39(4), 377–397.

Lim, H.L. and Sudweeks, F. (2009). Constructivism and online collaborative group learning in higher education: a case study. In C.R. Payne (ed.), *Information technology and constructivism in higher education: progressive learning frameworks*. Hershey, PA: Idea Group, pp. 231–246.

Paechter, M. and Maier, B. (2010). Online or face-to-face? Students' experiences and preferences in e-learning. *Internet and Higher Education* 13(4), 292–297.

Ward, N.D., Finley, R.J., Keil, R. and Clay, T.G. (2013). Benefits and limitations of iPads in the high school science classroom and a trophic cascade lesson plan. *Journal of Geoscience Education* 61(4), 378–384.

Zhu, C. (2012). Student satisfaction, performance, and knowledge construction in online collaborative learning. *Educational Technology and Society* 15(1), 127–136.

Appendix C EDU 307 Website Evaluation S14

Credentials

Who wrote the page	Currency/last updated	Author's credentials	Contact information

Quality indicators

Links to resources/do they work? Too many?	Reproduced and sourced information complete/acknowledged

Purpose of website/evidence

4-second rule	Persuade	Explain	Share	Inform

Design

No clutter	Use of white space	Graphics/text in harmony	Use of color

Text

Logical info categories	Cogent text	Font consistency	Accuracy

Navigation

Descriptive links	Where am I?	Forward/back navigation	Link to home page

Content

All content as listed in the Website content doc is included

Overall rating [comment]

_____

_____

_____

_____

Appendix D Practical projects

Online Journal Project for Department of English – the project is to establish a website based on existing models for Dr Maya Kesrouany DOE.
Arduino microcontroller-based board website with videos, tutorials and other useful information so engineering students can use Arduino effectively in their senior design projects for Dr Aydin Yesildirek CEN EE.
GPA calculator website to calculate students' semester and/or cumulative GPA [major v total GPA] for CEN CE.
Website for the course EDU315 Emotional Intelligence for Dr Rana Raddawi DOE.
MATLAB Workshop of three plus a website/blog where the relevant material will be posted along with recorded lectures for AUS Student Council and Dr Hasan Mir CEN ELE.
Internship website for the CEN Civil Engineering Department to familiarize students with the internship procedure and its requirements for Dr Ghassan Abu-Lebdeh CEN, CVE.
Website resource for ENG207 poster preparation and presentation for Dr David Prescott DOE and faculty teaching ENG207.

3 Technology-enhanced language instruction
Are we in the loop?

Saleh Al-Shehri

Introduction

Several researchers in both educational technology and applied linguistics have critically evaluated the potential of technology in language teaching/learning. Technology evaluation was meant to explore the effectiveness of instructional technologies for improving language instruction outcomes and providing students with better opportunities to use the language inside and outside the classroom. In this chapter, we will review some of the previous approaches and studies that evaluated the potential of technology for language instruction. The study is also an attempt to investigate perceptions of both EFL (English as a Foreign Language) students and teachers about educational technology and language instruction. This study is also an evaluation of technology-mediated language learning at a tertiary institution in Saudi Arabia, and whether students and teachers benefited from the implementation of technology tools. An overview of participants' views about the optimal practices of educational technologies for language instruction is also provided.

Literature review

There have been several attempts by researchers and applied linguists to evaluate the potential of technology for language instruction. For example, the Technology Acceptance Model, or TAM, was implemented to investigate how users come to accept and use technology for language-learning purposes. TAM usually focuses on two major factors: perceived usefulness and perceived ease of use of technology (Davis, 1989). The model has been upgraded to TAM2 (Unified Theory of Acceptance and Use of Technology), which has more focus on intentions and behaviour of technology users (see Figure 3.1). TAM3 was also developed to include effects of trust and perceived risk on system use (Venkatesh and Bala, 2008).

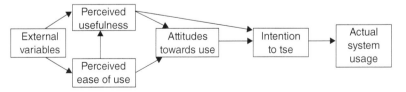

Figure 3.1 Technology Acceptance Model (adapted from Davis, 1989).

In language instruction, Cakir and Solak (2014) used TAM to understand the attitudes of Turkish EFL university students towards technology and to determine the impact of technology on their academic achievement. Cakir and Solak's study was conducted with 510 university students taking English through technology. Students benefited from videos, notes, files and so on prepared by language teachers in an e-learning context. The study revealed that anxiety towards technology had a negative impact on students' academic achievement. However, the study found that other factors had positive impact on students' achievement, such as perceived ease of use, attitudes, satisfaction and self-efficacy. The study concluded that intentions and continuity of EFL students could be improved by teachers' supervision and feedback when necessary.

Ng, Shroff and Lim (2013) also implemented a modified TAM to examine the benefits and challenges of field experience paper-based portfolios versus digital portfolios for EFL student teachers studying at the Hong Kong Institute of Education. The study was conducted with 77 participants using e-portfolios to demonstrate their language learning achievement and skills during field experience. Unlike paper-based portfolios, participants indicated that e-portfolios were more convenient, user friendly and organized. However, the study found that participants' willingness to use technology was lower than expected, and that there was a tendency among participants to use tools they were familiar with, i.e. paper-based portfolios.

In theory, there have been different attempts by several researchers to design evaluation approaches for educational technology, particularly in language instruction. Chambers (2010) reviewed three notable books that include specific sections on technology evaluation for language learning. These were *Computer-assisted language learning: context and conceptualization* by Michael Levy (1997), *Computer applications in second language acquisition: foundations for teaching, testing and research* by Carol Chapelle (2001) and *CALL dimensions: options and issues in computer-assisted language learning* by Mike Levy and Glenn Stockwell (2006). Chambers' review of the three books on evaluation is summarized in Table 3.1 below.

In particular, Chapelle (2001) conducted a comprehensive analysis of past and contemporary educational technologies used in second language instruction, where technology had a positive impact. Based on the analysis, Chapelle developed a set of six criteria that can be used to evaluate the potential of technology tools for second language instruction. The criteria include language learning potential, learners' fit, meaning focus, authenticity, positive impact and practicality. The criteria was used as an evaluation framework of technology implemented in the context of the study. The reason underpinning the choice of Chapelle's criteria was that they make a clear distinction between language learning and language use. In addition, it is more focused rather than simply creating opportunities for the students to use the language through technology. In addition, Chapelle's criteria would help in evaluating the usefulness of technology rather than focusing solely on the design of technology itself. Much research has been done on technology design and/or device rather than the demands of pedagogy and subject matter.

Table 3.1 Evaluation of technology for language instruction reviewed from three books (adapted from Chambers, 2010)

The book	Characteristics of evaluation
Computer-assisted language learning: Context and conceptualization	• Complexity of CALL (computer-assisted language learning) evaluation was recognized; evaluation was a multifaceted activity rather than a search for the perfect teaching tool • Discussion on developments in approaches to evaluation
Computer applications in second language acquisition: Foundations for teaching, testing and research	• A Focus on the need for principles and criteria for evaluation drawn from SLA (second language acquisition) research • Evaluation is a complex issue, involving a context-specific argument rather than a categorical judgment of effectiveness.
CALL dimensions: Options and issues in computer-assisted language learning	• Discussion on the difficult distinction between evaluation and research • Detailed guidance on methodology to CALL researchers • Devotion to the role of the designer-evaluator; deeper understanding of the learner context and learner needs

Notably, Chambers (2010) argues that the importance of technology evaluation comes as a result of its key position – '"at the interface between design, theory, research and practice' (p. 119). Thus, there have been different attempts by researchers and applied linguists to list different theories and learning approaches that they thought were relevant to language learning with technology (see, for example, Sharples, Taylor and Vavoula, 2005; Levy and Stockwell). The effectiveness of technology evaluation seemed impossible with no theoretical foundations. Relevant theories are grouped in five categories: 'psychology, artificial intelligence, computational linguistics, instructional technology and design, and Human–Computer Interaction studies' (Chambers, 2010, p. 117). Chapelle, as cited in Chambers (2010), lists only education, linguistics and psychology as the relevant fields to computer-assisted language learning. Mobile language learning and language learning with social media were two recent examples of new fields that still need theoretical foundations that can lead to effective evaluation. For example, Herrington, Herrington and Mantei (2009) developed a set of design principles that can be used as guidelines for mobile learning. Al-Shehri (2013) implemented these design principles with a design-based research approach to develop design principles for mobile language learning. Al-Shehri (2011) also implemented some principles of connectivism as guidelines for language learning with social media. Both studies illustrated the need for theoretical foundations for language learning with innovative technologies. Al-Shehri's studies also highlighted the potential of new technologies and social media tools to enrich the language learning experience. As mentioned, theoretical grounds are necessary for the evaluation of educational technology to be accurate and successful.

Methodology

This study is an evaluation enquiry of the potential of technology for language learning/teaching using Chapelle's criteria. Using a qualitative approach, 24 female students studying an English course with technology were surveyed. Female students had to interact with their classmates and English language instructor through Blackboard virtual classes. Moreover, 13 English language university teachers were surveyed. Data obtained from the surveys were analysed and discussed. An evaluation of the potential of technology for language instruction was then provided.

This study explored the following research questions:

1 To what extent has technology helped to transform language instruction in the university to be more student-centred and democratic, and to what extent can students see themselves as capable and independent?
2 After a decade, what strengths and weaknesses has the use of instructional technology highlighted?
3 Do innovative or traditional technologies have greater impact on language instruction, and does cost matter?
4 What are the optimal language learning/teaching environments, experiences and approaches that technology can enhance in Saudi Arabian and Gulf contexts?

Participants

This study was conducted with 24 female students studying Master of General Curriculum and Methodologies degrees and taking an English Terminologies course through Blackboard virtual classes. Students on the course practised different language learning skills like reading, writing, speaking, listening and translation. Students were also required to choose scientific texts and extract terminologies relevant to their field. It should be noted that gender-segregated education is practised at all Saudi public schools and universities, where male teachers are only allowed to interact with female students via audio channels or virtual classes; female students are not visible to their male teachers. As most of these female students' teachers were male, courses taught by male teachers were only available via virtual classes. All the students who participated in the study were believed to have excellent computer skills. Female students completed quizzes and homework through Blackboard, and were required to complete paper-based final exams at the end of the semester. Paper-based surveys were delivered to student participants and collected after being completed.

In addition, 13 EFL teachers participated in the study. Teacher participants of the study were both native and non-native speakers of English. Native speakers were of American, British and South African origins. Non-native speakers belonged to some Asian countries: Pakistan, India and Bangladesh. Most teachers held professional degrees in EFL education that ranged from diplomas to doctorates. The average years of experience for the teachers was 10, and ages ranged from 25 to 50. About 30 per cent of the teachers had taught at the university for more than 10 years, whereas the other 70 per cent had only 1–2 years' teaching experience at the university. Teachers with more experience had direct contracts with the university; other teachers with less experience worked for the university through a private operator. All teachers were working at the Preparation Year male campus, King Khalid University.

Context of the study

This study was conducted at the Preparation Year campus and postgraduate female students' campus, King Khalid University, Saudi Arabia. The university started an ambitious e-learning initiative in 2005 in an attempt to cope with innovative trends of educational technology. The Deanship of E-Learning is one of the most successful sectors and has won several excellence prizes locally and internationally. E-learning was launched in 2006 as an optional facilitative learning tool, with Blackboard® as the official university Learning Management System (LMS), and became compulsory for all students and teachers two years later. The university was the first Saudi institution to launch Mobile Blackboard in 2011, which enabled most students and teachers to access their learning/teaching material via their mobile devices. E-learning intensive training is available for all new students and teachers via both face-to-face and online courses. Wi-Fi networks are available for students, teachers and visitors at all campuses.

Procedure

Paper-based surveys were delivered to all female students who showed interest in participating in the study. Students' version of the survey include one open-ended question that enquired about the potential of technology for language learning, and what positives and negatives could be associated with educational technology. Surveys were collected after they were completed via the female students' coordinator.

The teachers' version of the survey was distributed to all teacher participants via their e-mail addresses. The survey included nine open-ended questions that asked about the participants' experience as EFL teachers, technology literacy, communication preferences, patterns of student–teacher communications, usage patterns and online interaction via Blackboard. All survey forms were completed within two weeks. Both student and teacher participants were informed that their participation was voluntary, and that their feedback would be used for research purposes.

Data analysis

Qualitative data obtained from the surveys was analysed and then categorized into common patterns and themes. Themes were classified into different areas that were initially investigated by the study comprising Chapelle's (2001) evaluation criteria of language learning technology: language learning potential, learner fit, meaning focus, authenticity, positive impact and practicality. Other themes that were covered by the survey were:

- the role of technology in maintaining student-centred language learning;
- strengths and weaknesses of technology for language learning;
- the impact of traditional vs. innovative technologies; and
- optimal environments, experiences and approaches that technology can enhance in similar language learning/teaching contexts.

Findings

Student participants were surveyed about their experiences with educational technology and asked to list advantages and disadvantages that could have been associated with the use of technology in language learning. Overall, most students indicated that technology had great potential for their language learning experience, and helped them to be active and positive learners: '

> Educational technology is one of important means that transforms learning from being indoctrinated into more creative, interactive, and skilful experience. Technology has helped to get information in shorter time and less effort.
>
> (Participant 433, p. 1)

As female students do not usually interact with their male teachers through face-to-face means, a student noted that technology was an effective learning channel in this respect:

> As female students, technology did not only allow us to learn and benefit from good male teachers, it has also helped us to easily communicate with our teachers, and exchange information and experiences with each other as a learning community.
>
> (Participant 812, p. 1)

In another student's words:

> We do not get the same benefits male students usually get through face-to-face interaction with their male teachers. Technology provided us with effective simulative language learning experience that can, to some extent, be matched with classroom learning experience.
>
> (Participant 871, p. 1)

Technology has also improved some skills beyond language learning:

> The use of technology in our learning experience improved our research skills [meant] it was easier for us to find relevant information and resources and benefit from available tools.
>
> (Participant 628, p. 1)

Technology offered many promises to the students at times and places convenient to them. This was true since most of the students were full-time teachers and/or had family commitments:

> Distance learning or e-learning have all enabled us to pursue our higher studies. Without technology, it would be impossible for most of us to manage our time and study.
>
> (Participant 875, p. 1)

Another student indicated that authentic language learning was maintained through technology:

> The use of technology helped to connect between our learning experience and the surrounding society and life. Some of the real-life experiments or sessions displayed through technology were not possible to be practiced in reality due to the risk or cost involved.
>
> (Participant 875, p. 3)

Most students favoured e-learning training sessions that were available via the university for all new students. They stated that such sessions made them aware of the potential of technology for their language learning experience.

Language learning with technology was not without limitations. Students listed some barriers to the full integration of technology into their language learning experience:

- The lack of awareness among some students and teachers of the potential of technology.
- The lack of readiness among some students to utilize group-work activities, or to share their work with others.
- Some students indicated that they needed more time to use technology for assessment and exam purposes, particularly for open-ended questions.
- Students may rely fully on technology and neglect the role of the teacher as a learning guide and facilitator.
- Older students or teachers were not so inclined towards technology as their younger counterparts.

Surveys delivered to teacher participants, on the other hand, enquired about sophisticated issues that were more relevant to Chapelle's evaluation criteria mentioned before (see Appendix 1). In general, teachers seemed to have excellent computer skills and had professional training; the use of educational technology was a requirement of the university. Teachers, particularly younger ones, indicated that they had used some basic technologies while they were students, including Microsoft Word and PowerPoint, Flash and Java technologies, overhead projectors and audio CDs at language labs. For their current teaching experience, teachers noted that they used tools that their students were familiar with, such as social media and WhatsApp as well as Blackboard:

> I think usefulness of technology in EFL contexts is beyond any debate. Thanks to the internet, social media, LMS, etc., learning has been freed from the four walls of classrooms and libraries.
>
> (Participant 2–1, p. 1)

The same teacher indicated that such innovative technology helped to maintain meaningful language learning experience for his students:

> Tools like LMS, YouTube and social media have made teaching easier and a lot more fun. They help to communicate and teach students in unconventional but effective ways, especially when it comes to skill teaching. Further, they offer options for students to choose the tool that suits their learning strategy.
>
> (Participant 2–1, p.1)

Another teacher felt that current practices of technology for language learning were more conservative:

> In my opinion, technology has helped a lot, but has not been utilized to its full potential. Teaching/learning is still classroom-centred and technological tools like Blackboard are occasionally used.
>
> (Participant 2–2, p. 1)

The same teacher indicated that using new technologies with which students were already familiar might have greater impact on language learning:

> Almost every day, new technologies are hitting the market. The newer and more innovative they are, the greater impact they can have on language instruction. According to me, cost does not matter, as technologies are getting cheaper day by day.
>
> (Participant 2–2, p. 1)

Another teacher emphasized that technology helped his students to be more capable and independent:

> Students can see themselves as independent to some extent in the teaching–learning process as they can try different online materials and learn at their own pace as and when time and resources permit.
>
> (Participant 2–5, p. 1)

Another teacher was in favour of technology in terms of maintaining student-centred and democratic language learning experience:

> Technology gives students learning freedom and decreases teacher's personal domination or influence.
>
> (Participant 2–7, p. 2)

Thanks to technology, the role of language teacher has considerably changed. In one teacher's words:

> Using technology effectively can shift the traditional role of the teacher to the challenging and much demanded new role of the teacher focusing on the students' learning rather than the instructor's teaching.
>
> (Participant 2–8, p. 2)

Teachers in general indicated that the use of technology in the university has improved language learning outcomes over time, and that today's students might have better language skills compared with previous students, when current technologies were not available:

> Blackboard is a very successful experience here at KKU. Actually, it makes the contact between the teacher and student easy and effective. It is an interesting learning tool, which makes the student loves what he is doing and becomes voluntary. His desire to study and participate is higher than before.
>
> (Participant 2–6, p. 2)

Whatever the potential of traditional technologies, one teacher stressed that innovative and affordable tools should be invested in for learning purposes:

> Innovative technology is getting more importance than traditional [methods]. Almost everyone is using smart phones and iPads. This actually reflects that their cost is not a significant issue.
>
> (Participant 2–7, p. 2)

Innovative technologies have also helped both students and teachers to maintain authentic and practical language learning experiences:

> Teacher–student face-to-face interaction is for a very short and limited time, but a student's mobile is always with her, and so authentic, reflective and real-world communication is maintained.
>
> (Participant 2–1, p. 2)

Another teacher indicated that social media could help to provide students with more authentic and human or simulative interaction that could foster language learning:

Social media can provide authentic and real-world interaction via video/audio media, as otherwise using text only communication takes away from actual feeling and disconnects from the human experience of engaging with another human.

(Participant 2-2, p. 2)

Teacher participants listed some factors that might have had negative impact on the integration of technology for language learning. Although the university provided professional training, teachers thought they, along with their students, were still in need of more training on how innovative and informal technologies could also be implemented for language learning:

In my opinion, current available technologies have great potential for English language learning if used properly and effectively. For that, teachers should be trained. Not only do they create an opportunity for students to learn independently, but they must also initiate a need on the part of teachers for their professional development – to keep in touch with the latest development in the use of technologies in the teaching–learning process.

(Participant 2-5, p. 2)

Concerns over exam reliability was noted by another teacher as a drawback of educational technology:

When an online quiz is given, we don't know whether the quiz was done by the particular student or by someone else, or by a group of students together. So, the reliability issue is there. The score of the online quiz isn't the same when it is conducted in the classroom.

(Participant 2-5, p. 2)

Technology dependency, as noted by a teacher, was also a concern:

The use of technology in language learning may develop technology dependency, e.g., students prefer to take a snap of the teacher's material on Blackboard rather than writing with their own hands.

(Participant 2-7, p. 2)

Teachers, older teachers in particular, were also concerned that the use of technology, particularly social media and mobile chatting, could affect their image:

Students may lose respect of teachers and assume they can bypass the classroom now as they have direct access to teachers.

(Participant 2-2, p. 2)

The same teacher suggested that too much involvement with students' own online chatting tools was not recommended. With his own students:

Personally, I chose not to involve myself in WhatsApp groups. It's important for the teachers to establish a good rapport with the student but at the same time he must exude authority and respect out of the students. As such, what I do is to encourage them to create such groups, and I only take one student's number, the one I trust the most, and ask him to pass my messages along to the group whenever needed.

(Participant 2-2, p. 2)

Delays in maintenance of lab computers and internet connections at some times were also listed as disadvantages that had affected the integration of technology for language learning. However, a teacher made a final and promising statement that the future of educational technology for language learning in Saudi Arabia is brilliant. He argued that cost affordability, availability of new trends of educational tools at universities and the encouragement of both policy makers and educators to utilize technology were all effective future enablers.

Discussion

Language learning potential

According to Chapelle (2001), language learning potential is determined by the degree of opportunity present for beneficial focus on form. Overall, it was obvious from both students' and teachers' responses that technology in this context had significant language learning potential. Both students and teachers indicated that meaningful language learning tasks were fulfilled with technology in terms of academic achievement and language use. This is consistent with many previous research works that identified several technological affordances for language learning (see, for example, Levy and Stockwell, 2006; Nah, White and Sussex, 2008; Kember, 2009; Golonka, Bowles, Frank, Richardson and Freynik, 2012; Vialleton, 2012). However, the focus on form rather than the language use is still questionable. This is true since most teachers noted that they use technology as a response to the university requirements. Students, on the other hand, are using technology to compensate for the missing face-to-face student–teacher interaction, or due to their work and family responsibilities.

Among the affordances of technology for language learning is the transformation into student-centred and collaborative learning, a learning experience where spoon-feed instruction and teacher dominance are diminished. However, it was shown in some responses that the cost factor did not matter. In other words, available or casual technology might have a greater impact on language learning than other tools that cost millions of dollars. Utilizing devices or tools with which students and teachers are already familiar is much more effective than devices and tools that need to be familiarized (Al-Adwan, Al-Adwan and Smedley, 2013; Lin, Huang and Chen, 2014).

Learners' fit

As mentioned, familiarity with the device or tool used in the language learning process is a crucial factor. Thus, technology of students' own preference would provide more opportunities to practise and use the language, as students are online most of the time. This is in line with Chapelle (2001), who asserts that learners' fit with educational technology is maintained by the amount of opportunity for engagement with language under appropriate conditions that cater for learners' characteristics. Again, it can be argued that technologies students are already using in their daily life, which are probably inexpensive or even free of charge, might imply more language learning opportunities and engagement. What is also needed is the motivation to use these casual tools for language learning purposes. Teachers, for instance, should receive adequate training and be aware of the potential of new trends in technologies and social media, and how they can be powerful language learning tools (Lin et al., 2014). Furthermore, the technological divide that usually exists between students and teachers should be narrowed down – both students and teachers would then be more mindful of the great potential of modern technologies.

Meaning focus

When language learners' attention is directed toward the meaning of the language, educational technology can be described as effective and successful (Chapelle, 2001). Alamir (2014) conducted an analysis of students' and teachers' online interaction and found that students were rarely found to correct their own errors or negotiate meaning. Alamir suggests that teachers' intervention is vital; teachers should revise online discourse to help students improve their language. In the present study, teachers seemed to focus on the task, for example, announcements, exams and so on, and neglect negotiation of meaning asserted by second language acquisition (SLA) theories. Students, on the other hand, focused on the pragmatic aspect of technology use, doing what is required by their teachers or the course profile in order to pass the exam. The language form and meaning were not of great importance to most students.

Authenticity

Most students indicated that the use of technology helped them to connect effectively between their language learning experience and the outside environment. As mentioned, female students do not usually have direct interaction with their male teachers. The same applies in the surrounding world, where some restrictions are found to hinder female–male interaction (except between relatives or family members). Hence, students found technology an effective channel that compensated for the limitedness of interaction. Moreover, students had the chance to connect with language activities that interested them. Similarly, Yang (2011) designed an online course that was able to enhance students' interest and involve them in authentic learning environment through peer- and small-group discussion. Yang also found that the teacher's interaction with the students improved their learning engagement and critical thinking, and helped them to correct their lexical errors. In this study, teachers preferred to perform these language learning processes via face-to-face interaction. They attributed this to students' lack of motivation to use technology to negotiate meaning or correct errors.

Positive impact

Language learning outcomes or language achievement was not the focus of the study; other investigations are needed to compare between outcomes of technology-based and traditional instruction in this specific setting. However, several studies have found that technology had a positive effect on learning achievement and students' attitudes (see for example, Godwin-Jones, 2011; Hwang and Chang, 2011; Lin et al., 2014). Hence, it was obvious in the present study that both students and teachers were in favour of technology, and that this helped to create language learning communities. Moreover, effective integration of local norms and cultural issues was also found to enhance students' interaction. A student, for instance, indicated that she found technology a motivating tool that decreased boredom and lack of interest found in traditional language learning settings. This is in line with Park's argument – 'e-learning self-efficacy may be considered an intrinsic motivational factor' that could effectively enable students to 'self-regulate their motivation on e-learning' (2009, p. 158).

Practicality

According to Chapelle (2001), practicality resides in the adequacy of resources to support the use of technology-based activities. Chapelle also claims that computers in the 1980s were seen as supplementary to rather than as replacements of classroom instructions. Similarly, most teacher participants indicated that their use of technology would never replace the role of the teacher. Concerns over losing the teacher respect and/or authority could be the reason for some teachers keeping blended learning characteristics. Female students, on the other hand, found in technology a powerful tool that, to some extent, compensated for the missing face-to-face student–teacher interaction. Technological concerns raised by some teachers could also be considered as unpractical factors that had negative impact of the use of technology in language learning.

Conclusion and limitations

Evaluation of educational technology can involve many aspects that a single study or an evaluation approach cannot adequately cover. Chapelle (2001), as cited by Chambers (2010), emphasizes that 'evaluation is a complex issue, involving a context-specific argument rather than a categorical judgment of effectiveness' (p.

120). This indicates that the process of Computer-Assisted Language Learning (CALL) evaluation should involve other factors that have contextual and cultural dimensions. Chapelle's criteria might have illustrated some deficiency in the use of technology at a Saudi Arabian tertiary context. However, another set of evaluation criteria might find that the use of technology in this language learning context is effective or at least is gradually improving.

At King Khalid University, English language instruction has benefited from the university's initiative to integrate the latest instructional technologies on par with international education institutions. Technology was, however, meant to be a successful tool to enhance student-centralism and to give students more independence and make them capable decision-makers. However, this study illustrated that significant factors still need more attention, including adequate training for both students and teachers. Students' and teachers' awareness of the potential of technology for language learning should also be improved.

The study revealed that the cost factor did not play a major role in determining what was best for language learning. Students might have found 'free' social media websites or mobile applications much more effective than institutional formal learning platforms. Teachers, on the other hand, were more conservative with new technologies that they might have thought of as less effective or even distracting.

Due to time restrictions, male students were not surveyed by this study, as the researcher did not have access to male students who already had good experience with educational technology – those in the Preparation Year were still under training. Another limitation was that teacher–student online interaction was not analysed due to privacy reasons; some teachers and students were not keen to share their interaction data.

References

Al-Adwan, A., Al-Adwan, A. and Smedley, J. (2013). Exploring students' acceptance of e-learning using Technology Acceptance Model in Jordanian universities. *International Journal of Education and Development Using Information and Communication Technology* 9(2), 4–18.

Alamir, A.H. (2014). Student–student versus instructor–student in online interactions: a study of second language performance and social presence of Saudi university English as Foreign Language learners. Unpublished doctorate dissertation, Monash University, Australia.

Al-Shehri, S. (2011). Connectivism: a new pathway for theorising and promoting mobile language learning. *International Journal of Innovation and Leadership on the Teaching of Humanities* 1(2), 10–31.

Al-Shehri, S. (2013). Design-based research: a tool to generate and refine instructional design principles for mobile language learning. *The International Journal of Design Education* 6(3), 1–12.

Cakir, R. and Solak, E. (2014). Exploring the factors influencing e-learning of Turkish EFL learners through TAM. *The Turkish Online Journal of Educational Technology* 13(3), 79–87.

Chambers, A. (2010). Computer-assisted language learning: mapping the territory. *Language Teaching* 43(1), 113–122.
Chapelle, C. (2001). *Computer applications in second language acquisition: foundations for teaching, testing, and research.* Cambridge MA: Cambridge University Press.
Davis, F.D. (1989). Perceived usefulness, perceived ease of use, and user acceptance of information technology. *MIS Quarterly* 13(3), 319–340.
Godwin-Jones, R. (2011). Autonomous language learning. *Language Learning and Technology* 15(3), 4–11.
Golonka, E.M., Bowles, A.R., Frank, V.M., Richardson, D.L. and Freynik, S. (2012). Technologies for foreign language learning: a review of technology types and their effectiveness. *Computer Assisted Language Learning*, 27(1), 70–105.
Herrington, A., Herrington, J. and Mantei, J. (2009). Design principles for mobile learning. In J. Herrington, A. Herrington, J. Mantei, I.W. Olney and B. Ferry (eds), *New technologies, new pedagogies: mobile learning in higher education* (pp. 129–138). Wollongong NSW: University of Wollongong.
Kember, D. (2009). Promoting student-centred forms of learning across an entire university. *Higher Education* 58(1), 1–13.
Levy, M. (1997). *Computer-assisted language learning: context and conceptualization.* Oxford: Clarendon Press.
Levy, M. and Stockwell, G. (2006). *CALL dimensions: options and issues in computer-assisted language learning.* Mahwah NJ: Lawrence Erlbaum Associates.
Lin, C.Y., Huang, C.K. and Chen, C.H. (2014). Barriers to the adoption of ICT in teaching Chinese as a foreign language in US universities. *ReCALL* 26(1), 100–116.
Ng, E.M., Shroff, R.H. and Lim, C.P. (2013). Applying a Modified Technology Acceptance Model to qualitatively analyse the factors affecting e-portfolio implementation for student teachers' in field experience placements. *Issues in Informing Science and Information Technology* 10, 355–365.
Park, S.Y. (2009). An analysis of the technology acceptance model in understanding university students' behavioral intention to use e-learning. *Educational Technology and Society* 12(3), 150–162.
Sharples, M., Taylor, J. and Vavoula, G. (2005). Towards a theory of mobile learning. In Proceedings of the mLearn 2005 Conference. Cape Town, South Africa.
Vialleton, E. (2012). Review of foreign language learning with digital technology. *Language Learning and Technology* 16(2), 27–30.
Venkatesh, V. and Bala, H. (2008). Technology acceptance model 3 and a research agenda on interventions. *Decision Sciences* 39(2), 273–315.
Yang, Y. F. (2011). Engaging students in an online situated language learning environment. *Computer Assisted Language Learning* 24(2), 181–198.

Appendix 1 Survey distributed to teacher participants

Dear Teachers,
Below is an evaluation of your experience as an EFL teacher at King Khalid University, Joint Programmes. This evaluation is intended to explore the effectiveness of technologies that have been implemented/should be implemented to improve EFL instruction at the Joint Programmes. Please be noted that your feedback will be used for research purposes, and that your participation is voluntary. Please answer the following questions carefully.

Many thanks,

******

1. How long have you been teaching English?
2. Did you use any technology tools in your previous study, including LMSs, Office, etc.? If yes, please elaborate.
3. To what extent has technology helped to transform language instruction in the university to be more student-centred and democratic, and to what extent can students see themselves as capable and independent?
4. How frequently do you use Blackboard for this process? And for what purposes?
5. After a decade of Blackboard implementation at King Khalid University, what strengths and weaknesses has the use of instructional technology highlighted?
6. How did you feel about current available technologies and their potential for English language learning? Any suggestions? What advantages/disadvantages have you encountered?
7. How effective were the tools you used in terms of creating a personally meaningful learning experience for yourself?
8. To what extent have innovative vs. traditional technologies had greater impact on language instruction? Does cost matter?
9. What are the optimal language learning/teaching environments, experiences and approaches that technology can enhance in Saudi Arabian contexts?

Thank you very much.

4 Blended learning
A promising learning and teaching approach for higher education institutions in the Arab States of the Gulf – a proposed open system model

Hend Mahmoud Merza

Introduction

In 1980, the Supreme Council for the Arab States of the Gulf resolutions asserted that higher education institutions of the Cooperation Council for the Arab States of the Gulf (GCC) nations should improve learning and teaching approaches and widen the use of technology in an attempt to help learners acquire knowledge. It suggested implementing new forms of education to cope with global political, social, economic and cultural changes (Cooperation Council for the Arab States of the Gulf, 2010).

To implement this resolution, Kuwait, Saudi Arabia, Bahrain and Oman opened branches of the Arab Open University (AOU) by 2003. The AOU is the first university in the Arabian Gulf region that adopts blended learning as a teaching and learning approach. By 2013, the total number of AOU branches reached eight (Arab Open University, 2013).

Some leading conventional higher educational institutions have partially implemented blended learning by:

1 Adopting various online Learning Management Systems (LMS) to enhance the teaching and learning process. Implementations include providing material in electronic format and discussions, communications and counselling through these systems.
2 Considering learning and teaching via online activities as complementary or supportive techniques to conventional in-class instruction methods.
3 Conducting educational research to assess the quality of e-learning courses or to test the effect of e-learning strategies on students' performance (Alsaidi, 2010; Al-Aonizi and Ally, 2014).

Part 1: What is blended learning?

Definitions of blended learning

There is a lack of consensus among researchers in defining the term blended learning. Various definitions exist. Fleck (2012) views blended learning as a mix of conventional face-to-face elements and online facilities. Singleton (2013) stated that it has many definitions in higher education today, but the most common is a course with online and on-campus components. Te@ch Thought (2014) defines blended learning as a relatively new tool where most professors use tools such as Blackboard and Moodle to access video of lectures, track assignments, interact with fellow professors and students, and to review other supporting materials.

Brady (2015) defined blended learning as a formal education programme in which a student learns at least in part through delivery of content and instruction via digital and online media with some element of student control over time, place, path or pace. However, he or she still attends a 'brick-and-mortar' school structure. There is confusion over the definition of blended learning here: these authors do not differentiate between personalized learning, adaptive learning, competency-based learning and individual rotation. Murphy, Snow, Mislevy, Gallagher, Krumm and Wei (2014) adopted Staker and Horn's (2012) conceptualization of blended learning, as it involves teaching and learning within a formal education programme, with some or all instruction delivered away from home.

Tolley (2014) stated that blended learning means many things to many people. Considering additionally educational technology companies, Knewton (as cited in Tolley, 2014, p. 1) suggests that a blended learning environment has six different models: face-to-face driver, rotation, flex, online lab, self-blend and online driver. Knewton also states that 'BL refers to any time a student learns, at least in part, at a brick-and-mortar facility and through online delivery with student control over time, place, path or pace.'

Vaughan and Garrison (2013) provide a definition of blended learning as the organic integration of thoughtfully selected and complementary face-to-face and online approaches and technologies. Garrison and Vaughan (2008) mentioned that the key assumptions of blended learning are thoughtfully integrating face-to-face and online learning, fundamentally rethinking the course design to optimize student engagement and replacing traditional class contact hours.

The Clayton Christensen Institute (2014) (www.christenseninstitute.org) asserts that blended learning involves leveraging the internet to afford each student a more personalized learning experience, meaning increased student control over the time, place, path and pace of his or her learning. The definition here is a formal education programme in which a student learns in part through online learning, with some element of student control over time, place, path and pace, in part in a supervised brick-and-mortar location away from home, such that the modalities along each student's learning path in a course or subject are connected to provide an integrated learning experience. In analysing these definitions of blended learning, the lack of consensus is obvious. For example, some scholars emphasize that blended learning is a type of formal education, whereas others focus on the use of technology. Others emphasize the element of student control over time, place, path or pace in the learning process, which is not considered in conventional face-to-face classroom instruction.

The author defines blended learning as formal education that integrates face-to-face conventional classroom instruction with online and digital media to provide learners with a well-planned, managed, structured and tutor-supervised interactive learning environment. High-quality content, activities and experiences are customized to the learners' needs, learning styles, places, times, paths and places. All of these processes and interactions lead to high-quality outcomes such as high levels of student achievement and development of advanced skills and attitudes. Blended learning is the smart use of pedagogy and technology for efficient learning processes and effective higher educational institutions.

Advantages of implementing blended learning

A number of researchers have investigated the effects of implementing blended learning on learners' skills, performance, achievement, interaction with peers and motivation. Gower (2006) asserts that blended learning provides flexibility to accommodate varied requirements of pedagogies, disciplines and course levels along with the needs of a wide variety of learners. Ally (2013) lists the advantages of implementing blended learning as a form of encouraging interaction among learners and their tutors, activating the learning process and accommodating different learning styles. Bryson and Jenkins (2015) report that 75 per cent of teachers surveyed in their study agreed that blended learning made them more effective and better able to meet the needs of their students and that it enabled teachers to make a fundamental shift toward higher-value responsibilities. The study also reported that blended learning affected the students in many ways through improved academic outcomes and increased student engagement and ownership of learning.

Woltering, Herrler, Spitzer and Spreckelsen (2009) investigated whether problem-based blended learning (PBL) increases students' motivation and supports the learning process. The findings revealed that motivation, subjective learning gains and satisfaction achieved significantly higher ratings from blended PBL students compared with students learning by conventional PBL.

Dickfos, Cameron and Hodgson (2014) conducted an online teacher survey and student interviews. Based on students' and teachers' perspectives, the findings suggest that blended learning technologies have facilitated flexibility in assessment by student self-reflection and fairness in assessment practices. On the other hand, Al-Aonizi and Ally (2014) investigated the effect of an electronic learning strategy on students' performance. The findings revealed that students who participated in the experiment experienced enrichment of knowledge and skill from to access to multiple learning resources, acquired effective communication skills and recognized the meaning of scientific documentation. When asked to evaluate the e-learning strategy, 95 per cent of participants responded favourably.

Fearon, Starr and McLaughlin (2011) explored students' views of blended learning in a university setting. The results proved that the blended learning approach is very flexible and preferable in many cases to traditional face-to-face learning.

Herlo (2014) explored the use of a blended learning strategy to support the teaching and learning process. The findings indicated that professors encouraged the students to become responsible and participate in forming knowledge, solving problems, research and applying what they gained in new and different contexts. In this way, professors worked directly and closely with students via face-to-face or e-learning for the highest purpose of student-centred learning.

Mahesh and Woll (2007) concluded that blended learning is a viable and cost-effective solution. It is neither simply adding the use of technology or e-learning, nor copying paper text books to CD or uploading them to a web page, nor lecturing through video conferences. It is an approach that uses pedagogy and technology for the sake of efficient learning processes and effective higher education institutions.

The flexibility of BL helps mature students to overcome time and place barriers; it enables them to access information, services and learning materials anywhere, at any time and through any device. Several studies reported that blended learning increased student motivation, improved academic outcomes and increased students' ownership of learning. The approach empowers teachers to maximize the quality of instructional time, differentiate learning, meet the different needs of students and have a greater impact on students, as well as increasing teacher retention.

Models of blended learning

Fleck (2012) discussed three common models of blended learning. The first, the correspondence and broadcast model, comprises four components: the use of external conventional faculty, broadcast lectures, correspondence printed material, and face-to-face tutorials and summer schools.

The second, the purpose-designed quality distance-education model, also comprises of four major elements: dedicated faculty focused on course design, course team-produced materials, structured support from associate lecturers (tutors) and professional logistics infrastructure for scale delivery.

The third is the learning community model, which is characterized by the creation of a learning community, emphasis on process and activities rather than content and assets, use of a wide range of specially designed assets, focus on student-driven learning, use of Web 2.0 and mobile devices to support communication, and design of face-to-face residential schools.

Bryson and Jenkins (2015) used a five-domain rubric to help teachers and school leaders to focus on key areas of blended learning:

Domain I: classroom culture that supports student learning and solving problems independently;
Domain II: management, which creates systems to maintain an effective blended learning environment;
Domain III: blended instructional planning and delivery;
Domain IV: blended assessments using multiple offline and online data sources to monitor students' academic performance;

Domain V: blended technology, which uses technology solutions to improve the blended learning environment.

Khan (2007) designed an eight-dimension framework for e-learning. The dimensions are pedagogical, technological, interface design, evaluation, management, resource support, ethical and institutional. Each of the dimensions comprises a number of items.

Al Hafez (2014) reviewed literature on e-learning and developed eight quality standards in the learning environment through the internet at higher education institutions. The standards are: 1. the quality in the aims of online learning; 2. physical elements and software; 3. human resources for online learning; 4. the tools of online learning; 5. the design of teaching material for online learning; 6. training and qualification of university lecturers; 7. guidance and tutoring of online learning students; 8. social and cultural relations for online learning and the physical environment for online learning.

Awadallha and Drarka (2014) conducted a prospective study to identify the contemporary international standard of e-learning. The study found that there is an agreement among experts regarding the importance of eight standards: 1. mission and the institutional effectiveness; 2. organization; 3. governance; 4. leadership; 5. academic programmes; 6. teaching methods; 7. faculty members, staff, students; 8. library; 9. learning resources; 10. infrastructure and technical support.

Based on research on college teaching and good practices, Chickering and Gamson (1987) identified seven principles that can help improve undergraduate education: 1. encouraging contact between students and faculty; 2. developing reciprocity and co-operation among students; 3. using active learning techniques; 4. giving prompt feedback; 5. emphasizing time on task; 6. communicating high expectations; and 7. respecting diverse talents.

When reviewing these models of blended learning, one notices that Fleck (2012) did not discuss his own model, but briefly described historical developments of blended learning over time. Bryson and Jenkins' (2015) model was very good in highlighting various components of blended learning, but did not focus on face-to-face tutorial or user training and induction as important elements. Khan's (2007) model is a checklist of e-learning content. The models of Al-Hafez (2014) and Awadallh and Drarka (2014) contain comprehensive standards that can be used as audit tools for monitoring the quality of existing e-learning systems. None of these models are visual, and none view the learning and teaching process as a system interacting with the external environment. Thus, the author has designed her own visual model, Merza's Open System Model of Blended Learning, which will be discussed in detail in the next section.

Part 2: Merza's Open System Model of Blended Learning

Figure 4.1 shows Merza's Open System Model of Blended Learning. The model comprises five elements: inputs, process, outputs, feedback and external environment.

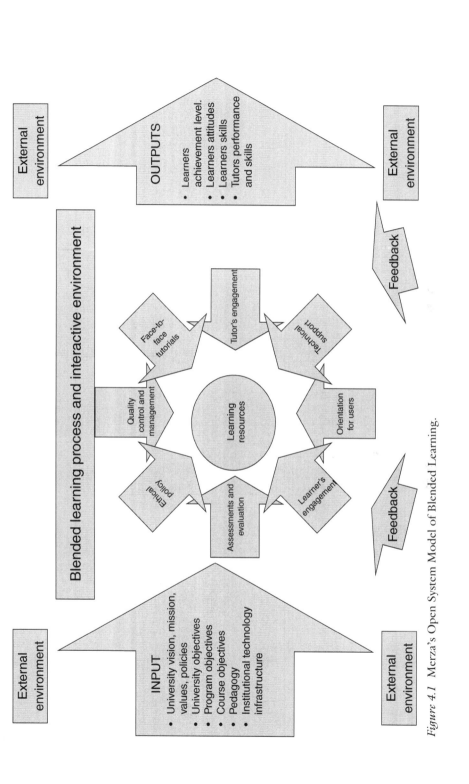

Figure 4.1 Merza's Open System Model of Blended Learning.

Blended learning inputs

University vision, mission and values

The majority of higher education students enrol in academic programmes without full awareness of the university's vision, values, mission and goals. These should be included in the course syllabi and communicated to students by various methods, emphasizing their relationship with course or programme objectives, activities and assessments.

University policies

The majority of higher education students enrol in academic programmes without comprehending the university's policies. The lack of awareness of policies may result in academic or administrative difficulties at later stages. Policies must be communicated to students by various methods, such as induction workshops, electronic manuals, etc.

Pedagogy

Pedagogy addresses issues such as content analysis, audience analysis, goal analysis, design, and methods and strategies that assess the principles and methods of teaching and learning. It addresses how the content of a course is designed, and identifies the learner's needs and how the learning objectives will be achieved. It might include a plan of blended options, for example that 70 per cent of course objectives will be delivered via online and or other technological formats, and 30 per cent will be delivered via face-to-face instruction. This element also addresses the delivery method for course activities and the appropriateness of the learning environment for achieving the learning goals of its intended audience. Interactive learning strategies in e-learning will engage and motivate students to learn so that they can finish their education rather than drop out of school.

Institutional technological infrastructure

Higher education institutions planning to implement blended learning methodology must ensure the readiness of supporting IT. The institution portal must be user friendly to allow access to information, services and learning materials from anywhere and at any time. The flexibility of access to the blended learning community from anywhere helps busy learners attend their online tutorials easily, at any time. The institutions must establish services and infrastructure to provide support to students from the time they register for courses or programmes to course completion or graduation. Students who use technology to complete their courses at a distance should be able to access institutional services virtually. The institute should also establish standards for tutor support to enhance student success, e.g. tutor response times to students' questions, feedback for students, etc. Social software should also be used to allow learners to communicate with each other so that they can support and help each other using peer tutoring.

Blended Learning processes and interactive environment

Quality control and management

Proper course management and quality control techniques should be used to make sure that blended learning course development is completed on time and that quality learning materials are developed. It is important that the course team members have the experience required to develop quality learning materials. Usually, blended learning materials are developed by a team of experts with different expertise. An important goal of the course manager is to make sure the team members work together to develop quality learning materials.

Another role of quality control and management of the BL environment is to provide a meaningful and successful BL environment, tutor training and continuous coordination with tutors to ensure tutors are effective in helping students with BL content and issues related to learning.

Quality control and management also requires handling attendance of learners and their interaction with peers and tutors. Quality control and management is involved in writing of comprehensive reports, extracting statistics about the course and consequently providing good feedback about the internal quality of the blended learning system.

Orientation and induction programme for users

Fleck (2012) cautioned that systematic training for effective use of technologies is necessary to take users beyond their customary habits. Also, Tolley (2014) mentioned that adopting a blended learning model does not mean immediate implementation, but students need to be carefully taught how to work in a blended learning environment.

Learning resources in the blended learning environment

Learning resources are the building blocks in the proposed model. E-learning platforms such as Blackboard or Moodle are suitable for delivering various learning resources including audio, video, printed materials, e-books, articles, encyclopaedias, social media, etc.

Fleck (2012) mentioned that the 'learning community model' uses of a wide range of existing and specially designed assets including the web, educational documentaries, open educational resources and open educational resources, which facilitate communication at any time. The blended learning community environment is a very rich platform with multiple modes of interaction among participants to achieve intended learning outcomes.

Technical support for users

Twenty-four-hour technical support should be provided for all concerned participants in case of problems with the technology or accessing the course materials.

Ethical policy

A no-rules blended learning environment is like a jungle. Tolley (2014) mentioned that to ease students into their roles as democratic participants a definition of a social contract should be provided, with clear expectations such as following ethical principles when using the technology to complete their lessons, not offending one another and not plagiarizing. Tutors must also use proper ethical guidelines when tutoring students. Developers of blended learning materials must follow proper copyright procedures. Proper privacy guidelines must be followed by a quality and management team to protect students' personal and sensitive data.

Learners' engagement

The blended learning approach is learner centred. Geçer (2013) pointed out that this is a flexible approach, which assists in the maintenance of education applications both in the face-to-face environment and on the web by developing technology. A learner who logs into the blended learning environment can engage in multiple learning activities such as viewing and downloading learning resources, logging in to a virtual library and asking questions. A learner may also take a rest and start a conversation at the virtual café to share thoughts and knowledge. Other activities can include assignments and feedback, dialogue with the facilitator and completing group assignments with colleagues. Ally (2013) added that a learner can also interview experts. Al Aonizi and Ally (2014) conducted an experiment and used various interactive e-learning activities with participating students, such as searching for both Arabic and English literature on specific topics, following up with local and international conferences, and facilitating students' registration in many electronic websites.

Tutors' engagement

Tutors' engagement is an important element in the proposed blended learning model, as their role is changed from that of a presenter of information to a tutor or facilitator of learning. Ally (2013) listed several new tutor roles in blended learning including to facilitate learning, motivate learners, help learners solve personal problems or problems with the content, share the different learning resources, such as handouts and recommended readings, and evaluate learners' performance. Further, Te@ch Thought (2014) stated that professors in blended classrooms use course management system platforms to communicate with students online. Through those platforms, students can access recorded lectures, track assignments and progress, interact with professors and peers, and review other supporting materials like presentations or scholarly articles.

Face-to-face tutorials

Face-to-face tutorials can be defined as scheduled lectures and meetings held on regular basis (e.g. weekly, bi-weekly).

Some claim that the blended learning methodology is similar to distance education, which does not require students to attend to face-to-face tutorials and consequently requires no direct contact between tutors and students. On the other hand, Fleck (2012) assured that face-to-face tutorial is an important element in the correspondence and broadcast model of the UK's Open University.

The objectives of conducting face-to-face tutorials are to overcome the isolation of distance learning, encourage interaction, exchange of ideas and learning experiences between students and tutors and among the students themselves, satisfy learners' social need for interaction, and to enhance the learning materials in a structured and supportive environment. The outcomes of these objectives improve the quality of the learning process and positively affect learners' achievement and performance.

Although learners are responsible for their learning in the blended approach, this does not mean the tutor has no role. The following advice, based on the author's personal experience in conducting face-to-face tutorials in the Saudi Arabia branch of the AOU, summarizes the facilitator's role before and during face-to-face tutorials.

- Careful planning of sessions will involve using a session plan or talk sheet.
- The objective of the session should be written.
- Suitable understanding activities that underline course topics should be designed
- Cover the most important points in the session, for example using concept maps.
- Arrive early to face-to-face tuition, spend the all of the time allocated for each meeting and do not merge sessions, regardless of the number of students present.
- Use various tutoring methods to achieve the required learning objectives for each concept: discussions, questioning, small groups and worksheets.
- Support the new students in the session.
- Encourage students to build their basic skills, e.g. reading, academic writing, etc.
- Encourage students to be responsible learners and actively participate.
- Ask questions, open up discussions and give examples that are relevant to course material.
- Consider having a five-minute break for an icebreaker.
- Use time effectively.

Face-to-face learning can be broken down as follows:

- Learn one quarter from the tutor.
- Learn one quarter from self-study.
- Learn one quarter from fellow learners.
- Learn one quarter while applying knowledge.

Tolley (2014) advised tutors to activate the learning process in face-to-face tutorials by breaking students into four groups. For example, one group of four to six students is actively working on research/homework, chatting occasionally, but largely on task. The second group is peer-editing one another's essays. The third group is at a whiteboard drawing a graphic depicting a concept from the course. The last group is seated around a small table with the teacher, discussing the unit's essential questions and devising new ones.

The studies of Weil, De Silva and Ward (2014) and Stewart and Nel (2009) revealed that learners value learning via digital media and online activities, but are unwilling to forgo the opportunities presented by face-to-face contact with peers and faculty members.

Assessments and evaluation

There is a quality assurance aphorism that says 'What gets monitored gets noticed; what gets noticed gets improved.' Assessments and evaluations should be conducted to determine the effectiveness of instructional design and delivery techniques. Learners should also be assessed to determine whether they accomplished the learning outcomes of the course using online and asynchronous assessment tools (Tolley, 2014). Ally (2013) mentioned several evaluation tools, such as online exams that are electronically marked according to a predefined ideal answer, supervised exams, e-portfolios, journalizing, forums, oral exams, assignments and blog formation. Software Secure Inc. (2015) is also using technology to provide remote proctoring. Bryson and Jenkins (2015) considered administering teacher-created and third-party assessments as a major element of the Blended Assessments Rubric to measure students' proficiency accurately.

The author recommends using recorded video as an evaluation tool of learner performance with respect to achieving learning outcomes. Videos can be uploaded into the blended learning management system for tutor review and grading. Although the blended approach depends heavily on online activities, the author recommends using traditional written tests as an assessment tool, i.e. where the learner sits in a classroom for a paper and pencil exam during a face-to-face session or scheduled exam period.

Blended learning outputs

The various findings of studies supporting the positive impacts of blended learning on learners are mentioned in detail in Part 1 of this chapter.

Blended learning external environment

The external environment is anything surrounding the blended learning system, e.g. the local community, social and economic factors, or stakeholders. When researching the literature on blended learning regarding the effect of the external environment, the author found only one resource. Thus, it is suggested that the effects of the external environment be considered when designing a blended programme or course. Also, when implementing blended learning systems, stakeholders such as parents and various interest groups should be kept informed of the benefits of applying a flexible approach. Tolley (2014) advised tutors always to capture the learners in their classroom via photo and video, and, wherever possible, share work online with parents and colleagues.

Feedback on blended learning

The results of Brew (2008) indicated that students were willing to provide detailed feedback and provided constructive criticism that proved useful in the evaluation process. Thus, the proposed blended learning model considers the feedback element as a source of improvement. There are two major sources of feedback – internal and external. Feedback about the internal quality of the blended learning programme or course can be collected via reports and various assessment data on students' performance. External feedback can be collected by contacting stakeholders.

Part 3: A proposal to implement Merza's Open System Model of Blended Learning in higher education institutes of the GCC

Part 1 of this chapter highlights that blended learning is an approach that uses pedagogy and technology for the sake of efficient learning processes and effective higher education institutions. Based on the advantages of blended learning, the author proposes that higher education institutions in the GCC nations implement this using Merza's Open System Model. Such implementation would achieve the following objectives.

- Putting into practice the resolutions for new forms of education taken by the Supreme Council for the Arab States.
- Improving the quality of higher education by speeding up the process of providing local markets with highly skilled workers holding higher education degrees.
- Responding to the increasing demand among working people in these countries for flexible higher education programmes to pursue professional development without giving up jobs
- Coping with global, political, social, economic and cultural changes.

What is primarily needed to implement Merza's Open System are some changes in policies and practices of the conventional universities in GCC nations, authorities and other parties. Blended learning should be recognized as a high-quality educational method; qualifications of graduates from both blended learning and conventional universities should be treated equally. Use of digital technologies and online learning communities should be considered a major element of the learning process rather than complementary. Other changes include approval of Merza's model for designing blended learning systems for existing conventional universities or brand new universities, implementation of professional training programmes for academic staff members, students and administrative staff to be able to use blended learning effectively, and hosting professional events to increase public awareness of it.

Conclusion

Blended learning is the smart use of pedagogy and technology for the sake of efficient learning processes and effective higher institutions. The advantages of implementing blended learning have been reported in many studies and include increased student motivation, improved academic outcomes and increased student ownership of learning. This approach empowers teachers to maximize the quality of instructional time, differentiate learning and meet the various needs of students. It also allows teachers to have a greater impact on students and increases teacher retention.

As Sloman (2007) stated, 'it seems beyond doubt that the concept of BL has arrived and is here to stay'. Thus, conventional higher education institutes in the GCC nations should shift to blended learning and consider it a major element of the teaching and learning process, alongside conventional classroom instruction. The author looks forward to approved implementation of her model in most or all conventional universities and in the newly opened universities of the GCC nations.

References

Al-Aonizi, S. and Ally, M. (2014). The use of e-learning in higher education (Dr Saudsite model). Paper submitted to the Global Forum for Innovation in University Teaching, Imam Muhammad bin Saud Islamic University, Riyadh.

Al-Hafez, M. (2014). Quality standards in the learning environment through the internet at higher education institutions. *Arab Journal of Quality Assurance in Higher Education* 7(15), 53–73. Retrieved from www.ust.edu/uaqe/count/2014/1/3.pdf

Ally, M. (2013). Managing, designing, and implementing "blended learning" for flexible delivery. Workshop handout at the first International Conference in Open Learning, Kuwait.

Alsaidi, E. (2010). Assessment of the quality of e-courses over the internet in the light of the standards of instructional design (King Abudaliza Model). Doctoral dissertation, Umm Al-Qura University, Makkah, Saudi Arabia. Retrieved from http://libback.uqu.edu.sa/hipres/FUTXT/12230.pdf

Arab Open University (2013). *A Decade of Success*. Office of Planning, Research, and Development, Kuwait.

Awadallah, A. and Drarka, A. (2014). The standards of e-learning at Taif University in the light of the contemporary international experiences: a prospective study. *Culture and Development* 77, 140–145. Retrieved from http://aou.opa.mandumah.com

Brew, L. (2008). The role of student feedback in evaluating and revising a "blended learning" course. *Internet and Higher Education* 11(2), 98–105. Retrieved from http://dx.doi.org/10.1016/j.iheduc.2008.06.002

Bryson, J. and Jenkins, A. (2015). Understanding and supporting 'blended learning' teaching practices. Retrieved from www.edelements.com

Chickering, A. and Gamson, Z. (1987). Seven principles for good practice in undergraduate education. *AAHE Bulletin*, 3–7. Retrieved from www.aahea.org/articles/sevenprinciples1987.htm

Cooperation Council for the Arab States of the Gulf (2010). The decisions of the Supreme Council of the Cooperation Council for the Arab States of the Gulf.

Dickfos J., Cameron C. and Hodgson C. (2014). 'Blended learning': making an impact on assessment and self-reflection in accounting education. *Education + Training* 56(23), 190–207. Retrieved from: http://dx.doi.org/10.1108/ET-09-2012-0087

Fearon, C., Starr, S. and McLaughlin, H. (2011). Value of 'blended learning' in university and the workplace: some experiences of university students. *Industrial and commercial training* 43(7). Retrieved from://www.emeraldinsight.com/doi/abs/10.1108/00197851111171872

Fleck, J. (2012). 'Blended learning' and learning communities: opportunities and challenges. *Journal of Management Development* 31(4), 398–411. Retrieved from: http://dx.doi.org/10.1108/02621711211219059

Garrison, R. and Vaughan, N. (2008). *Blended Learning in higher education: framework, principles, and guidelines*. San Francisco. John Wiley. Retrieved from https://books.google.ca/books?hl=en&lr=&id=2iaR5FOsoMcC&oi=fnd&pg=PR9&dq=garrison+vaughn+blended+learning+definition&ots=4CjbkVIGsC&sig=MzIucWdy9eM6531et8Xo0_Cy1Gk#v=onepage&q&f=false

Geçer, A. (2013). Lecturer–student communication in 'blended learning' environments. *Theory and Practice* 13(1), 362–367. Retrieved from http://search.ebscohost.com/login.aspx?direct=true&db=ehh&AN=85466206&site=ehost-live&scope=site

Gower, J. (2006). 'Blended learning' and online tutoring: a good practice guide. *Education + Training* 48(89). Retrieved from www.emeraldinsight.com/toc/et/48/8%2F9

Herlo, D. (2014). Benefits of using 'blended learning' in 'performer' education master program. *Journal Plus Education* Special Issue 10(2), 145–150. Retrieved from http://search.ebscohost.com/login.aspx?direct=true&db=ehh&AN=98932949&site=ehost-live&scope=site

Khan, B. (2007). *A framework for e-learning*. Retrieved from http://BooksToRead.com/framework/dimensions.htm

Mahesh, V. and Woll, C. (2007). Blended learning in high-tech manufacturing: a case study of cost benefits and production efficiency. *Journal of Asynchronous Learning*

Networks 11 (2), 43–60. Retrieved from http://search.ebscohost.com/login.aspx?direct=true&db=ehh&AN=27981725&site=ehost-live&scope=site

Murphy, R., Snow, E., Mislevy, J., Gallagher, L., Krumm, A. and Wei, Z. (2014). 'Blended learning' report. Michael and Susan Dell Foundation. Retrieved 20 January 2015 from www.sri.com/work/publications/blended-learning

Singleton, D. (2013). Transitioning to 'blended learning': the importance of communication and culture. *Journal of Applied Learning Technology* 3(1), 12–15. Retrieved from http://search.ebscohost.com/login.aspx?direct=true&db=ehh&AN=82474378&site=ehost-live&scope=site

Sloman, M. (2007). Making sense of 'blended learning'. *Industrial and Commercial Training* 39(6), 315–318. Retrieved from http://dx.doi.org/10.1108/00197850710816782

Slotkin, M., Durie, C. and Eisenberg, J. (2012). The benefits of short-term study abroad as a 'Blended Learning' experience. *Journal of International Education in Business* 5(2), 163–173. Retrieved from http://dx.doi.org/10.1108/18363261211281762

Software Secure Inc. (2015). Watchful eyes: a comparative look at online test proctoring models. Retrieved from www.softwaresecure.com/whitepaper-download/?CP

Stewart, A. and Nel, D. (2009). Blended and online learning: student perceptions and performance. *Interactive Technology and Smart Education* 6(3), 140–155. Retrieved from http://dx.doi.org/10.1108/17415650911005366

Te@ch Thought (2014). Retrieved from www.teachTe@ch thought.com/blended-learning-2/the-definition-of-blended-learning

Tolley, B. (2014). Creating successful blended-learning classrooms. Retrieved from: www.edweek.org/tm/articles/2014/10/08/ctq_tolley_blended_learning.html?qs=bill+tolley

Vaughan, N. and Garrison, R. (2013). *Teaching in blended learning environments*. Edmonton: AU Press. Retrieved from https://books.google.ca/books?hl=en&lr=&id=2iaR5FOsoMcC&oi=fnd&pg=PR9&dq=garrison+vaughn+blended+learning+definition&ots=4CjbkVIGsC&sig=MzIucWdy9eM6531et8Xo0_Cy1Gk#v=onepage&q&f=false

Weil, S., De Silva, A. and Ward, M. (2014). Blended learning in accounting: a New Zealand case. *Meditari Accountancy Research* 2(22), 224–244. Retrieved from http://dx.doi.org/10.1108/MEDAR-10-2013-0044

Woltering, V., Herrler, A., Spitzer, K. and Spreckelsen, C. (2009). Blended learning positively affects students' satisfaction and the role of the tutor in the problem-based learning process: results of a mixed-method evaluation. *Advances in Health Sciences Education* 14(5), 725–738. Retrieved from http://dx.doi.org/10.1007/s10459-009-9154-6

5 A conceptual model for the effective integration of technology in Saudi higher education systems

Abdulrahman M. Al-Zahrani

Introduction

For the last few decades, Saudi Arabia has boomed economically. As a rapidly developing Islamic country, it has willingly partaken in global digital technology developments. Largely through earnings linked with the petroleum industry, this wealth has aided health, public education, higher education and levels of consumption of technology (Joseph and Lunt, 2006; Hartley and Al-Muhaideb, 2007; Nelson, 2010; Ramady, 2010; Onsman, 2011). Despite the fact that Saudi Arabia has been considered a mono-cultural and conservative society, it provides significant insights into cultural change associated with the global competitiveness of the digital age (Onsman, 2011). Since its establishment, Saudi Arabia has played an important role in the Gulf region and the Arab world, as well as worldwide (Onsman, 2011). The speed of its development has been fascinating. For instance, Krieger (2007) expresses that 'Saudi Arabia has been developing at breakneck speed since the end of World War II, when oil production transformed this country of Bedouins into one of the richest polities in the world' (p. 1). The most dramatic changes have been observed in terms of the economy and social change (Ramady, 2010). Modern Saudi Arabia ranks first in the world in oil reserves, production and exports. The increasing economic role of Saudi Arabia allowed the state to join the World Trade Organization in 2005 and meet its obligations (Ramady, 2010).

The wide expansion of technological development in Saudi Arabia brings to the fore the need for the effective integration of new technologies, especially in higher education. However, despite the increasing consumption of technology, its integration, particularly in higher education, has been ineffective. According to Al Otaibi (2007), this inefficiency is mainly attributed to the lack of technology awareness among educational leaders and curriculum designers. Consequently, Saudi curricula traditionally focus on theory over practice and conventional methods of teaching rather than innovative use of technologies (Krieger, 2007; Al-Issa, 2009, 2010; Onsman, 2011).

Toward modelling the effective integration of technology

Modelling the effective integration of technology is problematic and considered very complex approach. As Smolin and Lawless (2007) argue, 'technology-based reform is especially challenging because it is a multifaceted endeavour' (p. 2). It is a 'terrain of complexity, multiplicity and interconnectedness' (Gale, 2007, p. 471). While this is so in developed countries, the case of the developing countries such as Saudi Arabia can be more problematic.

There are many perspectives on technology integration in higher education curriculum (Nkonge and Gueldenzoph, 2006; Polly, Mims, Shepherd and Inan, 2010). A review of the literature emphasizes three main perspectives, which are:

1 **The practitioner perspective**, which includes perceived concept, perceived self-efficacy and perceived awareness in terms of technology importance and usefulness.
2 **The pedagogical perspective**, which includes curriculum design, and technology-based pedagogical practices.
3 **The administration perspective**, which includes the role of the educational policies and the main functions of effective leadership such as infrastructure, training and support (see Figure 5.1).

First, the practitioners' perspectives

In the context of higher education, understanding technology practitioners' perceptions and beliefs related to digital technologies holds the key to improving their professional preparation and development (Wabuyele, 2003; Lee, Teo, Chai, Choy, Tan and Seah 2007; Northcote, 2009; Sang, Valcke, Braak and Tondeur, 2010). Beliefs also contribute to the successful integration of digital technologies in their future practices (Sang et al., 2010). Therefore, the focus here is on three main perceptions: perceived concept, perceived self-efficacy, and perceived awareness of technology importance and usefulness, as shown in Figure 5.2.

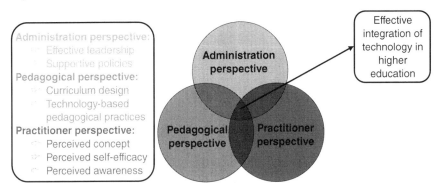

Figure 5.1 Effective integration of technology in higher education curricula.

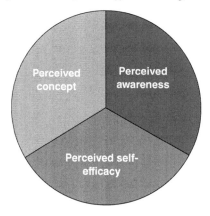

Figure 5.2 Practitioners' technology integration-related perceptions.

Perceived concept

Perceived concept can be defined as the constructed mind image that practitioners hold for the concept of technology integration. Shortly, 'a concept can be understood as an abstract object, abstractum, or a mental representation' (Bergman, 2010, p. 171). It is the way of understanding the world in accordance with Einstein (1936):

> The first step in the setting of a 'real external world' is the formation of the concept of bodily objects and of bodily objects of various kinds ... the concept owes its meaning and its justification exclusively to the totality of the sense impressions which we associate with it.
>
> (p. 4)

Accordingly, one significant challenge is how to conceptualize the integration of technology for effective implementation in higher education programmes (Pianfetti, 2005). Although a clear definition is needed to understand the wide implications of this concept in teaching and learning environments, there is currently no common definition or agreed conceptualization. Regardless, the most recent conceptualizations in terms of the effective integration of technology face the difficulty of establishing a common understanding. Hence, a diachronic perspective for the development of this concept shows certain changes in experts' perceptions from the application to more complex relevant concepts (see Table 5.1).

Table 5.1 Definition and concept of technology integration: a diachronic perspective

Definition	Concepts of the definition
Dockstader (1999): 'Technology integration is using computers effectively and efficiently in the general content areas to allow students to learn how to apply computer skills in meaningful ways... Integration is incorporating technology in a manner that enhances student learning. Technology integration is using software supported by the business world for real-world applications so students learn to use computers flexibly, purposefully and creatively. Technology integration is having the curriculum drive technology usage, not having technology drive the curriculum. Finally, technology integration is organising the goals of curriculum and technology into a coordinated, harmonious whole.' (p. 74)	• The effective use of computers • The efficient use of computers • Content areas • Computer Skills • Incorporation of technology • Enhancement of student learning • Support from private sectors • Real-world applications • Flexibility, purposefully and creativity in computers' use • Technology driven by curriculum • Coordinating technology and curriculum
Technology in Schools (2003): 'The incorporation of technology resources and technology-based practices into the daily routines, work, and management of schools. Technology resources are computers and specialized software, network-based communication systems, and other equipment and infrastructure. Practices include collaborative work and communication, Internet-based research, remote access to instrumentation, network-based transmission and retrieval of data, and other methods.' (No page number)	• Broad definition • Incorporation of technology and practice into daily routine, work and school management
Dawson (2006): 'Technology is a part of what is already happening in the classroom instead of apart from it'. (p. 268)	• Technology as a part of pedagogical practice in the classroom not apart from the physical classroom
Gale (2007): 'Terrain of complexity, multiplicity and interconnectedness'. (p. 471)	• Multiplicity and complexity
Dede (2011): 'we must reconceptualize technology integration not as automating conventional classroom processes—or even as innovating within the structure of industrial era schools—but instead as bridging to ways of teaching/learning so different that integration is no longer an accurate description'. (p. 4)	• Complexity of the issue • New meaning for teaching and learning practices with technology • Technology as powerful tools that may change the nature of teaching and learning

Perceived awareness

Another critical perception to the effective integration of digital technologies is the perceived awareness of the importance and the usefulness of technology. Existing literature has suggested that perceived awareness of the importance and usefulness of technology contributes to the integration of technology into higher education curriculum (Hall, Loucks, Rutherford and Newlove, 1975; Gregor et al., 2005; Nkonge and Gueldenzoph, 2006; Lee et al., 2007;; Robertson, Fluck and Webb, 2007; Smith and Kelley, 2007).

As a definition, Lee et al. (2007) state that 'perceived usefulness reflects the prospective users' subjective probability that applying the new technology will be beneficial to his/her personal and/or the adopting organisation's well-being' (p. 556). Therefore, raising technology awareness should be an initial phase in the educational change process model (Robertson et al., 2007). In this regard, Gregor et al. (2005) state that 'what you do is less important than how you do it and success requires ICT-awareness, persistence and being open to change' (p. 14).

Accordingly, determining the users' level of technology awareness seems to be a key factor for the effective integration of technology. Consequently, technology integration into the higher education curriculum has been influenced by the practitioners' level of technology awareness. Hall et al. (1975) emphasize four levels of technology awareness. These levels include:

- Non-use: technology users have no knowledge about technology.
- Awareness: users have limited knowledge. They are aware but need more skill training and support.
- Proficient: users have the skills to use technology, but their skills need to be expanded.
- Advanced: users are expert in the use of technology and have the ability to transfer this knowledge to others.

Perceived self-efficacy

One's self-efficacy influences the level of technology integration into higher education curricula. Bandura's theory of self-efficacy in the early 1970s is the key concept in the social cognitive theory, which has triangulated the relationship between one's personality, behaviour and environment (Chao, 2003).

A definition of self-efficacy is that it is the individuals' judgements of their abilities to execute a certain and conditioned course of behaviour(s) or to complete specified tasks (Bandura, 1997). In other words, self-efficacy can be defined as a concept of self-related perceptions in personality and social psychology interests (Bong and Skaalvik, 2003; Chao, 2003). Accordingly, self-efficacy is predicted to contribute to students' learning and academic performance as well as the general environment of educational institutions (Jungert and Rosander, 2010).

Students usually have different self-efficacy levels of cognitive, social and emotional engagement in their preparation (Bong and Skaalvik, 2003). Chao

(2003) stresses the influence of self-efficacy on technology integration in higher education by emphasizing that 'for many people, the ability to utilize computers is limited by an incapability of controlling or even using them. As for self-efficacy expectations, it may be the beliefs of an individual that results in the inability to use computers' (p. 414). According to Bong and Skaalvik (2003), there are different levels of self-efficacy among students. These differences in self-efficacy levels occur depending on several key questions, including the way they construe themselves, the attributes they think they possess, the roles they presume they are expected to play, the capabilities they believe they have acquired, the view they share in comparison with others and the way they judge that they are viewed by others.

Second, the pedagogical perspectives

It is assumed that innovative curriculum design combined with efficient technology-based pedagogical practices can create a better opportunity for the effective integration of digital technologies in higher education, as illustrated in Figure 5.3.

Curriculum design

It is a challenge to accommodate new technologies within the higher education curricula (Reimer, 2005; Altun, 2007; Peeraer and Van Petegem, 2011). Rogers (2007) emphasizes that there is great pressure on higher education institutions to integrate technology into their curricula.

Despite the fact that technology should be embedded in a curriculum for effective integration, it cannot be integrated into educational programmes and classrooms 'overnight' (Robertson et al., 2007, p. 115), and this can be 'a slow process' (Peeraer and Van Petegem, 2011, p. 981). Accordingly, technology integration into higher education curricula should be a systematic, collaborative approach between all related departments in higher education to gain the benefits of integrating technology behind this process. To do this, it is necessary to establish cooperative partnerships between educational technology units and initial preparation programmes (Shoffner, Dias and Thomas, 2001; Rogers, 2007).

Integrating technology into higher education curricula has many benefits, such as the exposure to new technology tools and applications. According to Roblyer and Edwards (2003), integrating technology into higher education curricula increases university lecturers' productivity, allows them to have

Figure 5.3 Pedagogical perspective of effective integration of technology.

Conceptual model for the effective integration of technology 73

convenient access to resource databases and information, and decreases the time needed for lesson preparation and the organization of materials for classes.

Nonetheless, higher education curricula seem to be less influenced by current sociological trends, such as the wide expansion of technology. Scholars such as Peeraer and Petegem (2011) and Pianfetti (2005) address the fact that, although the need for a new curriculum that integrates digital technologies is evident, higher education, particularly in developing countries, is still traditional and lacks effective integration of technology.

Technology-based pedagogical practices

In addition to effective curriculum design, there is always the need for extensive practice to establish effective integration of technology. It is essential for higher education students to bond their technological knowledge with real practice and experience so they can connect theory to practice (Robertson et al., 2007). In this regard, Vannatta (2007) argues that 'technology skills and fluency are essential to using technology; however, learning skills in isolation is not very exciting or motivating. Thus, all potential users should learn skills in the process of completing a task or project' (p. 136).

Increased technology practice in higher education offers great potential in enhancing communication and sharing pedagogical information that can authentically innovate the nature of higher education (Fabry and Higgs, 1997; Barnett, 2006). Fabry and Higgs (1997) stress that merely offering computer hardware and software in education does not mean effective integration; there must be a connection between technology and real pedagogical practice. Further, increased practice contributes to effective learning and reflects changed behaviour in the future (Robertson et al., 2007), as shown in Figure 5.4.

Third, the administration perspectives

Leadership plays a key role in facilitating an increased use and implementation of technology into practice, including the provision of adequate infrastructure, training, and professional and logistic support. When supported by proper and supportive polices that clarify the questions of what, when, how and why, this can create a better opportunity for the professional and effective use of technology. Figure 5.5 illustrates this concept.

Figure 5.4 Learning through practice: action and reflection (adapted from Robertson et al., 2007, p. 110).

Figure 5.5 The administration perspective of effective integration of technology.

The role of effective leadership

Effective leadership contributes to the effective integration of technology into higher education curricula (Fabry and Higgs, 1997; Culp, Honey and Mandinach, 2005; Lessen and Sorensen, 2006; Altun, 2007;; Robertson et al., 2007). Due to the fact that technology tools are a part of everyday life, leadership is essential in addressing the issue of technology integration, and it plays an extraordinary role in influencing educational institutions to develop strategic plans for the integration of technology (Reimer, 2005; Robertson et al., 2007).

To establish technology integration, effective leadership should consider this integration a priority in its pedagogical practices (Fabry and Higgs, 1997; Culp et al., 2005; Lessen and Sorensen, 2006; Robertson et al., 2007). Leadership in educational organizations must possess several important competencies to establish effective integration of technology. According to Anderson and Weert (2002), these competencies include 'critical thinking, generalist (broad) competencies, ICT competencies enabling expert work, decision-making, handling of dynamic situations, working as a member of a team, and communicating effectively' (p. 9).

Practically, Lessen and Sorensen (2006) identify four important key actions in which leadership can play a part in promoting the effective integration of technology. These four key actions include considering the use of technology as a priority, establishing an adequate technological infrastructure, maintain training and supporting opportunities for students and academic staff, and focusing on development processes. In terms of the affordability of financial resources, especially in terms of expensive technologies, Smith and Kelley (2007) point out that the establishment of appropriate, adequate and different funding resources to assist the effective integration of technology is an important key action for leadership. Moreover, Altun (2007) and Fabry and Higgs (1997) consider appropriate access and infrastructure with tutorials and training for both academic staff as priorities that leadership should maintain carefully and accommodate into their mission.

The role of policy

Leadership and policy are inseparable. While effective leadership contributes to the effective integration of technology, policies play a major role in the enhancement of the process of technology integration (Anderson and Glenn,

Conceptual model for the effective integration of technology 75

2003; Altun, 2007; Robertson et al., 2007; Smolin and Lawless, 2007). Policies are important due their action in expressing the what, how and why of the educational institutions and how they set their priorities in relation to pedagogical beliefs and practices (Robertson et al., 2007). According to Anderson and Glenn (2003), 'introducing change into a system is relatively easy; ensuring that change flows from policy to the classroom is a formidable challenge' (p. 19).

Nevertheless, integrating technology in diverse educational settings remains a concern of both practitioners and policy makers (Anderson and Glenn, 2003; Culp et al., 2005; Altun, 2007). According to Culp et al. (2005), the role of policies is to 'describe matches between specific capabilities of various technologies and persistent challenges to the delivery, management, and support of effective teaching and learning experiences' (p. 5). In this regard, 'one of the challenges to integrate technology in education is how to decide priorities between aims and how to accommodate these new opportunities within a curriculum' (Altun, 2007, p. 53). Bearing this in mind, Robertson et al (2007) state that 'purposes, policies and practices exist at, across and between all levels of any organization. Any system exists to help ensure the success of all its components, and thus the achievement of outcomes that match its goals and purposes' (p. 72) (see Figure 5.6).

However, in the technology era, while the role of policy making in education should be stretched from local to global, evidence shows that educational polices retain their local focus (Gale, 2005; Lingard, Rawolle and Taylor, 2005). To improve the quality of policy making in education, Culp et al. (2005) and Anderson and Glenn (2003) state that policy makers in education need to understand the relationship between the required educational changes and the process of integrating technology. Further, they must understand the challenges of the twenty-first century and encourage all parties to communicate, access information and learn how to implement emerging technologies effectively (Anderson and Glenn, 2003). In relation to this, Jhurree (2005) points out that effective integration of technology 'warrants careful planning and depends largely on how well policymakers understand and appreciate the dynamics of such integration' (p. 467).

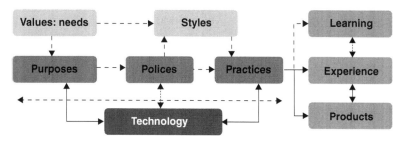

Figure 5.6 System alignment with technology (adapted from Robertson et al., 2007, p. 72).

Conclusion

The current chapter argues that the effective integration of technology, as a complex approach especially in developing countries, occurs in the intersection between the practitioner, the pedagogical and the administration perspectives. In developing countries, which are highly influenced by social, religious and traditional educational structures, the effective integration of technology in higher education can be seen from a different angle and requires duple efforts to occur. In short, the effective integration of technology in such contexts requires the intersection of the practitioner, the pedagogical and administration perspectives to occur in harmony.

Technology practitioners, including policy makers, instructors and students, should be technologically wise and positive. They should have a high level of pedagogical understanding of technology and its wide implications to the educational development in areas of administration, teaching and learning approaches. It is also fundamental to have an innovative technology-based curriculum that emphasizes the effective pedagogical practice of technology into teaching and learning. In other words, curriculum design should be globalized to be able to comprise the massive and rapid development of digital technologies as well as to meet the needs of learners, societies and labour markets in the twenty-first century. However, such theoretical assumptions need an umbrella of effective administration to be able to perform. Leadership has the core mission of translating theory into practice and ensuring the quality of planning, processes and outcomes. Part of this is the production of supportive policies that articulate a valid technological vision and ways of achieving it by the means of what, when, how and why.

References

Al-Issa, A. (2009). *Education reform in Saudi Arabia between the absence of political vision and apprehension of religious culture and the inability of educational administration.* Lebanon: Dar Al-Saqi.

Al-Issa, A. (2010). *Higher education in Saudi Arabia: the journey to find identity.* Lebanon: Dar Al-Saqi.

Altun, T. (2007). Information and communications technology (ICT) in initial teacher education: what can Turkey learn from range of international perspectives? *Journal of Turkish Science Education* 4(2), 45–60.

Anderson, J. and Glenn, A. (2003). *Building capacity of teachers/facilitators in technology–pedagogy integration for improved teaching and learning: final report.* Bangkok: UNESCO, Asia and Pacific Regional Bureau for Education. Retrieved from www.unescobkk.org/fileadmin/user_upload/ict/e-books/ICTBuidling_Capacity/BuildingCapacity.pdf

Anderson, J. and Weert, T. (2002). Information and communication technology in education: a curriculum for schools and programme of teacher development. France: Division of Higher Education.

Bandura, A. (1997). *Self-efficacy: the exercise of control.* New York: W.H. Freeman.

Barnett, M. (2006). Using a web-based professional development system to support preservice teachers in examining authentic classroom practice. *Journal of Technology and Teacher Education* 14(4), 701–729.
Bergman, M.M. (2010). On concepts and paradigms in mixed methods research. *Journal of Mixed Methods Research* 4(3), 171–175.
Bong, M. and Skaalvik, E.M. (2003). Academic self-concept and self-efficacy: how different are they really? *Educational Psychology Review* 15(1), 1–40.
Chao, W. (2003). Self-efficacy toward educational technology: the application in Taiwan teacher education. *Journal of Educational Media and Library Sciences* 40(4), 409–415.
Culp, K.M., Honey, M. and Mandinach, E. (2005). A retrospective on twenty years of education technology policy. *Educational Computing Research* 32(3), 279–307.
Dawson, K. (2006). Teacher inquiry: a vehicle to merge prospective teachers' experience and reflection during curriculum-based, technology-enhanced field experiences. *Journal of Research on Technology in Education* 38(3), 265–292.
Dede, C. (2011). Reconceptualizing technology integration to meet the necessity of transformation. *Journal of Curriculum and Instruction* 5(1), 4–16.
Dockstader, J. (1999). Teachers of the 21st century know the what, why, and how of technology integration. *T.H.E. Journal (Technological Horizons in Education)* 26(6), 73–74.
Einstein, A. (1936). Physics and reality. *Journal of the Franklin Institute* 221(3), 349–382. doi: 10.1016/s0016-0032(36)91047-5
Fabry, D.L. and Higgs, J.R. (1997). Barriers to the effective use of technology in education: current status. *Journal of Educational Computing Research* 17(4), 385–395.
Gale, K. (2007). Teacher education in the university: working with policy, practice and Deleuze. *Teaching in Higher Education* 12(4), 471–483.
Gale, T. (2005). Towards a theory and practice of policy engagement: higher education research policy in the making. *The Australian Educational Researcher* 33(2), 1–14. doi: 10.1007/BF03216831
Gregor, S.D., Fernández, W.D., Holtham, D., Martin, M.A., Stern, S.E. and Vitale, M.R. (2005). *Achieving value from ICT: key management strategies*. Canberra: Department of Communications, Information Technology and the Arts, Commonwealth of Australia 2005. Retrieved from www.dcita.gov.au
Hall, G.E., Loucks, S.F., Rutherford, W.L. and Newlove, B.W. (1975). Levels of use of the innovation: a framework for analysing innovation adoption. *Journal of Teacher Education* 26(1), 52–56.
Hartley, R. and Al-Muhaideb, S. (2007). User-oriented techniques to support interaction and decision making with large educational databases. *Computer and Education* 48, 268–284. doi: 10.1016/j.compedu.2005.01.005
Jhurree, V. (2005). Technology integration in education in developing countries: guidelines to policy makers. *International Education Journal* 6(4), 467–483.
Joseph, P.M. and Lunt, B.M. (2006). *IT in the Middle East: an overview*. Paper presented at the Proceedings of the 7th Conference on Information Technology Education, Minneapolis, Minnesota, USA. Retrieved 21 August 2014 from http://dl.acm.org/citation.cfm?id=1168821
Jungert, T. and Rosander, M. (2010). Self-efficacy and strategies to influence the study environment. *Teaching in Higher Education* 15(6), 647–659.

Krieger, Z. (2007). Saudi Arabia puts its billions behind Western-style higher education. *Chronicle of Higher Education* 54(3), 1–6.
Lee, C.B., Teo, T., Chai, C.S., Choy, D., Tan, A. and Seah, J. (2007). *Closing the gap: pre-service teachers' perceptions of an ICT-based, student-centred learning curriculum.* Paper presented at the ICT: Providing Choices for Learners and Learning Conference, 2–5 December. Proceedings ascilite, Singapore. Retrieved from www.ascilite.org.au/conferences/singapore07/procs/lee-cb.pdf
Lessen, E. and Sorensen, C. (2006). Integrating technology in schools, colleges, and departments of education: a primer for deans. *Change* 38(2), 44–46.
Lingard, B., Rawolle, S. and Taylor, S. (2005). Globalising policy sociology in education: working with Bourdieu. *Journal of Education Policy* 20(6), 759–777.
McCloskey, P. (2007). IT key to Saudi Arabia 25-year strategy for higher ed. 23 April. Retrieved 21 August 2014 from: http://campustechnology.com/articles/47614/
Ministry of Communications and Information Technology (2007). *The national communications and information technology plan: the vision towards the information society.* Riyadh, Saudi Arabia: Ministry of Communications and Information Technology. Retrieved from: www.mcit.gov.sa/arabic/NICTP/Policy/
Ministry of Economy and Planning. (2005). *The eighth development plan (1425/1426 – 1429/1430) A.H (2005–2009) A.D.* Riyadh, Saudi Arabia: Ministry of Economy and Planning. Retrieved from: www.mep.gov.sa/index.jsp;jsessionid=AF4528726 99B13F5814CDE7757C8FE75.alfa?event=ArticleView&Article.ObjectID=3
Ministry of Education (2005). *The executive summary of the Ministry of Education Ten-Year Plan 1425–1435 H (2004–2014)* (2nd ed.). Riyadh, Saudi Arabia: Ministry of Education.
Nelson, A.R. (2010). Education as a global commodity. *Nature* 464(7293), 1277–1280.
Nkonge, B. and Gueldenzoph, L.E. (2006). Best practices in online education: implications for policy and practice. *Business Education Digest* 15(XV), 42–53.
Northcote, M. (2009). Educational beliefs of higher education teachers and students: implications for teacher education. *Australian Journal of Teacher Education* 34(3), 69–81.
Onsman, A. (2011). It is better to light a candle than to ban the darkness: government-led academic development in Saudi Arabian universities. *Higher Education* 1–14. doi: 10.1007/s10734-010-9402-y
Peeraer, J. and Van Petegem, P. (2011). ICT in teacher education in an emerging developing country: Vietnam's baseline situation at the start of 'The Year of ICT'. *Computers and Education* 56(4), 974–982.
Pianfetti, E. (2005). An integrated framework used to increase preservice teacher NETS-T ability. *The Free Library*, 22 June. Retrieved 21 August 2014 from www. thefreelibrary.com/An%20integrated%20framework%20used%20to%20 increase%20preservice%20teacher%20NETS-T...-a0132711918
Polly, D., Mims, C., Shepherd, C.E. and Inan, F. (2010). Evidence of impact: transforming teacher education with preparing tomorrow's teachers to teach with technology (PT3) grants. *Teaching and Teacher Education* 26(4), 863–870.
Ramady, M.A. (2010). *The Saudi Arabian economy: policies, achievements, and challenges.* New York: Springer.
Reimer, K.L. (2005). Integrating technology into the curriculum. In M.O. Thirunarayanan and A. Perez-Prado (eds), *Integrating technology in higher education.* New York: University Press of America, Inc.

Robertson, M., Fluck, A. and Webb, I. (2007). *Seven steps to success with ICTs: whole-school approaches to sustainable change* (1st ed.). Camberwell: ACER Press.

Roblyer, M.D. and Edwards, J. (2003). *Integrating educational technology into teaching* (3rd ed.). Upper Saddle River NJ: Prentice-Hall.

Rogers, R.K. (2007). *Computer anxiety and innovativeness as predictors of technology integration*. Unpublished EdD, Texas Tech University, Texas.

Sang, G., Valcke, M., Braak, J.V. and Tondeur, J. (2010). Student teachers' thinking processes and ICT integration: predictors of prospective teaching behaviours with educational technology. *Computers and Education* 54(1), 103–112.

Shoffner, M.B., Dias, L.B. and Thomas, C.D. (2001). A model for collaborative relationships between instructional technology and teacher education programs. *Contemporary Issues in Technology and Teacher Education* [online serial], 1(3). Retrieved from www.citejournal.org/vol1/iss3/currentissues/general/article1.htm

Smith, D.W. and Kelley, P. (2007). A survey of assistive technology and teacher preparation programs for individuals with visual impairments. *Journal of Visual Impairment and Blindness* 101(7), 429–433.

Smolin, L. and Lawless, K. (2007). Technologies in schools: stimulating a dialogue. In L. Smolin, K. Lawless and N.C. Burbules (eds), *Information and communication technologies: considerations of current practice for teachers and teacher education* (vol. 2). Malden MA: Blackwell Publishing.

Technology in Schools (2003). Chapter 7: Suggestions, tools, and guideline for assessing technology in elementary and secondary education. Retrieved 10 June 2014 from http://nces.ed.gov/pubs2003/tech_schools/chapter7.asp

Vannatta, R. (2007). The intrepid explorer: a model of effective technology use for all educators. In K. Kumpulainen (ed.), *Educational technology: opportunities and challenges*. Oulu, Finland: Oulu University Press.

Wabuyele, L.C. (2003). *Understanding teachers' and administrators' perceptions and experiences towards computer use in Kenyan classrooms: a case study of two schools*. Unpublished PhD thesis, Ohio University, Ohio, USA. Retrieved from http://proquest.umi.com/pqdweb?did=766010831&Fmt=7&clientId=20828&RQT=309&VName=PQD

Part II
Practical applications

6 Mobile learning in Gulf Cooperation Council countries

Theory and practice

Hessah AlShaya and Afnan A. Oyaid

Introduction

Mobile technology is now an integral part of daily life. It allows users to do many things – connect with loved ones, play games, order food and manage money. The sheer breadth of tasks that can be achieved via mobile devices has prompted many to consider how they might be used for learning.

Curtis (2014) predicts that by 2016 more than two billion people globally will own a smartphone, increasing by more than half a billion to include around one in three of the world's population by 2018. Other mobile devices, such as tablets, laptops and MP3 players, are also hugely popular. People of diverse ages and backgrounds now have access to an unprecedented level of internet access and connectivity. This is an ideal time to explore the potential of mobile learning.

Research into mobile learning is increasing (Liu et al., 2014) and various mobile learning programmes are being used worldwide (Sharples, Arnedillo-Sánchez, Milard and Vavoula, 2014). The Gulf Cooperation Council (GCC) countries, namely Oman, Bahrain, Qatar, the United Arab Emirates, Kuwait and Saudi Arabia, are among the nations involved.

This chapter initially explores the concepts, advantages and issues surrounding mobile learning, then focuses on the implementation and advancement of mobile learning in GCC nations.

Definitions of mobile learning

Within the contexts of education and instructional technology, mobile learning (m-learning) can generally be defined as the use of mobile technology for the purposes of learning, at home or elsewhere (EDUCAUSE, 2010). Other definitions include the use of mobile devices to gain or share educational information in the form of non-physical learning resources of various media types (Mobil21, n.d.).

More precisely, mobile learning is the process of acquiring educational information and increasing knowledge, solely through the use of mobile technology, or mobile technology combined with other forms of information and communication technology (UNESCO, 2015). It can be undertaken in both formal learning contexts and more informally elsewhere, giving learners the chance to engage with other people and materials. Mobile learning also lets students build their own educational information and resources, thus facilitates dynamic learning (ibid.).

The role and nature of mobile learning can change with the user. This ability to mould to the user's preferences stems largely from the fact that mobile learning does not restrict the learner to the classroom; it has been explained in terms of the use of a mobile device to facilitate users' informational and social learning processes (Crompton, 2012).

Mobile learning – advantages and issues

Some describe this as the 'Age of Mobilism' (Norris and Soloway, 2011), where constant connectivity is an ideal. Such a context, where people demand constant access to information, regardless of location, is perfect for mobile learning, whereby students learn wherever they are. This gives great flexibility, permits interaction and can generate inspiration and the exchange of information without the burden of arranging meetings.

Mobile learning makes it easier for educators to reach students and to share resources. However, educators have yet to overcome some of the barriers to implementation.

Advantages of mobile learning

Crescente and Lee (2011) and Elias (2011) highlight the following advantages of mobile learning.

Accessibility: Mobile learning removes physical restrictions to the accessing of learning materials and information.

Productivity: Mobile learning has time management benefits; learners can use 'dead' time (commuting, etc.) to study.

Collaboration: Mobile learning lets students interact and share ideas, regardless of location.

Individual learning styles and speeds: Given the multiple means of accessing information online, mobile learning can flex to meet students' learning styles and speeds, so they learn at their own pace and in their own way.

Affordability: Mobile learning makes online resources affordable; most students find it easier to afford mobile devices than laptops or PCs. The overheads of face-to-face training are removed, so it is cheaper for learners to acquire new skills online.

Support: Mobile technology renders help and guidance constantly available.

More educated population: Mobile learning is increasing the number of young adults engaged in educational activities and helping to improve skills.

Streamlined learning: Mobile technology lets users consolidate educational information in one place, e.g. by downloading and uploading files and information.

Greater learner satisfaction: Some claim mobile learning is more fulfilling for students than conventional forms of education.

Issues in mobile learning

Nielsen (2009), Crescente and Lee (2011) and Elias (2011) highlight the following.

Technical hurdles

Battery and signal: Lack of signal or WiFi, or a flat battery, can interrupt mobile learning.

Size of device components: Mobile devices, especially those with small screens and keyboards, may be inappropriate for viewing large amounts of text, causing problems such as eye strain.

Device characteristics: Mobile devices quickly become obsolete. Sometimes, mobile devices become incompatible with certain software overnight, forcing users to upgrade. Mobile learning only works if the user's device can run required sites and applications, and such devices can be expensive. A Wi-Fi connection may be essential to access large amounts of information.

Other technical issues include:

- Mobile devices are limited in how much data they can store at once.
- Mobile platforms may not support all educational resources or content, so modifications to content are required to make them mobile-compatible.
- Mobile devices vary hugely in terms of operating systems, screen size and features.
- Mobile devices vary in their compatibility with certain materials.
- The multi-functional nature of mobile devices means that texts, e-mails, notifications and calls may interrupt learning.

Educational and social issues

- Time and energy must be spent planning the organization's transition to mobile learning, given the major implications for employees, educators and students.
- The costs involved – Wi-Fi connections, content creation etc. – must be planned and budgeted for.
- Mobile devices may be good for reading content, but less suitable for creating it.
- Teachers must ensure that learners can use mobile devices for learning in various settings.
- Learners must be able to apply content and save materials.
- There may be copyright and security concerns.
- The emerging 'mobile age' must be understood through appropriate theory.
- Differences between mobile leaning and electronic/online learning must be acknowledged.

Types of mobile learning activity

Mobile learning is acknowledged as a component of a larger learning scheme, thus mobile learning tasks are additional activities, not sole strategies. Naismith et al. (2004) propose the following frameworks for creation of mobile learning tasks.

Situated activities: Situated activities use authentic contexts to optimise learning. Lonsdale et al. (2004) and Rogers et al. (2002) state that mobile devices, like virtual learning environments, can generate realistic learning opportunities.

Collaborative activities: Collaborative activities focus on learner–learner interaction to enhance the learning process. Zurita and Nussbaum (2007), Cortez et al. (2004) and Zurita et al. (2003) suggest mobile devices be used to promote collaborative learning via information acquisition, storage and sharing, lesson management and the promotion of dialogue between learners. Mobile learning may generate novel approaches to educator–learner communication.

Informal and lifelong learning activities: Informal and lifelong learning activities occur largely outside the classroom. Mobile devices let learners acquire knowledge almost anywhere, at any time. Wood et al. (2003) found that informal learning via mobile devices allowed cancer patients to learn from and engage with each other, while Traxler (2003) claims that in the context of lifelong learning schemes mobile learning has great potential and attracts global interest.

Teaching and learning support activities: Teaching and learning support activities facilitate engagement between learners and educational materials. Corlett et al. (2004), Sharples et al. (2003) and Holme and Sharples (2002) claim that mobile devices offer educators many advantages, including alerts and reminders, allocation of material to learners and report generation.

Mobile learning programmes in GCC countries

Countries of the GCC have shown particular interest in mobile technology, including its use in education. This will now be discussed, with a particular focus on Saudi Arabia.

Saudi Arabia

Saudi Arabia has recently increased its focus on mobile learning, in line with improvements in and greater availability of mobile technologies and services. Smartphones, tablets and other 'smart' devices are very popular in Saudi Arabia.

National government has begun to shift its focus when it comes to supporting the growth of Saudi Arabia, moving away from the oil industry and towards expertise and specialization. Thus the Saudi Arabian government is generous in its funding of mobile learning programmes and IT in schools.

Saudi Arabia has implemented both mobile- and distance-learning programmes. To meet the needs of modern, technology-oriented learners, it has invested in the provision of appropriate learning and teaching methods in educational settings, including universities. Young people in Saudi Arabia show a particular appreciation of mobile devices and technologies; Al-Shehri (2013) claims that Saudi Arabian youth is the most active of all Arab populations on mobile social media.

Recent figures show that most Saudi Arabians own one or more contract mobile phones, and that of all mobile phone owners 15 per cent own a 3G phone (Arab News, 2013). Alhumaidan (2013) quotes figures from statcounter.com, which suggest that IOS phones are so popular in Saudi Arabia that it is the third-placed Arab nation in terms of iPhone consumption. Further, Saudi Arabia has more BlackBerry users than any other country. Ease of access enhances the potential of mobile learning.

Statistics on Saudi Arabia (SAGIA, 2015) suggest that per capita income will reach $33,500 in 2020. This puts the country among very few nations experiencing reasonably strong per capita income and rapid development. Healthcare and education are free of charge for all residents, and university students receive a monthly allowance.

While the world has begun to increase its focus on learner centred practices, Saudi Arabia has taken significant steps. Most universities have now established e-learning deanships, and official agreements between themselves, global organizations and e-learning logistics firms. In the case of deanships, mobile learning has long been a primary emphasis. University students are given mobile devices such as iPads to enhance their learning experience and technological skills. Students and lecturers engage via social media, and all understand how to combine official and social media channels to improve communication.

Saudi Arabian internet use

Over the past decade, internet use in Saudi Arabia has soared. Meanwhile, there has been steady and continuing growth in ICT. Figures show growth of 13.9 per cent in the Saudi ICT sector for 2012, with investment of SAR 94 billion. In 2013, growth was around 14 per cent, with SAR 102 billion investment, and by 2017 spending will exceed SAR 138 billion and the compound annual growth rate (CAGR) of the ICT market will reach 8.1 per cent.

The number of people using tablets and smartphones in Saudi Arabia is booming. Users engage strongly with mobile entertainment, music, video, social networking sites and apps. Increasingly, companies let employees use their own devices at work to maximize the advantages of mobile technology, enhance customer service and build a mobile-savvy workforce.

In just five years (2007–2012) the average Saudi Arabian subscribed to 1.82 wireless networks, with total wireless network subscriptions increasing from 28.4 million in 2007 to 53 million in 2012. Subscriptions to mobile broadband increased even more over that time, rising from 0.2 per cent to 42.1 per cent, and in 2012 mobile sector income was 55.91 billion SAR, a rise of 68 per cent from 2007.

Researchers from King Saud University, Saudi Arabia, used questionnaires to assess students' views on the application of mobile technology to learning (Al-Fahad, 2009). One aim of the study was to clarify how undergraduates at King Saud University could be encouraged to use mobile technology in their degree studies. The findings suggest that mobile learning could be beneficial to students' learning, and tutors' teaching, experiences and that this could in turn benefit student retention.

The same study gathered opinions from 131 undergraduates on the technological issues around mobile learning, as well as the perceived effectiveness and potential benefits of the technique. At least three out of four students favoured mobile learning, and in particular students liked using mobile devices to interact with other students, to access information at any time and to learn in ways that suited their own preferences.

Mobile and distance-learning schemes and establishments introduced by Saudi Arabia's government include the Saudi Centre for Support and Counselling (SANEED), the Saudi Electronic University, the Saudi Digital Library, the learning management system JUSUR and the National Centre for E-Learning and Distance Education.

Qassim College of Medicine is credited with having pioneered the Saudi higher education sector's use of mobile learning (Garg, 2013); subsequently, in 2011, the 'mobile blackboard' was established by King Khalid University, which had already used iPads to conduct tests and enhance learning experiences. Al-Shehri (2012) claims that King Khalid University taught students to link their mobile blackboard to Facebook to receive alerts and updates – an innovative approach that built on recognition of students' engagement with social media. Many Saudi universities provide Wi-Fi.

Al Fahad (2009) investigated use of mobile learning in medicine and arts courses, using a sample of female students undertaking these degrees. The researcher found that almost all subjects owned an advanced smartphone, highlighting the potential for mobile learning. Al Fahad suggested that many Saudi Arabian students engaged with social networking sites and the internet using mobile phones, but noted that the cost of consuming mobile data was a potential barrier for students.

In another study (Chanchary and Islam, 2011), participants, who were students from Najran University, expressed a preference for blended learning techniques. This study suggests a reluctance to shift entirely to mobile learning, and also perhaps that students were confused about the role and benefits of this approach.

Nassuora (2012) sought to understand what influences the adoption of mobile learning in higher education and used the Unified Theory of Acceptance and Use of Technology (UTAUT) framework with participants from Alfaisal University, a private establishment in Saudi Arabia. This revealed that while most subjects viewed the concept and idea of mobile learning favourably, very few understood it.

Seliaman and Al-Turki (2012) used a similar framework to study the concept of students using mobile technologies to engage in information exchanges, internet searches, essay completion and reading educational content. This study did not find any strong positive relationship between students' opinions of the effectiveness of mobile learning and their opinions on the impressive or novel qualities of the mobile learning concept. Thus, while university students may be savvy consumers of mobile technology and devices, they may not wish to use these as their sole or primary means of learning.

In another study (Al-Shehri, 2012), the author – a PhD student at King Khalid University – sought to clarify the benefits of mobile technology in simulating 'real-life' learning environments. Further, he investigated the benefits of mobile learning for students studying English as a Second Language. Al-Shehri's findings highlight a number of technology-based issues, including a preference for carrying out learning tasks on PCs and laptops. Interruption of learning by non-educational content on social media sites and inability to access mobile networks in some locations were also issues, although it is suggested that mobile technology could enhance learning through its provision of authenticity.

The literature suggests that although many students and lecturers in the tertiary sector have favourable perceptions of mobile learning, many students are yet to properly understand the benefits it may offer them. However, some researchers suggest that mobile learning will become increasingly popular and prominent over time (Al-Shehri, 2012).

Al Hamdani (2015) investigated Saudi students' use of tablets and mobile phones to share information, search the internet, complete projects and read content. In order to use student opinion to evaluate the effectiveness of mobile learning, Al Hamdani used the Technology Acceptance Model (TAM). The initial findings from that study suggest that students' views of mobile learning's effectiveness do not evidently increase in line with their views on the value of mobile technologies.

The following section explores mobile learning practices in other GCC countries.

The Gulf

The provision and popularity of e-learning courses has surged in the Arab world recently. The Arab Open University (AOU) is a leading online course provider in the region, serving Oman, Bahrain, Lebanon, Jordan, Egypt, Saudi Arabia and Kuwait. Its students can study both online and in physical locations; there is heavy use of mobile learning. The AOU is at the forefront of mobile learning in higher education, and in 2007 it established a Java-based online resource database for students. The AOU currently has more than 50,000 students in the GCC region alone, with enrolment increasing by 20 per cent or more annually. The popularity of the AOU and other universities offering online-only study represents an important shift in the region's higher education sector, since until recently there was no access to online courses for GCC students.

Kuwait

The Ambient Insight Premium Report (2013) states that the Kuwaiti government aimed to launch mobile learning in all schools by 2013 in an 'e-education' drive. The scheme was piloted in secondary schools during 2011, with online materials and learning technologies allocated to students and teachers. The following year, provision was rolled out to middle, primary and nursery schools, which all received mobile learning tools and saw all textbooks adapted to e-book format by October 2012.

Qatar

All of Qatar's primary and secondary school students – around 100,000 – were given their own mobile device by 2014, to facilitate interaction with teachers, other students and learning materials both inside and outside the classroom. This was part of a 2012 government incentive scheme, which gave teachers similar devices.

Qatar's government committed to converting all course materials used by public schools into digital format by 2014, and to publish all learning content in both English and Arabic to develop Qatar's competitive advantage in the global education sector.

Workers in the Qatari domestic energy sector are shortly to trial a mobile training application that is being developed by Qatar University in collaboration with Athabasca University, Canada. The parties aim to provide a mobile learning application for use in various industries; indeed, such an approach is already being taken in the oil and gas sector, as well as with students of English as a Second Language. One of the Qatar University researchers working on the app says that Qatar has not used this type of application for training purposes before, thus it is a truly innovative project.

Ansari (2013) describes the scheme as part of the government's drive to improve Qatar through its 'National Vision 2030' strategy, the aim of which is to encourage long-term economic development and improve the population's quality of life while retaining Qatar's cultural history and norms.

Oman

Despite having just 3,632,000 citizens, Oman has made impressive progress in mobile learning. Government focus has shifted from the energy industry towards the importance of supporting economic growth through knowledge and expertise. Oman has only had a public schooling system for four decades and lacks a solid education sector, so has some way to go build the educated population that it aims to create.

Both males and females in Oman can attend primary and secondary education, and increasing numbers are entering university. More than 5,000 undergraduate and postgraduate students are enrolled at Oman's Sohar University. Seven out of ten university students are female, revealing Oman's increasingly progressive nature.

Sohar University is also leading the way in the implementation of technology. Lecturers are encouraged to adopt the leading Learning Management System (LMS) Moodle (SULMS). Most Sohar students own mobile phones and many also own laptops or PCs. However, the university has yet to establish a framework for mobile technology in the classroom, and because lecturers lack guidelines mobile devices are not generally used in lectures.

Despite the relative lack of official policy, Sohar University students have proven eager and active in the use of independent mobile learning. Students on the university's Communicative Language Teaching (CLT) course can use mobile learning techniques in the classroom and feedback from those students reveals that mobile learning has encouraged critical thinking and helped students to deal with course content.

Sarrab et al. (2014) studied students' opinions and understanding of mobile learning in a user-centred participatory study with science and engineering students from Sultan Qaboos University. In phase one of the study, mobile learning was explained to the students. In phase two, students provided basic information about themselves and shared their knowledge and opinions of e-learning and mobile learning, along with suggestions for the researchers. The findings showed students to be highly enthusiastic about mobile learning and the prospect of engaging in mobile learning activities. The concept of mobile learning was widely accepted.

Another study (Al-Mamari, 2009), which sought to establish the success of Oman's mobile learning implementation in higher education, focused on the listening skills of students. Findings showed that students learning English showed a marked increase in listening ability when mobile phones were used as a learning tool. Students viewed mobile learning very favourably.

Today, Oman's citizens represent 2.1 per cent of the world's internet users, according to global internet usage reports. By the end of 2013, more than 2.1 million Oman residents had internet access, a penetration rate of 66.4 per cent. By mid-2014, almost 98 per cent of Oman's fixed dialup internet contracts had been upgraded to ADSL, WiMAX and line leases.

Just 8.8 per cent (around 495,700) of Oman's mobile phone users have a contract mobile, but a huge 91.2 per cent (over 5.1 million users) have prepaid (PAYG) subscriptions. By the end of 2012 there were 119,398 internet users in Oman, which increased by almost 33 per cent to number 158,678 users in 2013. Household penetration in 2013 was 39.4 per cent, and fixed internet penetration was 4.4 per cent. By the end of 2013 mobile broadband penetration was 67.4 per cent, with more than 2.4 million users.

United Arab Emirates

A national iPad incentive during academic year 2012/13 benefited all of the UAE's state-owned universities, and all public schools are to be supplied with learning technologies. The UAE has released some 7,000 digital copies of educational materials and lessons in order to help teachers, and has provided schools with advanced ICT systems. The Ambient Insight Premium Report (2013) states the UAE government aims to give all schools students access to a learning device by 2017.

In 2012, the UAE's Ministry of Higher Education allocated iPads to all foundation course students and teachers (Gitaski, 2013). Whilst many universities have yet to implement a formal learning device protocol, many lecturers do, to some extent, use mobile learning activities.

April 2012 saw the launch of the Mohammad Bin Rashid Al Maktoum Smart Learning Program, to provide 4G internet access via tablet for all of the UAE's students by 2017. Consequently, the UAE government will give state schools more than 200,000 tablets.

The UAE's first online-only university, Bin Mohammad e-University (HBMeU), was established in 2009; it now provides educational materials for consumer-oriented mobile learning VAS (value-added service) subscriptions.

The UAE and Apple collaborated on the globally ground-breaking Federal Higher Education Mobile Learning Initiative. First-year students from selected universities were given iPads, the government providing 14,000 devices during the first year of the scheme. A strong focus was placed on English as a Second Language, and all iPads had educational applications pre-installed. By 2017 more than 55,000 university students should have their own iPads.

By July 2013, the UAE had the highest proportion of smartphone use in the world, with 73 per cent of mobile phones being smartphones (eMarkter, 2015).

Bahrain

Bahrain has one of the most advanced education systems in the Gulf, and has consequently effectively developed and applied IT in the classroom. King Hamad bin Khalifa Al Khalifa established the King Hamad Schools of the Future to facilitate mobile learning and online collaboration between schools.

Bahrain's schools already apply mobile learning. In a study by Al-Ani et al. (2013), a questionnaire was given to 107 students at the University of Bahrain's Information Technology College. Participants were asked which factors influenced their willingness to embrace mobile learning, their views on its effectiveness in their own learning and their beliefs about its ease of use. According to the findings, these factors were all positively associated.

Arinakou and Giousmpasoglou (2014) surveyed 45 participants from 4 state and private universities and concluded that complete implementation of mobile learning strategies in Bahrain's universities is likely to take some time, even though most lecturers surveyed reported that they already made some use of mobile learning techniques and that they understood it.

This study also showed that lecturers tend to use mobile learning for navigation and interaction, thereby failing to maximize its benefits (although lecturers acknowledge these). However, the researchers predict that full implementation of mobile learning should be achieved by 2020. This study (Arinakou and Giousmpasoglou, 2014) offers a helpful framework for educators, highlighting the influence that mobile learning can have on knowledge acquisition and encouraging educators to adopt a more learner-based approach. The results suggest that universities should focus on technological development and employee training, and show the importance of implementing mobile learning in higher education to the development of Bahrain's economy.

Improving mobile learning in practice

The paragraphs above, which consider mobile learning in GCC countries, raise the questions of why these schemes and incentives have worked, and how they can underpin development of mobile learning. It seems that in mobile learning projects success is facilitated by widespread, good-quality internet access and sufficient investment in technology, e.g. the provision of devices. Educational content that has been well thought out, clear learning goals and effective teacher training also seem to help.

Expectations for the development of mobile learning

Technology is likely to become easier to access and more affordable in the coming decade, which is important for mobile learning. This itself is no guarantee that a mobile learning strategy will succeed; while technology is important, too little is known about students' opinions on technology and their use of it to perform given tasks.

The technological arena of 2025 is relatively easy to foresee, but the development of mobile learning is less certain. However, the work of Shuler, Winters and West (2013) does describe the expectations of UNESCO regarding mobile learning, which are worthy of more detailed exploration.

Technological predictions

UNESCO holds that future technology will allow users to perform multiple functions, will be reasonably priced and available to most. Users will be able to collect, sync and evaluate large amounts of information via mobile device(s) and learning will be enhanced by new forms of mobile information. As a result, learners will have a more realistic, meaningful and tailored learning experience.

Better mobile translation applications will help second language learners, allowing students' access to materials in a wider range of languages. Mobile audio translation is a real possibility. UNESCO has predicted that developments in Google Glass and other innovations (e.g. folding screens) will address current issues of screen size and allow users to watch 3D content, view content in higher resolution and magnify in a way that cannot now be achieved on mobile devices. Battery life and charging speeds will probably increase, overcoming key barriers to greater adoption of mobile learning.

Educational predictions

UNESCO suggests that blended learning will becoming increasingly popular and mobile learning will become a core facet of teaching practice. The current contextual benefits of mobile learning will be enhanced, students will be able to learn almost anywhere and mobile learning affiliations will probably involve galleries, factories, agricultural sites – any site of educational interest. Users will be able to learn more at a greater distance and student-centred learning will be key, because mobile learning will offer tailored activities and applications to suit individual students.

The technology used in mobile learning could allow educators and universities to quantify the impact of mobile learning projects, by tracking students' use of them. Learners may benefit from the connective capacity of mobile technology, connecting with their peers worldwide.

Conclusion

This chapter has explored the concept, advantages, issues and implementation of mobile learning, focusing on the advancement of mobile learning in GCC countries. Its ultimate aim was to provide the reader with a detailed account of mobile learning in GCC countries, supported by contemporary literature and statistics.

References

Al-Ani, M.F., Hameed, S.M. and Faisal, L. (2013). Students' perspectives in adopting mobile learning at University of Bahrain. Available at: http://dl.acm.org/citation.cfm?id=2585862

Al-Fahad, N. (2009). Students' attitudes and perceptions towards the effectiveness of mobile learning in King Saud University, Saudi Arabia. *The Turkish Online Journal of Educational Technology – TOJET* 8(2), article 10.

Al Hamdani, D. (2015). Mobile learning: a good practice. Paper published in the 13th International Educational Technology Conference.

Alhumaidan, A. (2013). Saudi Arabia ranks first in terms of BlackBerry users. *Aleqtisadiah Newspaper* 7120. See also website: www.aleqt.com/2013/04/09/article_745979.html

Al-Mamari, K. (2009). *The effect of mobile learning technologies on students' listening skills in higher education in the Sultanate of Oman*. Unpublished MA thesis, Sultan Qaboos University, Muscat, Oman.

Al-Shehri, S. (2012). *Contextual language learning: the educational potential of mobile technologies and social media*. Unpublished doctoral dissertation, University of Queensland, Australia.

Al-Shehri, S. (2013). An outlook on future mobile learning in Saudi Arabia. Paper to mLearn 2013, 22–24 October, Doha, Qatar.

Ambient Insight Regional Report (2013). The 2012–2017 Middle East Mobile Learning Market.

Ansari, Kalim (2013). Qatar University develops mobile learning application to improve training. See also website: www.qatarchronicle.com/education-2/46436/qatar-university-develops-mobile-learning-application-to-improve-training-3/

Arab News (2013). Most Saudis have at least one mobile subscription. See also website: www.arabnews.com/news/445567

Arinakou, E. and Giousmpasoglou, C. (2014). M-learning in higher education in Bahrain: the educators' view. Paper for the 6th e-Learning Excellence in the Middle East Conference – Leadership, Design and Technology for the 21st Century Learning, Dubai, 3–5 March.

Chanchary, F.H. and Islam, S. (2011). Mobile learning in Saudi Arabia – prospects and challenges. See also website: www.nauss.edu.sa/acit/PDFs/f2535.pdf

Corlett, D., Sharples, M., Bull, S. and Chan, T. (2004). Evaluation of a mobile learning organizer for university students. 2nd IEEE International Workshop on Wireless and Mobile Technologies in Education, Jung Li, Taiwan.

Cortez, C., Nussbaum, M., Santelices, P., Rodriguez, P. and Zurita, G. (2004). Teaching science with mobile computer supported collaborative learning (MCSCL). Paper presented at the 2nd IEEE International Workshop on Wireless and Mobile Technologies in Education.

Crescente, Mary Louise and Lee, Doris (2011). Critical issues of m-learning: design models, adoption processes, and future trends. *Journal of the Chinese Institute of Industrial Engineers* 28(2), 111–123.

Crompton, H. (2012). M-learning definitions. In Z.L. Berg and L.Y. Muilenburg (eds), *Handbook of mobile learning*. New York: Routledge.

Curtis, S. (2014). Quarter of the world will be using smartphones in 2016. 11 December. www.telegraph.co.uk/technology/mobile-phones/11287659/Quarter-of-the-world-will-be-using-smartphones-in-2016.html

EDUCAUSE (2010). 7 things you should know about mobile apps for learning. www.educause.edu/library/resources/7-things-you-should-know-about-mobile-apps-learning

Elias, Tanya (2011). Universal instructional design principles for mobile learning. *International Review of Research in Open and Distance Learning* 12(2), 143–156.

eMarketer (2015). United Arab Emirates leads Middle East and Africa in mobile phone penetration. See more at: www.emarketer.com/Article/United-Arab-Emirates-Leads-Middle-East-Africa-Mobile-Phone-Penetration/1011971 #sthash.O1Gmt2HK.dpuf

Gitaski, C.R.-C. (2013). A research agenda for the UAE iPad initiative. *Learning and Teaching in Higher Education: Gulf Perspectives* 10(2). Retrieved from http://lthe.zu.ac.ae

Grag, V. (2013). The emergence of mobile learning for higher education in Kingdom of Saudi Arabia. Upside Learning Blog. See also website: www.upsidelearning.com/blog/index.php/2013/01/15/emergence-of-mobile-learning-for-higher-education-in-kingdom-of-saudi-arabia/

Holme, O. and Sharples, M. (2002). Implementing a student learning organiser on the pocket PC platform. Proceedings of MLEARN2002, European Workshop on Mobile and Contextual Learning, Birmingham, UK, pp. 41–44. http://arxiv.org/ftp/arxiv/papers/1504/1504.01139.pdf   www.nauss.edu.sa/acit/PDFs/f2535.pdf

Liu, M., Scordino, R., Geurtz, R., Navarrete, C., Ko, Y. and Lim, M. (2014). A look at research on mobile learning in K–12 education from 2007 to the present. *Journal of Research on Technology in Education* 46(4), 325–372.

Lonsdale, P., Barber, C., Sharples M., Byrne, W, Arvanitis, T., Brundell, P. and Beale R. (2004). *Context awareness for MOBIlearn: creating an engaging learning*

experience in an art museum. Conference paper MLearn 2004, conference proceedings.
Mobile21 (n.d). Basics of mobile learning. www.mobl21.com/Basics_Of_Mobile_Learning.pdf
Naismith, L., Lonsdale, P., Vavoula, G. N. and Sharples, M. (2004). *Mobile technologies and learning.* Futurelab.
Naismith, L., Lonsdale, P., Vavoula, G. and Sharples, M. (2004). *Literature review in mobile technologies and learning.* London: University of Birmingham Publications Press.
Nassuora, A.B. (2012). Students' acceptance of mobile learning for higher education in Saudi Arabia. *American Academic and Scholarly Research Journal* 4(2). Retrieved from www.naturalspublishing.com/files/published/5z8b9f97ju9k98.pdf
Nielsen, J. (2009). Mobile usability. Message posted to www.useit.com/alertbox/mobile-usability.html, 20 July.
Norris, C.A. and Soloway, E. (2011). Learning and schooling in the age of mobilism. *Educational Technologies* 51(6): 3–10. Retrieved 6 November 2012 from http://cecs5580.pbworks.com/w/file/fetch/50304204/Soloway%20Ed%20 Tech-Learning%20and%20Schooling%20in%20the%20Age%20of%20 Mobilism.pdf
Rogers, Y., Price, S., Harris, E., Phelps, T., Underwood, M., Wilde, D., Smith, H., Muller, H., Randell, C., Stanton, D., Neale, H., Thompson, M., Weal, M. and Michaelides, D. (2002). Learning through digitally augmented physical experiences: reflections on the Ambient Wood project. *Equator Technical Report.* Retrieved 25 August 2014 from: http://users.mct.open.ac.uk/yvonne.rogers/papers/Rogers_Ambient_Wood2.1.pdf
Sarrab, M. (2014). M-learning in education: Omani undergraduate students' perspective. Paper published in the IETC.
Saudi Arabian General Investment Authority SAGIA (2015). Investment climate in Saudi Arabia. https://www.sagia.gov.sa/Investment-climate/Some-Things-You-Need-To-Know-/Investment-Incentives/
Seliaman, Mohamed E. and Al Turki, M.S. (2012). Mobile learning adoption in Saudi Arabia. *World Academy of Science, Engineering and Technology* 6, 20 September. See also website: www.waset.org/publications/11339
Sharples, M., Arnedillo-Sánchez, I., Milrad, M. and Vavoula, G. (2014). Mobile learning. *Cambridge handbook of the learning sciences* (pp. 1513–1573). New York: Cambridge University Press.
Sharples, M., Chan, T., Rudman, P. and Bull, S. (2003). Evaluation of a mobile learning organiser and concept mapping tools. Proceedings of MLEARN 2003: Learning with Mobile Devices. London, UK: Learning and Skills Development Agency, 139–144.
Shuler, C., Winters, N. and West, M. (2013). The future of mobile learning: implications for policy makers and planners. UNESCO, available at: http://unesdoc.unesco.org/images/0021/002196/219637e.pdf
Traxler, J. (2003). M learning: evaluating the effectiveness and the cost. Proceedings of MLEARN 2003: Learning with Mobile Devices. London, UK: Learning and Skills Development Agency, 183–188.
UNESCO (2015). ICT in Education, Mobile Learning. www.unesco.org/new/en/unesco/themes/icts/m4ed/

Wood, J., Keen, A., Basu, N. and Robertshaw, S. (2003). *The development of mobile applications for patient education: designing for user experiences.* San Francisco: Dux.

Zurita, G. and Nussbaum, M. (2007). A conceptual framework based on Activity Theory for mobile CSCL. *British Journal of Educational Technology* 38(2), 211–235.

Zurita, G., Nussbaum, M. and Sharples, M. (2003). Encouraging face-to-face collaborative learning through the use of handheld computers in the classroom. In *Human-Computer Interaction with Mobile Devices and Services* 2795 (pp. 193–208). Udine, Italy: Springer Verlag.

7 PresentationTube
A network for producing and sharing online video lectures at Sultan Qaboos University

Alaa Sadik

Multimedia applications are increasingly popular among instructors because they provide powerful tools for creation of instructional materials in conventional universities. When used appropriately, these applications can support face-to-face teaching and extend traditional lectures in valuable ways. In traditional lecture settings, multimedia applications allow lecturers to create and manipulate presentations in a wide variety of contexts that enhance students' interests and engagement (Mills and Roblyer, 2006). Using multimedia, instructors can incorporate multiple types of media formats (e.g. tests, diagrams, photos, drawings, audio etc.) that cannot be easily integrated together into one single medium such as printed materials.

Students are attracted to multimedia presentations because of the graphical, transactional, aesthetic and interactive features they provide. Parette, Blum, Boeckmann and Watts (2009) suggested that, regardless of such concerns related to the effectiveness of multimedia tools, it is no longer an issue of whether to use them or not. Instead, instructors must focus on how they can successfully use these tools inside and outside of their lectures.

When deciding how to support learners who are beyond the boundaries of the lecture hall, the literature emphasizes the importance of considering the possibilities that a video presents (Cunningham and Friedman, 2009). Proponents of using videos argue that there is increasing interest in providing university students with video materials, which have been demonstrated to be an expanding channel for presentation tools (Sturmey, 2003). Videos are used to support face-to-face, online or blended learning. Students can choose when and where to use the video material and can spend as much or as little time on each learning activity as they like (Whatley and Ahmad, 2007). Video is socially acceptable, widely used and supported by multimedia mobile devices and portable media players. Therefore, it is a powerful link between the instructor and students.

Research describes many advantages of using online video presentations in conventional universities (Dey, Burn and Gerdes, 2009; Fernandez, Simon and Salan, 2009; Zue and Bergom, 2010). For example, video presentations allow students to review material at their own pace and location, they are useful for international students, they provide an opportunity to reorganize teaching time and they are helpful for 'equation-heavy' disciplines. Video lectures allow students to catch up if they miss a face-to-face lecture and help instructors to adopt more flexible, student-centred and collaborative learning approaches.

Producing and sharing video lectures

Today, videos of face-to-face lectures are growing in popularity within higher education institutions. The review of the existing video technologies available revealed that there is a wide range of presentation recording or lecture capture systems available. Lecture capture systems refer to the methods of recording university face-to-face lectures that are made available to students after the lecture. Lecture capture systems allow instructors to record what happens in their classrooms and make this available digitally. The term is used to describe a wide array of software and hardware options (EDUCAUSE, 2008). It includes multimedia content, such as audio and video, and the visual aids that support the instruction, such as slides and whiteboards (Figure 7.1). Traditionally, a

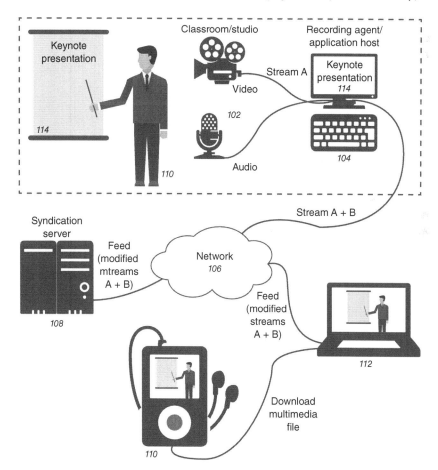

Figure 7.1 Diagram of lecture capture systems (Lane, 2008).

videotaped lecture involved directing a video camera toward the lecturer and whiteboard or screen, whereas a more advanced setup includes recording the lecturer and displaying PowerPoint slides in a separate frame alongside the video.

The majority of these solutions are sophisticated applications intended for large-scale recording and distribution. Wilson (2010, p.1) argued that 'even when a basic level of sophistication has been decided on, there are many offerings with very similar feature sets that make choosing one somewhat difficult'. Fortunately, recent developments in digital recording and internet technology make the utilization of recording technology and delivery of video via the web easy (McClure, 2008). These technologies range from very simple desktop video recording applications to highly sophisticated lecture capture and streaming stations with multiple cameras and dedicated servers.

Whatley and Ahmad (2007) distinguished between two different approaches for producing video presentations. The first is using lecture capture systems that make video available without editing the original footage. However, when using video captured from a lecture, much of the interactivity (e.g. students' questions and comments) should be cut out because of the low quality of sound and lighting. The second approach is recording a 'summary presentation' of the lecture in an office or studio. The lectures recorded in offices are superior to those recorded in the lecture for a number of reasons: the material can be rehearsed, sound and lighting levels are more controllable, there is less extraneous noise, unnecessary movements are avoided and the quality of sound is better (Whatley and Ahmad, 2007).

Principles for selecting lecture recording tools

Review of the available literature revealed many important guidelines for selecting or designing lecture recording tools. One finding from this body of research is that overcoming the limits of learners' working memory requires presenting part of the information being taught in a visual mode and part of it in a verbal mode (Mayer, 2001; Homer, Plass and Blake, 2008). Presenting lesson information in both visual and verbal formats helps learners construct their own knowledge and easily retrieve information. According to Mayer and Anderson (1991), video can enable improved communication of learning material and aid the retention of verbal information. Mayer (2001) provided a practical set of research-based principles that help reduce cognitive load in PowerPoint-based video materials. For example, he argued that learners understand a multimedia explanation better when the words are presented as narration rather than on-screen text.

A second finding emphasized the concept of video presence and personalized narration within multimedia environments. Research indicates that although displaying the video of the instructor along with the slides creates a visual distraction, taking the audience's attention away from the visual information in the slides, presence of the instructor view is important in giving the learner a sense of interaction with the instructor while watching the video, and may improve understanding, even while adding to cognitive load (Mayer and Moreno, 1998;

Homer et al., 2008). Indeed, Gunawardena (1995) found that social presence is necessary to support participants in technology-based learning environments.

A third finding highlighted the technical design and usability of presentation recording solutions. Zhu and Bergom (2010) indicated that the skill level required to record a presentation and make it available should be minimal and without the need of significant support services. In addition, the solution should make videos available for submission without further manipulation or editing before they are available for viewing (Wilson, 2010). Copley (2007) and Dey et al. (2009) each emphasized that the system must capture and combine audio, video (via digital camera or webcam) and PowerPoint slides simultaneously into a single video frame to preserve the entire presentation experience.

The need

At Sultan Qaboos University (SQU) in the Sultanate of Oman, faculty members are challenged to support student learning by providing new ways to present curriculum materials, illustrate concepts that are less easily explained through traditional media, support new types of learning opportunities and provide enrichment activities for students in traditional face-to-face lectures or through e-learning environments. Faculty at SQU deal with many barriers regarding the selection and use of learning materials, such as students' needs, quality of content, language, social considerations and appropriateness to curriculum objectives. Many of these barriers could be avoided through a system that easily encourages SQU instructors to produce and share course materials on their own.

At SQU, the author observed that multimedia presentation applications, particularly Microsoft PowerPoint, are the dominant tool because they are readily available and easy to use for the majority of instructors. Although PowerPoint presentations are shared with students on a daily basis via e-mail and online slide-sharing applications, PowerPoint slides are designed for delivery by instructors in lectures and need to be paired with the use of LCD projectors and large screens. The design includes the lecturer guiding the students through the slides, explaining the content to them, keeping their interest and attracting their attention. In other words, slide content and visual features are not a substitute for the guidance an instructor delivers. When the students are not seeing and listening to the instructor, learning from the slides in isolation is less valuable and more difficult.

At the same time, although video hosting and streaming solutions such as YouTube provide great solutions for hosting and sharing video content with learners, they do not provide instructors with the tools for producing quality video content based on classroom presentations. Therefore, the identified need was to design, develop and implement a simple and easy-to-use tool to help faculty produce and share quality video tutorials with their students based on their existing PowerPoint presentations.

Importance of the network

Like many other universities around the world, SQU has utilized technology as a way to better prepare students and help them to achieve their learning objectives. The Centre for Educational Technology (CET), a special centre within SQU, was formed to coordinate SQU's efforts to infuse technology in daily teaching and learning practices. According to CET, infusion of technology implies development in improving the performance of students and increasing the capacities of technology use in the university. A new system helps CET, faculty members and students by providing an easy-to-use facility for producing and sharing video content those results in a shift in technology utilization. Much can be learned from this project in terms of pedagogy and technology of online video tutorials to better facilitate the use of technology in similar higher education institutions and blended learning environments.

Design and development of the network

Motivation and assumptions

At SQU, none of the lecture capturing solutions mentioned were available or supported by CET. This situation placed an emphasis on the need to find a simple but effective solution for producing and sharing effective video lectures at SQU. The solution required leveraging existing technology that is directly administered by instructors – without the need of significant support services – and accommodating the technical differences among SQU instructors. In addition, this system had to meet the pedagogical and psychological principles of multimedia design for university students.

The general design principles of the system were derived from the literature, the author's experience, and grounded in the review of existing online video sharing solutions. The reviews included many important assumptions for consideration in designing the proposed system outlined below.

1. Minimal skills required to produce instructional videos and make them available and no need for significant additional technical support.
2. Videos are available as early as possible before or after lectures without the need for further manipulation or editing, because most students need to watch the video right after the lecture (McClure, 2008).
3. Multimedia research emphasized the importance of combining the presenter's video footage with slides simultaneously into a single video frame (Mayer and Moreno, 1998).
4. The solution synchronizes visual aids such as PowerPoint slides with handwriting and drawings.
5. The video output is produced in both standard- and high-quality video formats that are compatible with the majority of operating systems and students' mobile devices.

6 The presence of the instructor is important to give students a sense of interacting with him or her while watching the video lesson and may improve learning outcomes (Mayer and Anderson, 1991).
7 Overcoming the limits of working memory requires presenting lesson information in both visual and verbal formats, which helps students to construct their own knowledge and retrieve information more easily in the future (Mayer and Anderson, 1991).

Media capture and acquisition techniques

The main intention was to design and build the appropriate capture technique to acquire and synchronize visual aids simultaneously. In traditional lecture-capture settings, the lecturer uses a large wall screen and a whiteboard and wants to video everything, including him or herself. But if the camera is pointed at the screen or play area, the audience cannot read text from the video because of the quality of the video output (e.g., small font size, low contrast, reflective surfaces, glare, shadows, limited area, positioning, etc.). Therefore, the need to develop a tool to assist instructors with automating the process of synchronizing and recording video lectures using their own desktop computers was important. This tool would take advantage of the concept of screen recording and synchronize all screen and audio activities in the instructor's computer, such as webcam footage, PowerPoint slides, text editor and drawing board (Figure 7.2).

Microsoft Visual Studio, a high-level object-oriented graphical user interface-driven development platform for Windows, was used to design user interfaces and to code the screen recording tool. The primary output of this phase was a

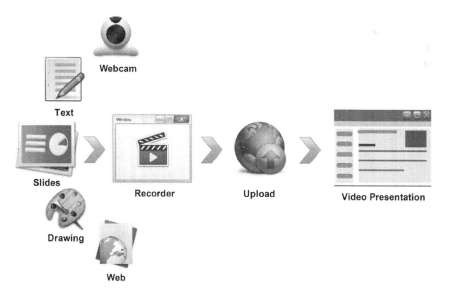

Figure 7.2 The design of the video presentation recorder.

complete code, a fully functional beta version (prototype) of the video presentation recorder (called 'PresentationTube Recorder'). The software has two major aspects: display and capture. The software process involves displaying content in a small window within the software window (Figure 7.2), which allows the instructor to display, manipulate and narrate the content the same way as in full-screen mode. Using navigation buttons, the instructor can navigate forward and backward through slides and employ other features, including slide transitions, text and graphic animation, slide timing, mouse movement, audio effects, embedded video and pen annotation (Figure 7.3).

The same window is used as a camera viewer to show the presenter's video footage using an integrated or external webcam. Additionally, more than one camera may be connected to give views of the scene periodically. The instructor can generate professional-looking video presentations by switching between multiple camera views, which is an important aspect of creating attractive video materials. The instructor can merge and display the camera video footage inside the content window (picture in picture) or add the video footage beside the content window (side by side).

With visual aids such as the drawing board, instructors can draw lines, curves, graphs and shapes on the screen to emphasize or clarify their ideas and make the demonstration as clear as possible. The whiteboard allows instructors to type text using the keyboard while presenting, making it an ideal tool to add more details or explain equations using words, numbers and symbols. This display window allows the instructor to switch between slides, whiteboard, drawing board and webcam while recording, which simplifies the capture process and avoids the problems of managing different visual aids and media (Figure 7.2). The final output of the video presentation recorder is a video file in .ASF or .WMV format. The .ASF file is uploaded to the online platform to create the video with slide navigator, as shown later.

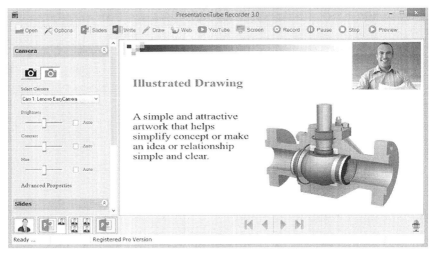

Figure 7.3 View of the presentation recording tool.

To determine whether the prototype met the needs and expectations of instructors and to collect user performance and satisfaction data, the rapid applications development (RAD) model offered a framework within which the software was designed, developed and tested on time and within budget (Rushby, 1997; Scacchi, 2001). The RAD model allowed the developer to construct early or primitive versions of the recorder rapidly for user evaluation. A series of usability testing tryouts were conducted using one-to-one and small groups of academicians at SQU (n = 16). The computer experience of the participants varied. During tryouts, the researcher noticed some user-interface interaction problems, and collected useful suggestions from the participants in the second round of software development.

The online platform

Typically, educational institutions stores videos on local servers, and students can connect to stream them from their browsers whenever they want. It is also possible to use a free or paid video streaming network, such as YouTube, Vimeo, Wistia, ustream or dailymotion, to make the videos available on demand. Some of these video streaming services, particularly YouTube, allow media developers to upload videos directly from their websites using advanced programming techniques called application programming interfaces (API). YouTube's API allows developers to upload videos directly to the PresentationTube channel without the need to have a separate account for each instructor. For example, when an instructor signs in to the PresentationTube network and uploads a video presentation, the video is uploaded directly from PresentationTube servers to YouTube media servers for encoding and optimization and then for embedding in the PresentationTube platform. For these reasons, YouTube was the optimal solution for uploading, hosting and streaming video presentations for this project.

One problem of online video is the prescribed rate of viewing, meaning one minute of video content is consumed per one minute of watching time in a prescribed direction. This prevents learners from learning at their own pace and their own arrangement. Although YouTube's video player allows learners to easily skip forward and backward on the video streamline to locate relevant content, the video player does not provide a solution to integrate the video with the slide content. Therefore, the PresentationTube platform offered a new way to combine the video content with the presentation slide thumbnails.

The slide thumbnails, or slide navigator, are similar to the slide sorter view in PowerPoint. Thumbnails are arranged in vertical view to allow the learner to browse and navigate through the video content and to control both the player and sequence of video presentation. In addition, this association helps to break the forced pace and linear consumption of video content, allowing the learner to move to the respective video content and control both the time and progress of video presentation. For example, if the learner needs to watch the instructor's explanations on the fifth slide, the learner clicks on the 'Slide 5' thumbnail to skip directly to the video part associated with this slide. Furthermore, video presentations are augmented by a discussion forum to enable some asynchronous interaction with the lecturer, who is able to elaborate on issues that might arise from the material presented in the video or respond to students' questions (Whatley and Ahmad, 2007).

PresentationTube network was made available online for SQU faculty members at www.presentationtube.com in January 2013.

Implementation

A three-stage implementation methodology was adopted in this study. The first stage was a series of orientation seminars and training workshops to identify implementation requirements. The second stage was implementing the project with a small group of 15 faculty members at SQU. The third stage consolidated participants' perceptions and examined their online activities throughout the network.

At the beginning of the implementation, Autumn 2013, participants attended five orientation seminars and training workshops organized by the SQU's Centre for Educational Technology and the assistant deans for training and community services at the College of Education and College of Arts. Topics discussed in the training included producing and sharing video presentations, the applicability of online video presentations to current teaching contexts at SQU and the associated advantages. In addition, daily information and success stories about using the PresentationTube recorder and network were offered via the PresentationTube blog and Facebook group. The workshops emphasized the importance of cooperation among the developer and faculty members for the success of the project and the benefit of the students.

Overall, participants performed well after training and continuous monitoring and support, and they were able to use the video presentation recorder and the network successfully. However, instructors faced certain challenges at the beginning of the implementation. Among these challenges were adopting new video-based instructional strategies and selection of topics, class management and student attendance. In addition, instructors faced the challenge of creating a balance between face-to-face teaching duties and videoing all necessary content within a fixed schedule. By the end of the fall 2013 semester, more than 120 video presentations had been produced and shared with students in various subjects and courses.

A usability questionnaire and individual interviews provided very encouraging feedback regarding the usability of PresentationTube network at the end of the semester. The initial results showed that instructors favoured the video presentation recorder and found it helpful in producing video presentations as well as easy to use and satisfactory. Davis (1989) argued that perceived usefulness and ease of use of a system are each highly correlated with self-reported use and future use. The importance of the PresentationTube's ease of use is that it has a significant positive relationship with future adoption of the network in the university. In addition, Rogers (1995) found that the relative advantage, in terms of the usefulness as perceived by instructors, is positively related to the innovation's rate of adoption. In other words, faculty members are more likely to use PresentationTube if they perceive it is easy to use and helpful for producing and publishing video presentations for their students.

Informal and initial analysis of students' feedback indicated that they found PresentationTube videos produced by their own instructors useful for their understanding and review of lectures. They also found PresentationTube effective on occasions when they had missed a lecture, when they needed some help to understand a topic or when they needed help putting the material into perspective. In addition, addressing learners using personalized narration allows them to feel they are active participants in the video presentations, thereby improving learning and possibly motivation.

Discussion and recommendations

Faculty members have professional and ethical responsibilities to provide their students with quality content and resources to support their learning. At SQU, the needs emerged to develop and implement an online network to help faculty members produce and share quality video presentations with their students. To meet these needs, the author developed PresentationTube network offering a video presentation recording application and online video sharing platform. This recording application allows instructors to narrate and annotate PowerPoint slides and synchronize a variety of visual aids, including webcam video footage, whiteboard, drawing board and web browser. The platform uses the YouTube API to upload videos and integrate them with scrollable slide thumbnails, allowing students to move to the respective video content and control both the progress and length of the video presentation.

The possibilities for future development and research in this project are exciting. Future research will investigate whether PresentationTube actually improves students' learning and how instructors' personalized narration can influence comprehension of presentations. Feedback from instructors and students will provide useful guidelines about which features need to be improved or added. For example, participants faced some challenges during the implementation period, namely, creating balance between face-to-face teaching duties and videoing all necessary content within a fixed schedule. Many instructors were not able to shift to more student-centred classes and identify how to adopt the new video presentations to both meet their students' needs and enhance instructor–student interaction inside and outside their classrooms. Therefore, instructors may need more training on how to utilize PresentationTube video presentations to the fullest potential.

In addition, further research is needed to investigate the design of content and develop principles for the design of effective video presentations consistent with what students need and how they learn from online video presentations. In addition, more investigation is required on the role of PresentationTube video presentations in improving student learning. Comparisons of how students learn from these videos versus face-to-face classes need more investigation. Lastly, more studies are needed to determine which learning approaches and environmental settings result in good learning outcomes when PresentationTube is used.

References

Copley, J. (2007). Audio and video podcasts of lectures for campus-based students: production and evaluation of student use. *Innovations in Education and Teaching International* 44(4), 387–399.

Cunningham, A. and Friedman, A. (2009). Captivating young learners and preparing 21st-century social studies teachers: increasing engagement with digital video. In I. Gibson et al. (eds), *Proceedings of society for information technology and teacher education international conference 2009* (pp. 1797–1803). Chesapeake VA: AACE.

Davis, D. (1989). *A technology acceptance model for empirically testing new end-user information systems: theory and results*. Unpublished doctoral dissertation. Cambridge MA, MIT Sloan School of Management.

Dey, E.L., Burn, H.E. and Gerdes, D. (2009). Bringing the classroom to the web: effects of using new technologies to capture and deliver lectures. *Research in Higher Education* 50(4), 377–393.

EDUCAUSE. (2008). Seven things you should know about lecture capture. EDUCAUSE Learning Initiative. Retrieved from https://net.educause.edu/ir/library/pdf/ELI7044.pdf

Fernandez, V., Simon, P. and Salan, J. (2009). Podcasting: a new technological tool to facilitate good practice in higher education. *Computers and Education* 53, 385–392.

Grabe, M. and Grabe, C. (2007). *Integrating technology for meaningful learning* (5th ed.). New York: Houghton Mifflin Company.

Gunawardena, C. (1995). Social presence theory and implications for interaction and collaborative learning in computer conferences. *International Journal of Educational Telecommunications* 1, 147–166.

Homer, B., Plass, J. and Blake, L. (2008). The effects of video on cognitive load and social presence in multimedia-learning. *Computers in Human Behavior* 24, 786–797.

Lane, S. (2008). *Apple filing takes podcasts to the next level*. Retrieved from http://appleinsider.com/articles/08/07/17/apple_filing_takes_podcasts_to_the_next_level

Mayer, R. (2001). *Multimedia-learning*. New York: Cambridge University Press.

Mayer, R. and Anderson, R. (1991). Animations need narrations: an experimental test of a dual coding hypothesis. *Journal of Educational Psychology* 83(4), 484–490.

Mayer, R. and Moreno, R. (1998). A split-attention effect in multimedia-learning: evidence for dual processing systems in working memory. *Journal of Educational Psychology* 90, 312–320.

McClure, A. (2008). Lecture capture: a fresh look. *University Business* 11(4), 57–60.

Mills, S.C. and Roblyer, M.D. (2006). *Technology tools for teachers: a Microsoft Office® tutorial* (2nd ed.). Upper Saddle River NJ: Pearson Merrill Prentice Hall.

Parette, H.P., Blum, C., Boeckmann, N.M. and Watts, E.H. (2009). Teaching word recognition to young children using Microsoft PowerPoint coupled with direct instruction. *Early Childhood Education Journal* 36, 393–401.

Rogers, M. (1995). *Diffusion of innovation* (4th ed.). New York: The Free Press.

Rushby, J. (1997). Quality criteria for multimedia. *Association for Learning Technology Journal* 5(2), 18–30.

Scacchi, W. (2001). Process models in software engineering. In J. Marciniak (ed.), *Encyclopedia of software engineering* (2nd ed.). New York: Wiley.

Whatley, J. and Ahmad, A. (2007). Using video to record summary lectures to aid students' revision. *Interdisciplinary Journal of Knowledge and Learning Objects* 3, 185–196.

Wilson, M. (2010). *Lecture capture overview*. ComETS 2010 Symposium, Iowa State Memorial Union, 18 February.

Zue, E. and Bergom, I. (2010). Lecture capture: a guide for effective use. Tomorrow's Professor, e-mail newsletter 1018.

8 Initiatives to innovate education to prepare Qatar for the future

Mohamed Ally, Martha Robinson and Mohammed Samaka

Introduction

The State of Qatar occupies a small peninsula in the Arabian Gulf, sharing its border with Saudi Arabia. Over the past 20 years, Qatar has experienced exponential growth in income and population, thanks to the development of the nation's huge oil and gas reserves. The combination of natural resources and a massive foreign labour force has resulted in the world's highest per capita income and lowest unemployment (Central Intelligence Agency, 2015). In 2012, however, Qatari nationals made up only 6 per cent of the economically active population aged 15 and over (Qatar Information Exchange, 2015) and by 2014 foreign nationals comprised 88 per cent of the national population (Snoj, 2014).

With a view to utilize Qatar's economic and human potential effectively and recognizing that dependence on hydrocarbon reserves is unsustainable, in 2008, the General Secretariat for Development and Planning published Qatar National Vision 2030 (General Secretariat for Development and Planning, 2008), which charted a course for national development across various sectors. The first pillar of the National Vision is the development of human capital in Qatar, which aims to prepare the Qatari people to participate more actively in an internationally competitive knowledge-based economy. This will be accomplished through a modern, world-class education system that provides innovative training to prepare Qatar nationals for an increasingly technical world. The system also aims to develop analytical and critical thinking skills and to encourage creativity and innovation (GSDP, 2008). In pursuit of such ambitious goals, educational institutions in Qatar have undertaken to identify innovative technologies and practices that address the particular needs of the local population so that they can be educated for the twenty-first-century world. This chapter will describe the use of innovative learning technologies in Qatar to prepare students and workers to contribute to Qatar's National Vision and strategic goals.

A strategy for development

Just as the patrons of early Arab–Muslim science like Harun Al Rashid and Al Mamun in Baghdad, Al Hakim in Cairo and the Umayyads in Al Andalus sought to create states that encouraged research and development of ideas and products that would in turn serve the world and its people, so is Qatar embarked on a modern campaign to do the same (The Vision of Qatar, n.d.).

Qatar National Vision 2030 (GSDP, 2008) provides the roadmap for this campaign in an effort to balance the needs and objectives of diverse stakeholders as the Gulf State of Qatar moves from a dependence on hydrocarbons to full participation in a knowledge-based economy. This vision rests on four pillars: human, social, economic and environmental development. Towards the goal of human development, Qatar aims to develop a world-class educational system that encourages analytical and critical thinking, creativity and innovation in preparation for a complex twenty-first-century workplace.

A 2014 survey conducted by Qatar's World Innovation Summit for Education (WISE) predicted that education systems will undergo major changes by 2030. Of 645 participants representing the global WISE community, 93 per cent favour schools that implement new teaching approaches and creative processes and only 7 per cent anticipate that schools will return to fundamental values and traditional teacher-centred tools and pedagogy (World Innovation Summit for Education, 2014). About half of the respondents said that the source of knowledge will come from online content. Most of the respondents said that content will be personalized to meet individual student needs. Overall, participants expect a continued shift in the role of teachers from deliverers of consistent and standardized content to guides and mentors of increasingly online and personalized content.

The march towards innovative, transformative education was also highlighted recently by Maha Khamis Al Sulaiti, Senior Research Analyst at Qatar Foundation:

> Qatar is striving to bring about the national vision 2030 and move our economy toward a sustainable knowledge based economy and move away from carbons. Education will help to create this for the nation and be the instrument of transforming people and a nation. Moreover, innovation in education is the key for success of the educators and the students in this ever-changing global market place.
>
> (Rahbek-Nielsen, 2015)

A connected society

Recent years have brought extensive adoption of information and communication technologies (ICT) throughout the State of Qatar. The recently established Qatar Foundation Research and Education Network (QFREN) will link educators and researchers in Qatar and the Gulf countries and allow them to conduct and share best practices to innovate education. The Measuring the Information Society 2014 report (International Telecommunication Union, 2014) included Qatar on its lists of most dynamic countries – those showing greatest change in rank between 2012 and 2013 – in terms of access (up 6 to 22), use (up 8 to 30) and overall ranking (up 8 to 34) out of 166 nations surveyed. Qatar's ICT Landscape 2014 (ictQatar, 2014c) reports mobile subscription over 100 per cent and an increase to 100 per cent internet access, from 38 per cent in 2008. This survey also found that all segments of Qatar's resident population have access to internet-enabled ICT devices and traditional mobile phones, though newer devices such as smartphones and tablets have not penetrated the transient labour population. For the mainstream population, ownership of ICT devices such as mobile phones and laptops more than doubled between 2012 and 2013, while desktop use has remained flat due to the growing demand for mobility. Qatar's ICT Landscape 2014 further reports that consumers in Qatar increasingly need and want the ability to log on to the Internet 'anytime, anywhere'.

Qatar's first National Broadband Plan (ictQatar 2013) is intended to promote broadband infrastructure deployment and market development, resulting in improved broadband services, especially in terms of speed and affordability of both fixed and mobile services by 2016. Targets include:

- affordable, high-quality broadband services of at least 100Mbps download/50Mbps upload to 95 per cent of households;
- high-quality access to at least 1 Gbps effective symmetrical speeds for all businesses, schools, hospitals and government institutions;
- digital literacy across all the mainstream population;
- guarantees of user digital privacy, protection of personal data and freedom of opinion and expression.

In addition, to meet the increasing demand for faster and more secure networks and overall ICT access, work continues on a FTTH (fibre-to-the-home) network that will enable universal access to high-speed broadband (ictQatar, 2014c). To provide controls and guidelines for broadband infrastructure provisioning within Qatar, the Broadband Infrastructure Security Policy aims to ensure availability, resilience, security and privacy in broadband services and internet infrastructure (ictQatar, 2014b).

Qatar's residents rank highly in their perception of access to basic services (1), ICT use and government efficiency (3) and internet access in schools (15) out of 148 countries in the World Economic Forum's Global Information Technology Report (World Economic Forum, 2014). Though residents across the education spectrum access social networking (93 per cent), VoIP and other basic internet services, however, there remains room for improvement among the population in the area of advanced ICT skills and knowledge that will drive future innovation and economic success. The Ministry of Information and Communication Technology (ictQATAR) is currently implementing digital literacy and IT skills programmes in an attempt to address this shortfall (ictQatar, 2014c).

Institutional support

Guided by the National Vision 2030, several national institutions promote technological and educational innovations in Qatar.

Ministry of Information and Communication Technology (ictQATAR)

Restructured and rebranded in 2013 from the Supreme Council of Information and Communication Technology established in 2004, ictQatar is responsible for overseeing and developing the ICT sector to support a diversified economy that will benefit all residents, including a competitive ICT investment environment, next generation of infrastructure and driving innovation as an agent for human, social, economic and environmental change (ictQatar, 2014a). It also administers the Qatar National e-Learning Portal (QNEP), which provides online access to courses in IT and business.

In the past, ictQatar participated in the development of the 'School's e-Maturity Tool', intended to measure and compare the performance of individual schools with regard to their e-readiness and e-effectiveness. The council was also instrumental in developing the Knowledge Net (K-Net), a learning management system that allowed collaboration, communication and resource sharing between teachers, students and parents around the country, as well as promoting best practices in ICT education, holding pedagogical workshops for teachers, and recognizing student initiative and excellence in the use of ICT through the Digital Star Competition.

Events organized by ictQatar include the 'Everything Mobile Forum' in 2012, which explored mobile from a business, consumer and regulatory perspective. Specific topics addressed included m-commerce and finance, mobile, culture and mobile, mobile entertainment and games, mobile software and hardware, mobile public services, m-content, location-based services, social media and apps (ictQatar, 2012b). The Digitally Open: Innovation and Open Access Forum in 2010 examined digital content rights, open source, open cloud, openness in science and technology, government and culture (ictQatar 2010a). Also in 2010, ictQatar partnered with Carnegie Mellon University – Qatar to present ICT Pedagogical Workshops on Digital Content to help teachers assess quality digital content and create their own content (ictQatar, 2010b).

From 2009 to 2011, ictQATAR and the College of the North Atlantic – Qatar sponsored the Digital Star contest open to students and teachers throughout Qatar. In the student competition category, students were asked to submit digital projects based on lessons taught in their schools showing how the lessons could be improved through the use of technology. In the lesson plan category, teachers were asked to submit lessons plans that integrate ICT (ictQatar, 2011).

Since restructuring in 2013, the ministry has shifted its focus away from formal education practices and towards research, policy development, and informal and public education initiatives. Current programmes include:

- Digital Literacy, including a Cyber Safety Awareness campaign and SafeSpace website (safespace.qa), which provides guidance and resources for parents, teens and educators on safe and effective use of the internet.
- ICT Skills Development: Tumuha TEC promotes ICT as a career choice to young people, raising awareness and providing opportunities for youth to

enhance ICT skills. Its activities include school visits, lectures, competitions, workshops, internships and production of resource material. The national e-Learning Portal, discussed in the section on workforce training, provides workplace training for employees and the general public.

- Digital Impact and Emerging Technologies (Rassed) monitors the effects of ICT and the internet on society by conducting research and measuring change over time. It monitors and communicates technological and digital developments with internal and external stakeholders to facilitate effective decision-making at the local and regional level (ictQatar, n.d b).

Educational research and innovative learning awards in Qatar

Established by Qatar Foundation in 2006 to build a research culture in the nation, the Qatar National Research Fund (QNRF) aims to foster original, competitively selected research in areas of national interest and to encourage dialogue and partnerships between stakeholder institutions in Qatar and abroad (QNRF, 2015). Funding is provided under four separate categories: research programmes, capacity building and development programmes, K-12 programmes and special programmes.

Research programmes

As the primary research programme of the QNRF, the National Priorities Research Program (NPRP) supports research in the areas of engineering and technology, physical and life sciences, medicine, humanities, social sciences and the arts. Participating institutions are encouraged to develop collaborations with international academic institutions and with government and the private sector. Of twenty-three research projects in the field of Educational Science since 2008, however, only four explore the adoption of emerging technologies to enhance learning outcomes and develop twenty-first-century skills.

Capacity building and development programmes

These programmes support upcoming researchers and provide a stage on which to develop their research and collaboration skills and to disseminate their work.

The **Undergraduate Research Experience Program (UREP)** seeks to stimulate undergraduate research in order to contribute to workforce training. It promotes hands-on activities under a faculty mentor, whereby students gain experience in research methods and procedures and in collaboration with various other members of academia. UREP solicits proposals from Qatar's academic institutions and provides funds for the purchase and management of supplies and equipment, as well as travel, accommodation and stipends where required. Though most research takes place at the academic institution that receives it, funding allows for faculty-mentored projects carried out in government or private industry. The programme further provides continuity and institutional memory of projects, a raised awareness of research opportunities in Qatar and increased collaboration.

The **Graduate Student Research Award (GSRA)** will promote the development of graduate studies and further contribute to the building of Qatar's human capital by supporting outstanding graduate students to undertake graduate research-based studies towards doctoral degrees at approved institutions within Qatar. It helps ensure continuity of research-based doctoral education and awareness of local research opportunities.

The **Postdoctoral Research Awards (PDRA)** support postdoctoral scholars to work within Qatar-based research groups located in areas of national priority as outlined in the Qatar National Research Strategy (QNRS). These awards provide funds to pay for postdoctoral salaries, travel and other personal expenses.

The **Junior Scientists Research Experience Program (JSREP)** supports junior scientists to initiate or lead their own research and to fund research that is aligned with QNRS. It provides incentives for institutions to build the organizational infrastructure needed to support researchers and helps promote knowledge and technology transfer.

K-12 programmes

In order to encourage early interest and skill in science and research, the following innovative education programmes have been developed.

The **Secondary School Research Experience Program (SSREP)** is conducted in collaboration with the Scientific Research Skills (SRC) Development Team of the Supreme Education Council. SSREP promotes hands-on research activities as effective methods for secondary school education. Candidates conduct and document their research on their projects and submit the results and recommendations through SSREP.

The **Science Challenge for Middle School Program (SCMSP)** nurtures scientific creativity at the middle-school level and prepares students for the Secondary Schools Research Experience Program (SSREP). This challenge requires students to design and build an object according to specified guidelines, using limited resources. This activity encourages students to think creatively.

Following positive feedback from a highly successful science competition, the **Middle School Science Challenge Program (MSSCP)** was developed in order to encourage the practical application of scientific principles taught in the classroom.

Primary education

The establishment of the Supreme Education Council (SEC) in 2002 laid the foundation for the development and advancement of the education sector and for national educational policy to meet the objectives of Qatar National Vision 2030. The SEC's strategic goals include the provision of diverse learning opportunities, effective educators, and sufficient and appropriate education infrastructure to meet these objectives (SEC, 2015c). The Chairman of the SEC, in an inaugural address at the first International Conference on Education in Doha in 2015, emphasized the need to adopt creative strategies and innovative practices in education and promote a culture of excellence in educational institutions, encouraging creativity and innovation with the aim of sustainable human development (SEC, 2015a). Towards this end, the SEC launched an e-learning initiative, which provides integrated technological support for educational processes and services. The objectives of the initiative include:

- to increase the positive trend and to raise the community awareness about 'ICT' and its impact on both of the teaching and learning process;
- to provide an exciting learning environment that increases the students' motivation and encourages them to be creative;
- to enable students to learn anytime and from anywhere;
- to develop the spirit of independence and self-reliance among students, which promotes research skills and self-directed learning.

This initiative includes a learning management system (LMS), e-library, e-content and a one-to-one tablet programme. The LMS aims to create an effective link between students, teachers, parents, school management and the SEC. It enables teachers to develop and publish lessons for students to use anytime and anywhere. The LMS allows students to access content, activities and teacher support electronically and facilitates direct and convenient communication between parents or guardians and the school. The e-library enables consistent access to appropriate resources and information to support learning. The e-content component will provide schools with easily accessible digital sources consistent with the standards of the national curriculum. These will include downloadable e-books and online media and resources approved by the SEC. The one-to-one tablet initiative has entailed the distribution of 100,000 tablets to students in independent schools throughout the country (SEC, 2012).

Besides such sector-level initiatives, individual organizations in Qatar have also promoted innovative practices. In 2015, the Qatar National Committee for Education, Culture and Science sponsored a Mobile Applications Competition for applications in education, culture, science and educational games (SEC, 2015b). The National Robot Olympiad (NRO) is hosted by the College of the North Atlantic – Qatar (CNA–Q), with sponsorship from private corporations, to encourage the development of programming and problem-solving skills. Teachers receive training at CNA–Q and in turn train students to build and program robots in order to solve a challenge. To further encourage this initiative, the World Robot Olympiad was held in Qatar in 2015, with support of the same private and education organizations (NRO, n.d.)

A recent study by Nasser (2014) investigated the effect of using mobile devices to assign and support homework completion on the actual return rates and subsequent student achievement. The findings showed an increase in the return rates of the homework among students with high-frequency reminders, with a high and positive trend compared to students in other groups. In terms of the achievement scores, students with high-frequency reminders scored higher than both the low-frequency and traditional groups. Though differences were not significant, the evidence of increasing scores in the fourth and fifth weeks of the trials provide evidence that getting students to persist even marginally more in homework can result in higher academic achievement.

Higher education

Colleges and universities in Qatar are regulated by the Supreme Education Council's Higher Education Institute, which dictates licensing and accreditation requirements. Beyond this, however, there is substantial diversity, as the majority of higher education institutions are affiliated with parent institutions in other countries, and bring with them many of the learning philosophies and approaches of parent institutions.

Qatar University (QU) has invested in a range of instructional technologies in recent years. A Blackboard LMS has been utilized since 2008. A significant number of QU classrooms are equipped with video capture systems and video conferencing capabilities are available in many meeting rooms across the campus. The Information Technology Systems division in the university provides a number of IT tools that can be utilized for various innovative instructional purposes. In 2014, discussions began on a formalized Technology Enhances Learning (TEL) strategy, and the strategy team has been exploring TEL facets that might be appropriate for students, faculty and the community (M. Samaka, personal communication, 22 June 2015). The proposed strategy targets:

- learner success: develop success skills and twenty-first-century competencies; demonstrate objective gains in mastery; support flexible learning and engaging lifelong learning to increase student retention
- modernizing QU now and into the future: develop the organizational capacity to introduce and sustain change; prepare and support the academic community for emphasis on TEL
- expanding the university's visibility and leadership: lead the region in educational innovation and in the provision of TEL-competent educators; promote a culture of open education
- extended learning opportunities to outside audiences

To date, several pilot projects have been conducted under this initiative. A blended learning approach consisting of 30 per cent face-to-face and 70 per cent online interaction was evaluated with various sessions of one course. Learning outcomes from blended learning and face-to-face learning were compared for males and females in segregated classes and, in a later class, results from blended learning were compared between male and female students. In another pilot, the use of a flipped classroom model resulted in higher student satisfaction, deeper learning and sustained higher attendance over the length of the course. MOOCs (massive open online courses) have also been introduced to enhance course offerings. To date, short MOOCs have been designed for a local audience, and MOOCs from other institutions worldwide have been offered at QU. Further planned pilots include a fully online course, the provision of iLabs for the completion of experiments remotely, online professional development provision and further engagement of the community. To address the targets of expanded visibility and leadership and of extending opportunities to outside audiences, QU has adopted an Open Access Strategy, which will provide open access to lectures and seminars of benefit to the Qatar community, thus strengthening engagement and cooperation between students, faculty and the community.

At the College of the North Atlantic–Qatar (CNA–Q), the Advanced Learning Technologies Center (ALTC) coordinates, facilitates and supports instructors in using new and existing technologies that enhance teaching and learning. The centre manages the college's Desire2Learn (D2L) LMS and provides support and advice around digital and blended learning (CNA–Q, n.d.). Every classroom has a data projector, interactive software and interactive whiteboard. Given the high adoption of mobile technology among youth in Qatar, the college has undertaken a number of initiatives that exploit this characteristic, including the implementation of a comprehensive Bring Your Own Technology (BYOT) plan, including policies and procedures documentation and staff support. Other uses of mobile technology in various programme areas include:

- Quick response (QR codes) to access mobile reusable learning objects (RLO) for learning basic computer hardware terminology and functions in English (Information Technology) and to simulate x-ray image critiques for radiography students (School of Health Sciences).
- iPads are used to record simulations of radiographic procedures for use as RLOs in courses developed for the D2L learning management system.
- EFL students use iPads to access e-books and other locally produced learning objects.
- Emergency Medical Technician students use body cameras (GoPro) to record simulation activities as part of their training assessment portfolios.
- Augmented reality learning objects are being developed for use by Engineering Technology students to aid in safety training, and training on the maintenance and repair of petrochemical refinery equipment (R. Power, personal communication, 8 June 2015).

Opened in September 2010, the Community College of Qatar (CCQ) arose from the need for college-level courses for academic transfer, critical job training, and corporate and continuing education. CCQ is a Qatari college that serves only citizens of Qatar. Students pursue studies in foundation courses (English, maths, office skills), in core courses for university transfer (English, maths, sciences, social sciences and humanities) and in short-term workforce certificates and corporate training courses (CCQ, n.d.). Currently, technology is used at the college primarily to support administrative functions. Banner has been chosen as the student information system and the college uses the Blackboard LMS. To date, most teaching and learning has followed a traditional teacher-led model, and implementation of Blackboard functionalities in individual courses has varied depending on the experience and interest of the instructor. There remains the opportunity to further explore innovative approaches and exploit the available technology to enhance the teaching–learning process. Such initiatives could potentially arise as a result of demand from incoming students from innovative secondary schools, who have come to expect and value the added opportunities for research, communication, collaboration and creativity afforded by varying educational approaches.

Virtual simulation is a growing field for training and continuous professional development in medicine and healthcare. In the Middle East and North Africa (MENA) region, virtual simulation in healthcare education has consisted mostly of technical training for surgical residents and nurses, in countries like Saudi Arabia, Kuwait and Turkey. There has also been discussion of the potential of virtual reality to replace the use of cadavers for anatomy training (Umoren et al., 2014). In Qatar, Umoren et al. report a lack of collaborative inter-professional education activities, despite a need in medical, nursing and pharmacy programmes. They suggest that virtual simulation may provide a means for such activities to mitigate limitations due to geography and scheduling challenges.

One effort that addressed this need was the Global Forum on Innovations in Medical Education, hosted by Weill Cornell Medical College in Qatar (WCMC–Q) early in 2015. The forum brought together medical and educational experts from all over the world for debate on both evolutionary and disruptive innovations that have the potential to transform medical education in the region and beyond (WCMC–Q, 2015).

In late 2013, Texas A&M at Qatar invited faculty to present projects that showed promise in improving learning outcomes. The three projects that were brought forward harnessed innovative technologies to engage students, encourage exploration of ideas in new ways and allow for real-time assessments:

1   active learning via smart student response system in an engineering classroom;
2   interactive and collaborative mobile learning platform for engineers;
3   software visualization tool for learning 3D objects (Texas A&M, 2013).

The Educational Technology department at Texas A&M at Qatar is responsible for various resources and initiatives, including multimedia equipment, classroom media, e-learning, audio-visual technology and computer lab management (Texas A&M, n.d.). The university is transitioning to a new centralized learning management system (LMS), eCampus (powered by Blackboard Learn), which promises easy navigation, communication and e-Portfolios, and mobile access to courses and grades. This major IT project is a significant undertaking that will ultimately affect a large number of courses at the university, whether they are taught partially or fully online. Lecture halls, classrooms and conference rooms are equipped with a range of tools, including audio-visual (AV) systems, interactive tools and a podium system designed to facilitate teaching, note-taking, presentations, recording, accessing and projecting online content, and video conferencing. DyKnow software fosters interaction through collaborative note-taking, student response tools, content replay and anywhere-anytime access. Faculty can instantly transmit content to student screens on desktops, laptops, tablet PCss, etc. in fixed, mobile or distance environments. It also acts as a classroom management tool, allowing faculty to monitor and/or block content and activity on student screens.

To facilitate a hands-on approach to the practical skills required by the engineering profession, Texas A&M at Qatar students have access to 25 engineering teaching labs to run simulations, record observations and write reports while running experiments. Labs are set up with specialized instruments that interface with a computer to allow data acquisition and control. Engineering research labs provide extensive facilities and resources. The university has a sophisticated computer numerical controlled (CNC) five-axis machine, coupled with a titanium 3D printer and a port plastic maker (PPM), which provides Texas A&M at Qatar the capability of making 3D models and components. There are 32 labs with a variety of equipment, including data capture and experiment control software and general simulation, visualization and productivity software for use by researchers working on research project. Also available is a 3D Immersive Visualization Facility (IVF) to enable understanding and presentation of results in visual form. This 120° curved screen allows the viewer to be immersed in the visualization, and the stereo projection capabilities enables 3D visualization.

Research

A recent research project funded by the Qatar National Research Fund (QNRF) investigated the use of mobile technology for workplace English training in Qatar (Ally et al., 2014). The client organization, the national petrochemical corporation, depends on a multi-national labour force, most of whom are non-native English speakers. Due to the nature of the industry, employees are dispersed in several centres throughout the country and offshore. Initial training is normally carried out in the classroom for several months. However, recurrent training requires employees to be absent from their worksites for varying amounts of time. This limits the amount of classroom-based recurrent training that is feasible. The mobile approach was selected over traditional e-learning due to the flexibility it offered for a workforce that is dispersed across the country in urban and rural settings, onshore and offshore, often with limited internet access. The decision to create a free-standing mobile application rather than depending on web-dependent content arose from this reality.

In the first year of implementation, content for three courses was developed and programmed for use on mobile devices, based on corporate training materials and input from English instructors and workplace supervisors. Data was collected relating to learner usage of expository content and practice materials. Pre-tests, post-tests, questionnaires and follow-up interviews provided data on the

Initiatives to innovate education 121

participants' achievement and experience with the technology and content. After each implementation, supervisors and/or instructors supplied feedback regarding employee use of and response to m-learning.

To date, m-learning has been used in two different training settings. As part of a blended learning approach, it offers reinforcement of content covered in class. For example, the content in the 'Presentation Skills in English' m-learning course is based on the curriculum of the classroom-based five-day course. It reviews concepts learned in class and provides interactive activities to reinforce learning. It also provides the means for a student to record and assess his or her own presentation in an effort to improve practice. While this content may be used during the five-day course as in-class independent practice or after-hours review, it can also be available to the employee once he or she returns to normal duties, as a refresher the next time he or she has to make a presentation.

The second use of m-learning has been with firefighters on the job. Once the initial training period is completed, it is challenging to gather firefighters in a formal learning setting to review basic English skills. The 'Pumps and Primers' course reviews content from the initial training and combines it with English skills – such as forming proper sentences, questions and commands – which are used on the job in relation to the firefighting content (Figure 8.1). Employees are encouraged to use the application during downtime on shifts and on days off. Other forms of motivation have been discussed, such as tracking use or success rates on practice activities or regular questions or reminders sent out to the mobile handsets that require users to look up the information.

The economies of scale offered by m-learning allow English training and support to be offered more extensively throughout the company, beyond only the Qatari trainees, thus improving English skills throughout the organization, with little added cost.

Another research study funded by the Qatar Foundation is in the area of problem-based learning (PBL). Most traditional education is passive and teacher-centred, where the teacher presents the information to students. As a result, most students are not motivated to learn, and they tend to achieve low-level skills. To

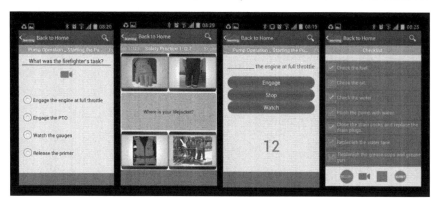

Figure 8.1 Mobile learning interface for firefighters' training.

address these issues, there need to be a shift from teacher-centred education to learner-centred education. One learning strategy is to use the PBL approach so that learners are actively solving relevant problems. As they solve the problems they acquire relevant knowledge and at the same time achieve high-level knowledge and skills. The PBL project in Qatar is developing a PBL system that teachers and professors can use to develop PBL lessons. The PBL system has a web-based graphical PBL authoring tool, which the teacher can use to develop the PBL lesson (Miao et al., 2014). The system is web-based so that the teacher can develop the PBL lessons at any time and from anywhere.

Rutgers University, Northwestern University and Qatar University have teamed up to investigate the use of mobile media for innovative content in Qatar and the United Arab Emirates. The study will analyse big data to study patterns in mobile media use in Qatar and the UAE. The project will use location-based data on usage patterns as well as content analysis of social media, user surveys and interviews to inform the production a model of potential mobile-media content innovation, which can guide public education and engagement via mobile media, among other business applications (Pavlik, Dennis and Mersey, n.d.)

Conclusion

Qatar is using its 2030 National Vision to focus innovations in education and research activities. A wide range of innovative educational initiatives that exploit emerging technologies are being explored. This is important, since the young generations of Qataris are using emerging technologies and they will expect education to be delivered using this more engaging approach now and when they are in the workforce. The country's resources must be used efficiently to contribute to the future of Qatar. Because of rapid innovations in technology and information explosion, a concerted effort and commitment will be required to remain abreast of innovations in technology and education if they are to be effectively exploited to meet the needs of the people of Qatar. Existing infrastructure must be analysed to determine if there are any gaps and a model or strategy must be developed that maximizes the opportunities provided by technologies to provide culturally appropriate content and delivery for students, workers and the community at large in order to achieve the goal of human development and prepare the people of Qatar for the twenty-first century.

Acknowledgement

This chapter was made possible by NPRP Grant # 4-125-5-016 from the Qatar National Research Fund (a member of Qatar Foundation). The statements made herein are solely the responsibility of the authors.

References

Ally, M., Samaka, M., Impagliazzo, J., Mohamed, A. and Robinson, M. (2014). Workplace learning using mobile technology: a case study in the oil and gas industry. In M. Kalz, Y. Bayyurt and M. Specht (eds). *Mobile as a mainstream: towards future challenges in mobile learning.* Proceedings of 13th World Conference on Mobile and Contextual Learning, mLearn 2014, Istanbul, Turkey, 3–5 November.

Central Intelligence Agency (2015). Qatar. In The World Factbook. Retrieved from www.cia.gov/library/publications/the-world-factbook/geos/qa.html

College of the North Atlantic – Qatar (n.d.). Centre for Teaching, Learning and Educational Innovation [web page]. Retrieved from www.cnaqatar.com/CTLEI/Pages/welcome.aspx

Community College of Qatar (n.d.) About CCQ [web page]. Retrieved from www.ccq.edu.qa/index.php?option=com_content&view=article&id=111&Itemid=695

General Secretariat for Development and Planning (GSDP) (2008). Qatar National Vision 2030. Doha, Qatar.

International Telecommunication Union (ITU) (2014). Measuring the Information Society Report 2014. Retrieved from www.itu.int/en/ITU-D/Statistics/Documents/publications/mis2014/MIS2014_without_Annex_4.pdf.

Lonzer, J. (2015). Qatar's Innovative Health Education Campaign, Sahtak Awalan, to be showcased at WISH 2015. Accessed at http://nuviun.com/content/qatars-innovative-health-education-campaign-sahtak-awalan-to-be-showcased-at-wish-2015

Miao, Y., Ally, M., Samaka, M. and Tsinakos, A. (2014). Towards pedagogy-driven learning design: a case study of problem-based learning design. Berlin, Heidelberg: Springer-Verlag, pp. 1–11.

Ministry of Information and Communication Technology (ictQATAR) (2010). Digitally Open: Innovation and Open Access Forum. Retrieved from www.ictqatar.qa/en/news-events/event/digitally-open-innovation-and-open-access-forum

Ministry of Information and Communication Technology (ictQATAR) (2010). ICT Pedagogical Workshops: Digital Content. Retrieved from www.ictqatar.qa/en/news-events/event/ict-pedagogical-workshops-digital-content

Ministry of Information and Communication Technology (ictQATAR) (2011). Digital Star Competition. Retrieved from www.ictqatar.qa/en/news-events/event/digital-star-competition

Ministry of Information and Communication Technology (ictQatar) (2012). Blended Learning Workshop. Retrieved from www.ictqatar.qa/en/news-events/event/blended-learning-workshop

Ministry of Information and Communication Technology (ictQATAR) (2012). Everything Mobile Forum. Retrieved from www.ictqatar.qa/en/news-events/event/everything-mobile-forum

Ministry of Information and Communication Technology (ictQATAR) (2012). Tumuha TEC's ICT Workshops. Retrieved from www.ictqatar.qa/en/news-events/event/tumuhatec%E2%80%99s-ict-workshops

Ministry of Information and Communications Technology (ictQatar) (2013). National Broadband Plan of the State of Qatar. Retrieved from www.ictqatar.qa/en/file/documents/qatar-national-broadband-plan-enpdf

Ministry of Information and Communication Technology (ictQATAR) (2014). About us. Retrieved at www.ictqatar.qa/en/about-us

Ministry of Information and Communication Technology (ictQATAR) (2014). Broadband Infrastructure Security Policy. Retrieved from www.ictqatar.qa/en/file/documents/broadbandbroadband-infrastructure-security-policy

Ministry of Information and Communications Technology (ictQatar) (2014). Qatar's ICT Landscape 2014: Households and Individuals. Retrieved from www.ictqatar.qa/en/file/11006

Ministry of Information and Communication Technology (ictQatar) (n.d.). e-Learning: learning anytime, anywhere. Retrieved from www.ictqatar.qa/en/digital-society/ict-skills-development/e-learning-portal

Ministry of Information and Communication Technology (ictQatar) (n.d.). Rassed: Exploring digital impacts on society [web page]. Accessed at www.ictqatar.qa/en/rassed/about, 21 June 2015.

Nasser, R. (2014). Using mobile devices to increase student academic outcomes in Qatar. *Open Journal of Social Sciences* 2, 67–73. Retrieved from www.scirp.org/journal/jss

National Robot Olympiad – Qatar (n.d) [website]. Accessed at http://webit.cna-qatar.edu.qa/nro/welcome.php

Pavlik, J., Dennis, E. and Mersey, R. (n.d.), Content Innovation Strategies for Mobile Media in Qatar [research project]. Retrieved from www.qatar.northwestern.edu/research/projects/content-innovation-strategies/index.html

Qatar Information Exchange (2015). Labour force: economically active population (15 years and above) by nationality, sex and occupation. Retrieved from www.qix.gov.qa/, 21 June 2015.

Qatar Mobility Innovations Center (QMIC) (2012). About. Accessed at www.qmic.com/about/

Qatar National Research Fund (QNRF) (2015). Vision and Mission. Accessed at www.qnrf.org/en-us/About-Us/Vision-Mission, 21 June 2015.

Rahbek-Nielsen, T. (2015). Workshop brings innovative ideas in teaching and learning to post-secondary educators in Qatar. 6 May. Retrieved from www.qatar.ucalgary.ca/about/news/may2015/workshop-brings-innovative-ideas-in-teaching-and-learning-to-post-secondary-educators-in-qatar

Snoj, J. (2014). Population of Qatar by nationality, BQ Doha. Retrieved from www.bqdoha.com/2013/12/population-qatar.

Supreme Education Council (SEC) (2012). One hundred thousand tablet devices will be distributed to independent schools [press release]. Retrieved from https://www.education.qa/en/AboutTheProgram/News/Pages/News1.aspx

Supreme Education Council (SEC) (2015). HE Prime Minister inaugurates education conference 2015 [press release]. Retrieved from www.sec.gov.qa/En/Media/News/Pages/NewsDetails.aspx?NewsID=3637

Supreme Education Council (SEC) (2015). May 15 closing date for submitting nominations for the ALECSO mobile apps competition [press release]. Retrieved from www.sec.gov.qa/En/Media/News/Pages/NewsDetails.aspx?NewsID=3654

Supreme Education Council (SEC) (2015). Supreme Education Council Reviews 2015–2022 Strategy [press release]. Retrieved from www.sec.gov.qa/En/Media/News/Pages/NewsDetails.aspx?NewsID=3652

Texas A&M (2013). Texas A&M University at Qatar hosts teaching innovation with technology competition [press release]. Retrieved from www.qatar.tamu.edu/

newsroom/university-news/2013/12/texas-am-university-at-qatar-hosts-teaching-innovation-with-technology-competition/
Texas A&M (n.d.). Services and Resources [web page]. Retrieved from http://it.qatar.tamu.edu/services/Pages/services.aspx
The vision of Qatar (n.d). Arab science: a journey of innovation. Retrieved from www.grouporigin.com/clients/qatarfoundation/chapter4_2.htm
Umoren, R., Stadler, D., Gasior, S., Al-Sheikhly, D., Truman, B. and Lowe, C. (2014). Global collaboration and team-building through 3D virtual environments. *Innovations in Global Medical and Health Education*. Retrieved from www.qscience.com/doi/full/10.5339/igmhe.2014.1
Weill Cornell Medical College in Qatar (WCMC–Q) (2015). WCMC–Q hosts global forum on innovations in medical education [press release]. Retrieved from http://qatar-weill.cornell.edu/media/reports/2015/IGMHE.html
World Economic Forum (2014). Global information technology report 2014. Accessed at http://reports.weforum.org/global-information-technology-report-2014/#section=10th-pillar-social-impacts
World Innovation Summit for Education (WISE) (2014). 2014 WISE survey: 'school in 2030'. Accessed at www.wise-qatar.org/sites/default/files/wise-survey-school-in-2030.pdf
World Innovation Summit for Health (WISH) (2015). Innovation showcases. Accessed at http://wish.org.qa/summit/2015-summit/innovation-showcases-2015

9 Use of social media in technology-enhanced learning

Ali S. Al Musawi

Introduction

The Arab States of the Gulf Cooperation Council (GCC) should keep pace with the tremendous influence and speed of change that social media exerts on their people's lives. Data showed that the three most used social media are Facebook, Twitter and YouTube, with Facebook in the lead. According to Reyaee and Ahmed (2015, p.23), '[the] Internet has the potential to be a multi-vocal platform through which every segment of the society can have their voices heard'). Expanse of social media usage has been strong in Saudi Arabia and the United Arab Emirates (UAE), with users growing over 50 per cent (Dubai School of Government, 2013). Some GCC states have taken tangible steps in adopting social media through government departments and fulfilling the ministry's duties and communication with their citizens. Some public figures use social media to gauge public opinion on government issues (Al-Badi, 2013).

However, research on using social media for educational purposes is limited. Researchers need to investigate the use of social media by learners and publish the results so that others can be informed of best practices. This chapter analyses research in this area to determine the patterns of students' use of social media in learning and exchange of information.

Data analysis approaches

1. Analysis approach

By analysis, we mean a quantitative form of education-related literature review of earlier research with shared statistical measure (e.g. effect size and research quality) to identify the effect or relationship of interest. The method and procedures involve the following steps (Hunter et al., 1982; Schmidt, 1984):

a   locate all relevant and usable studies containing information about the effect of interest;
b   code each study for characteristics that may be related to the size of the effect obtained in the study;

c   calculate estimates, variance and means of effect sizes for variables across studies;
d   determine the amount of variance in effect sizes;
e   if a sufficiently large percentage of variance across studies can be attributed to the preceding artefacts, the meta-analysis ends;
f   if a large percentage of variance across studies is unaccounted for by statistical artefacts, determine whether study characteristics can account for the residual variance.

The research studies reviewed on the use of social media in education in the GCC states are listed in Table 9.1. Other articles and documents are, however, used to support the research arguments.

2. Online ethnography approach

Online ethnography is ethnographic study based on the digital methods and interactions using Facebook, Twitter, blogs, websites and forums specifically within the educational online format. The methods and procedures combine quantitative (e.g. frequencies of word use) and qualitative (dialogue analysis) techniques. The procedure is adapted making cultural entrée, data collection, analysing data and conducting ethical research contingencies and provide sets of specific guidelines (Kozinets, 2006). Online ethnography enables the researcher to access huge datasets with the possibility for collaboration and direct participant input from variety of sources and platforms. To achieve the objective of online ethnographic study, a Facebook study group from the Evaluation in Educational Technology course designed and taught at Sultan Qaboos University was selected for analysis purposes.

Table 9.1 Research accounts on social media use in education

Research Domain	No of Manuscripts	Authors
Academic application	8	Al-Otaibi (2011); Al-Qahtani (2012); Al-Shehri (2011); Mansour (2015); Martin (2012); Mehmood and Taswir (2013); Paliktzoglou and Suhonen (2014); Reyaee and Ahmed (2015); Xanthidis and Alali (2014).
SM adoption	2	Al-Badi (2013); DSG (2013); Al-Mukhaini (2014).
Design/training	2	Al-Shoiei (2012); Amasha, M. and Al Shaya. H. (2009).

Social media in education

Lenhart et al. (2010) conducted a survey for the Pew Research Center Project on Social Media and concluded that teens and young adults are the two groups who go online using wireless internet or cell phones. They found that Facebook and YouTube are the most used social media among students. Transforming the students' learning to improve their academic performance with social media should be a future goal for educational institutions, especially with new generations of learners, whose technology skills develop at an early stage in their lives.

According to the literature, educational application of social media seems to be mostly effective (Curcher, 2011; Liu and Stevenson, 2012), although other literature shows no impact for their use (e.g. Kolek and Saunders, 2008; Pasek et. al., 2009; Hamat et. al., 2012). Literature shows that spread of social media such as Facebook and Twitter can support traditional classroom communication (Lugano, 2008). Oradini and Saunders (2008) suggest that educational institutions need to have their own closed social media system.

Zaidieh (2012) states that social media in education are beneficial for their 'flexibility, repeatable, convenience, and accessibility'. The following is a list of benefits that are mentioned by researchers (Hiltz, Coppola, Rotter and Turoff, 2000, cited in Yang and Tang, 2003; Firpo, 2009; Boyd, 2007, cited in Flad, 2010; Eller, 2012):

1 helping the students to express themselves and construct knowledge;
2 making learning more interactive;
3 sharing information and the multimedia environment, and;
4 providing the students with authentic experiences and increase their understanding of shared knowledge.

Schlenkrich and Sewry (2012) listed the following factors for the successful use of social meida in education:

- fast internet connection;
- privacy and security measures for all users;
- legal and acceptable activities;
- current and controversial issues, checking suspect information;
- separation of personal and professional activities;
- professional and ethical content; and,
- positive attitude toward the use of social media and other users.

Social media in education at GCC states

Background to technology in GCC states' education

The development of digital technologies has presented the world of education with new methods in the delivery of teaching and learning. GCC states are no exception to this global transformation process – they too have begun to establish e-government, education portals and education technology programmes (Al Musawi, 2010). In addition, educational institutions in the GCC states, especially at higher education level, highlight the importance of technology in supporting students by the introduction of wireless connections, fully supported multimedia laboratories and ongoing training programmes.

Instructional technologies are implemented in teaching where teaching rooms are connected to the internet and students use Moodle as a learning management tool. In Omani basic education in particular, teaching and learning technology is considered the most important factor that contributes to achieving effective learning, using appropriate teaching aids along with appropriate education strategies and good implementation and timing to achieve goals. Students increasingly use the internet and social media, but there is little research evidence of its use in fields of learning, specifically in the Arab educational environment (Al Musawi, 2013).

Al Musawi and Ammar's (2015) findings show that Omani students use the internet and email several times per day, with the minimum use of the internet being one to two days per week. They find that wireless connections and mobile technologies spread quickly among the students and wire-based connections are used from their homes. Research also shows that Saudis increasingly use social media and prefer blended education (Amasha and Al-Shaya, 2009).

A research case study conducted by Porcaro and Al Musawi (2011) demonstrates that the outcomes of applying Computer Supported Collaborative Learning environments include:

- enhanced course content knowledge;
- increased confidence in applying course knowledge and skills;
- stronger collaboration skills (arguing ideas, making decisions, providing solutions);
- greater ability to create instead of simply consume knowledge;
- added benefits of leadership and presentation skills.

Social media in GCC states' education

1. Pedagogical concerns

It seems that there is a demand to use social media in learning at GCC educational institutions due to its ease of use and flexibility. Paliktzoglou and Suhonen (2014) find that the use of Facebook as a learning tool had a positive impact on Bahraini students. Amasha and Al Shaya (2009) find that that schools' administrators prefer to communicate with the educational planners using social media. Martin (2012) states that SM, if used wisely, can provide a good avenue for learning for Omani students. He concludes that:

    a   Social pressure could affect educators' and students' intention to use Facebook group in e-learning;

 b Educators and students who are frequent and/or heavy users of Facebook are more likely to use the group in e-learning;
 c Educators and students believe that Facebook group will be more useful if there will be interactive communications between educator and students and among students; and,
 d Educators and students feel that Facebook group is interesting and fun to use in e-learning.

However, a 2013 Arab social media report series states that:

> social media has become common place and can act as a tool that improves the efficacy of learning and assists teachers, parents, academics, students and educational institutions ... To reach social media's potential in educational environments; the prerequisites include reforms in curricula, technological infrastructure, educational institutions and national policies.
> (DSG, 2013, p.3)

Mansour (2015) study shows that the Kuwaiti faculty members are in general agreement about the effectiveness of social media, especially for disseminating and sharing information, communication and informal collaboration. The following are the main findings of this study.

1 Social media users among faculty members tend to be males, aged between 41 and 50 years, PhD holders, ranked as assistant professors, full-time faculty members, specialists in information technologies and relatively new to teaching, with experience ranging from one to five years.
2 No significant differences were found between the academic rank, teaching status and teaching experience of faculty and their use of social media.
3 YouTube, Twitter, Facebook and blogs respectively were used mostly by faculty members, but Twitter, Facebook and YouTube were the most well-known social media on which they have profiles.
4 SM was mainly used for the purpose of communicating with others and finding and sharing information with peers and students.
5 Tasks performed on social media by faculty members were mostly communication related – sending/receiving messages – and finding general and specific information.

Al Musawi and Ammar's (2015) findings on using social media in education indicate that the Omani students use these for educational purposes and activities on a weekly basis. Mehmood and Taswir (2013) find that Omani students have started using social media for academic purposes, with a high percentage utilising social media as an avenue to search for information, join educational networks and look for career opportunities. Al Aamri (2012) suggests Omani educational institutions empirically value and utilize the pedagogical assets of Facebook and blogs technology in teaching and urges both practitioners and teachers to implement Facebook and blogs tools in the learning environment and composition classroom effectively.

Research indicated that using social media improves Saudi students' achievement, skills and talents (Al-Otaibi, 2011; Al-Qahtani, 2012). Al-Qahtani (2012) recommends that Saudi educational institutions should encourage faculty staff to make the best use of social media applications in teaching. Al-Shoiei's study (2012) reported positive attitudes among Saudi students towards using social media in education. Al-Shehri (2011) substantiated this result, stating that the mobile application of Facebook was preferred by Saudi learners when completing their study assignments. It contributed to improving their academic performance and opened 'friendly' communication channels with their instructors (Xanthidis and Alali, 2014). DSG (2013) shows that social media could enhance students' competencies in several areas, including technological competency, creativity, collaboration, research skills, soft skills, communication skills and job skills. More specifically, social media would be useful for the integration of students with special needs within the education system. Social media can become a tool that can enhance the learning experience, whether in the classroom by promoting more interactive discussion, or by creating opportunities to learn remotely through distance learning. Findings regarding using social media in education indicate that Omani students use search engines perhaps to look for information, and that they do not use email applications for learning purposes. Most use social media for educational purposes and activities on a weekly base. Interestingly, however, findings prove that using social media can teach students IT skills, but does not develop their thinking skills (Al Musawi and Ammar, 2015).

Older Omani basic education students learn to create animations, web pages and to program what the computer does using advanced programming languages. They plan their enquiries using shared information space and social media, where they can post their ideas and provide positive and constructive feedback to the ideas of other students. Collaboration through social media may lead to insights that might not have been possible without the benefits of discussion and interaction.

Online ethnographic analysis shows that students seem to use SM in their courses for communication and chat, sharing files and resources, and discussing instructional assignments. The students find that their interaction level through Facebook lessons is vital nowadays and the visual materials make these lessons easier, lively and accessible. They express their opinion on their ability to apply what they learn through practising in their own time and at any location. They think social media are better for delivering content and other materials and the Facebook course is good example of their benefits in education. One student opined that after three courses of Facebook use 'I believe more courses should be presented in social media as effective online environment through which instructors and students can communicate easily.'

2. Socio-cultural and technological concerns

Al-Otaibi (2011) finds that Facebook use spreads among Saudi students with more positive effects in terms of improving cultural, social and academic level. In Oman, young students in schools are encouraged to build virtual worlds with Etoys and SimStories using the same educational software environment as students in Brazil, Canada, Germany, Japan and the USA. Collaborating with other students and outside experts is also encouraged through dedicated software such as Journal Zone.

Students' use of social media is mostly characterized by the need to establish relationships and continue to communicate with friends. However, Al Musawi and Ammar (2015) find that Omani students are culturally bound to their way of approaching new social media with 'caution', specifically in terms of language and cultural differences. In addition, there is a high level of awareness of disruptive and potentially negative aspects of social media use (e.g. distraction and inappropriate behaviour) in the classroom, acknowledging the need for parental and teacher supervision (DSG, 2013).

Al Musawi and Kelso (2015) state some other GCC 'culturally' related factors that may hinder modern technologies' use in education. These are:

- doubts about the real need for e-learning in traditional educational institutions, which were founded and equipped to support face-to-face education and provide students with their human, financial and physical resources and facilities;
- faculty members who have their own technophobia originating from the fear that e-learning can replace them;
- lack of infrastructure and internet accessibility;
- scarcity of technical expertise and human resources;
- lack of legal frameworks and/or precise criteria for the academic evaluation;
- impact of technology on Arabic identity, specifically in terms of using Arabic language versus other languages;
- existence of 'digital divide' between those who use e-learning applications and those who do not use them among lecturers and students and males and females.

The online ethnographic analysis shows that students think that social media use in education makes their instructors more accessible and friendlier in communications and in providing them with various materials and resources. They think that social media such as Facebook enhance communication between students themselves and their instructor. They perceive that social media increase the interaction with students who are too shy to participate in the classroom.

In terms of technological needs, Mehmood and Taswir (2013) found that technical issues such as low speeds and poor connectivity may obstruct SM use and cause gaps in communication. Mansour's study (2015) revealed that the time, technology training and skills were the most important barriers that social media Kuwaiti instructors faced. Barriers like interest in social media as well as awareness and trust of them were respectively the most important barriers to non-users. Al-Mukhaini et al. (2014) recommend that non-users should be provided with necessary assistance to foster their skills towards social media usage. The online ethnographic analysis substantiated these findings by showing the need for more technical support and multimedia infrastructure. The students thought that a persistent need exists to train the lecturers to design and integrate social media in their courses. The online ethnographic analysis also shows that students use various social media such as Facebook, Moodle, WhatsApp, google+, blogs, Instagram, Wikis, YouTube, SlideShare, PresentationTube, Google Maps, Dropbox, Twitter, Google Docs and Prezi.

3. Research concerns

The Arab social media survey examines the satisfaction with and quality of education systems, technology and social media use in the classroom, and perceptions about social media use in the classroom (DSG, 2013). It investigates the adoption of social media in relation to student performance, teacher quality, mentorship, the learning environment, and access to information and knowledge sharing. The reviewed research investigates the motives for the use of social media by higher education students, the impact on students of using them and the benefits of using social media as tools for developing a new style of learning. These and other research recommend conducting the following research in the future:

a   Al-Mukhaini et al. (2014):
- Examine aspects of using social media among faculty members that may affect their use, such as the technical, legal, ethical and intellectual aspects.
- Gather more information to investigate why some faculty members do not use social media especially for educational purposes.

b   Mansour (2015):
- Study qualitatively the perception and opinions of faculty members about their use of social media.
- Specify the relation between the use of social media and each area of study separately.
- Compare experiences of faculty members and students regarding the use of social media in educational practices.

Conclusion

From what has been said above, the following can be concluded in terms of using SM in education at GCC states academic/educational institutions.

a Students' and faculty members' attitudes are positive towards social media benefits and use in education due to their potential for sharing knowledge and supporting students' competencies and teacher quality.
b It is widely thought that social media reduces time and cost with ease of access.
c It is believed that social media has potential in fields of distance education, e-learning and for students' with special needs.
d There are some impediments that need to be approached and resolved for better implementation.

Implications and best models

For an educational institution to implement social media in its educational institutions/system, the best models are those combining 'blended' learning and taking advantage of the existing classroom/schooling and online social networking platforms promoting students' interaction by building a systematic Computer Supported Collaborative Learning Environment. Figure 9.1 below visualizes this model, which constitutes six components, namely:

1 The educational system of the institution, including its vision, mission and philosophical approaches.

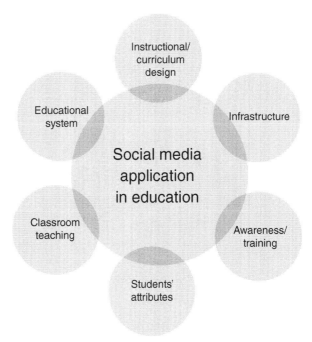

Figure 9.1 Social media application in education at GCC states' educational institutions.

2 Classroom teaching: development of instructional delivery techniques in the classroom such as interaction, discussion, moderation, demonstration, tutorials, simulations, role-playing, modelling, debate, field trips, case studies, and lectures presentations.
3 Students' attributes: know their demographic information, academic levels, geographic distribution, prior knowledge and anxiety levels.
4 Awareness and training.
5 Infrastructure: analyse the institution technical/financial/administrative infrastructure.
6 Instructional/curriculum design: determine learning content best to be delivered and analyse it in line with the pre-determined learners' characteristics.

The model shown in Figure 9.1 on the macro level can be followed with the next steps, derived from ASSURE Model (Al Musawi, 2011).

1 Analyse institutional and pedagogical contexts: blended learning designers should analyse the preparedness of the institution in terms of technical/financial infrastructure (e.g. hardware, software, servers, bandwidth, security), administration and personnel, and ethical/political philosophy (e.g. copyright regulations, admissions procedures and course offerings).
2 Select appropriate instructional modes and forms: blended learning designers should develop their blended delivery techniques in ways that enable every learner to go through the same experience of the blended components.
3 Select appropriate technology and resources: blended learning designers, at this stage, need to create blended environment and tools of delivery and select from myriad combinations of technologies that can be used in blended learning environments and best fit the learning prescribed modes/forms.
4 Use resources and methods: At this stage, the management of the blended learning should be conducted. Infrastructure, facilities and logistics to use and implement blended delivery modes should be secured.
5 Request interaction/participation: At this stage of the blended instructional process, activities should focus on learners' engagement through reports, presentations, discourses, small group debates and threaded discussions.
6 Evaluate and review: at this stage, instructors should qualitatively and quantitatively assess their students' achievement of learning outcomes, performance, participation in the discussions, contribution to activities and understanding of concept explained.

Acknowledgement

Thanks to Dr Alaa Sadik, instructor at Sultan Qaboos University, for allowing the author to view/analyse the online Facebook courses.

References

Al Aamri, K. (2012). Using Web 2.0 technologies to enhance academic writing proficiency among EES students in Sultan Qaboos University: an example of Facebook and blogs. Paper presented at the 2nd International Conference on the Future of Education, June, http://conference.pixel-online.net/edu_future2012/common/download/Paper_pdf/66-ENT60-FP-Alaamri-FOE2012.pdf

Al-Badi, A. (2013). The adoption of social media in government agencies: Gulf Cooperation Council case study. *Journal of Technology Research* 1(5), 1–26.

Al-Mukhaini, E., Al-Qayoudhi, W. and Al-Badi, A. (2014). Adoption of social networking in education: a study of the use of social networks by higher education students in Oman. *Journal of International Education Research* 10(2), 143–151.

Al Musawi, A. (2010). The Instructional and Learning Technologies Department (ILT) in the College of Education, Sultan Qaboos University. In M. Orey et al. (eds), *Educational media and technology yearbook* (vol. 35, pp. 101–116). Retrieved from AECT.

Al Musawi, A. (2011). Blended Learning. *Journal of Turkish Science Education* 8(2), 3–8.

Al Musawi, A. (2013). Current aspects and prospects of ICT in the Arab higher education sector: literature review. In F. Albadri (ed.), *Information systems applications in the Arab education sector* (vol. 1, pp. 1–22). Retrieved from IGI.

Al Musawi, A. and Ammar, M. (2015). Students' use of the internet and social networking sites for learning and other activities at Sultan Qaboos University. *International Journal of Social Media and Interactive Learning Environments* 3(2), 142–161.

Al Musawi, A. and Kelso, M. (2015). Issues and implications of Integrating e-learning at Arab universities. In M. Ally and B. Khan (eds), *International handbook of e-learning* (vol. 2, pp. 257–270). Retrieved from Routledge.

Al-Otaibi, J. (2011). Saudi universities' male and female students' use of Facebook: practical study. Unpublished Master's thesis, King Saud University, Saudi Arabia.

Al-Qahtani, M. (2012). The effect of using social networks in teaching English grammar on the achievement of the female students in Al-Imam Muhammad Ibn Saud Islamic University. Unpublished master's thesis, Al-Imam Muhammad Ibn Saud Islamic University, Saudi Arabia.

Al-Shehri, S. (2011). Context in our pockets: mobile phones and social networking as tools of contextualizing language learning. Paper presented at the 10th World Conference on Mobile and Contextual Learning, October. http://mlearn.bnu.edu.cn/source/ten_outstanding_papers/Context%20in%20our%20pockets%20Mobile%20phones%20and%20social%20networking%20as%20tools%20of%20contextualising%20language%20learning.pdf

Al-Shoiei, M, (2012). Design a training program for the development of educational applications use of Web 2.0 and social networks with learning resources specialist and attitudes towards them. Paper presented at the 13th Conference of the Egyptian Society of Education Technology – Contemporary Issues and Trends, Cairo, Egypt, 11–12 April.

Amasha, M. and Al Shaya, H. (2009). Educational administration using Web 2.0 technologies: field study on Al-Qaseem Saudi principals. Paper presented at the 12th Conference of the Egyptian Society of Education Technology – e-Learning Technologies and Future of Education, Cairo, Egypt, 28–29 October.

Curcher, M. (2011). A case study examining the implementation of social networking technologies to enhance student learning for students learning in a second language. *Education, Business and Society: Contemporary Middle Eastern Issues* 4(1), 80–90.

Dubai School of Government (DSG) (2013). *The Arab social media report series: transforming education in the Arab World: breaking barriers in the age of social learning 2013.* Retrieved from www.arabsocialmediareport.com/UserManagement/PDF/ASOCIAL MEDIAR_5_Report_Final.pdf

Flad, K. (2010). *The Influence of social networking participation on student academic performance across gender lines.* Master's thesis, State University of New York, New York, USA. Retrieved from http://digitalcommons.brockport.edu/cgi/viewcontent.cgi?article=1030&context=edc_theses

Hamat, A., Embi, M. and Abu Hassan, H. (2012). The use of social media among Malaysian university students. *International Education Studies* 5(3), 56–66.

Hunter, J.E., Schmidt, F.L. and Jackson, G.B. (1982). *Meta-analysis: cumulating research findings across studies.* Beverly Hills CA: Sage.

Kolek, E. and Saunders, D. (2008). Online disclosure: an empirical examination of undergraduate Facebook profiles. *Student Affairs Administrators in Higher Education (NASPA) Journal* 45(1), 1–25.

Kozinets, R.V. (2006). Netnography 2.0. In Russell W. Belk (ed.), *Handbook of qualitative research methods in marketing* (pp. 129–142). Cheltenham UK and Northampton MA: Edward Elgar.

Lenhart, A., Purcell, K., Social Mediaith, A. and Zickuhr, K. (2010). Report on social media and mobile internet use among teens and young adults: prepared for the Pew Internet and American Life Project. Retrieved from http://web.pewinternet.org/~/media/Files/Reports/2010/PIP_Social_Media_and_Young_Adults_Report_Final_with_toplines.pdf

Liu, M. and Stevenson, M. (2012). Learning a language with Web 2.0: exploring the use of social networking features of foreign language learning websites. *The Computer-Assisted Language Instruction Consortium (CALICO) Journal* 27(2), 233–259.

Lugano, G. (2008). Mobile social networking in theory and practice. *First Monday Journal* 13(3). Retrieved from http://firstmonday.org/htbin/cgiwrap/bin/ojs/index.php/fm/article/viewArticle/2232/2050

Mansour, E. (2015). The use of social networking sites (SNSs) by the faculty members of the School of Library and Information Science, PAAET, Kuwait. *The Electronic Library* 33(3), 524–546.

Martin, R. (2012). Factors affecting the usefulness of social networking in e-learning at German University of Technology in Oman. *International Journal of e-Education, e-Business, e-Management and e-Learning* 2(6), 498–508.

Mehmood S. and Taswir T. (2013). The effects of social networking sites on the academic performance of students in College of Applied Sciences, Nizwa, Oman. *Asian Social Science* 8, 11–17.

Oradini, F. and Saunders, G. (2008). The use of social networking by students and staff in higher education, online learning development. Retrieved from www.eife-l.org/publications/proceedings/ilf08/contributions/improving-quality-of-learning-with-technologies/Oradini_Saunders.pdf

Paliktzoglou, V. and Suhonen, J. (2014). Facebook as an assisted learning tool in problem-based learning: the Bahrain case. *International Journal of Social Media and Interactive Learning Environments* 2(1), 85–100.

Pasek, J., More, E. and Hargittai, E. (2009). Facebook and academic performance: reconciling a media sensation with data. *First Monday Journal* 14(5). Retrieved from http://ojs-prod-lib.cc.uic.edu/ojs/index.php/fm/article/view/2498/2181

Porcaro, D. and Al Musawi, A. (2011). Lessons learned from adopting computer-supported collaborative learning in Oman. *EDUCAUSE Quarterly (EQ)* 34(4). Retrieved from www.educause.edu/EDUCAUSE+Quarterly/EDUCAUSEQuarterlyMagazineVolum/LessonsLearnedfromAdoptingComp/242681

Reyaee, S. and Ahmed, A. (2015) Growth pattern of social media usage in Arab Gulf states: an analytical study. *Social Networking* 4, 23–32. http://dx.doi: 10.4236/sn.2015.42003.

Schlenkrich, L. and Sewry, D. (2012). Factors for successful use of social media in higher education, *South African Computer Journal* 49, 12–24.

Schmidt, F.L. (1984). Meta-analysis: implications for cumulative knowledge in the behavioral and social sciences. Paper presented at the 92nd Annual Meetings of the American Psychological Association, Toronto, Ontario, 24–28 August 1984.

Xanthidis, D. and Alali, A. (2014). Effects of social media on e-learning development in the GCC case study: Saudi Arabia. Paper presented at World Symposium on Computer Applications and Research (WSCAR2014). http://dx.doi.10.1109/WSCAR.2014.6916787.

Yang, Heng-Li and Tang, J. (2003). Effects of social network on students' performance: a web-based forum study in Taiwan. *The Journal of Asynchronous Learning Networks (JALN)* 7(3). Retrieved from http://nccur.lib.nccu.edu.tw/bitstream/140.119/27390/1/v7n3_yang.pdf

Zaidieh, A. (2012). The use of social networking in education: challenges and opportunities. *World of Computer Science and Information Technology Journal (WCSIT)* 2(1), 18–21.

10 Student-centred learning analytics dashboards to empower students to take responsibility for their learning

Naif R. Aljohani, Hugh C. Davis, Mohamed Ally and Syed Asim Jalal

Introduction

Learning analytics dashboards usually provide a dashboard to report and visualize the analytics results for different intended users, such as teachers and managers (Leony, Pardo et al., 2012; Verbert, Duval et al., 2013; Verbert, Govaerts et al., 2013). These include, for example, Teacher ADVisor (Kosba, Dimitrova et al., 2005), Classroom View (France, Heraud et al. 2006), Moodle Dashboard (Podgorelec and Kuhar, 2011) and LOCO-Analyst (Ali, Hatala et al., 2012). However, most of these dashboards are intended to be used by teachers (Aljohani and Davis, 2013; Verbert, Duval et al., 2013). Therefore, this chapter will clarify theoretically the significance of directing the analytical results to students, which will be delivered to their student-centred learning analytics dashboard to empower students to take responsibility for their learning.

Learning analytics dashboards can be classified differently, based on many considerations. However, for the purpose of this chapter, learning analytics dashboards are divided into teacher-centred dashboards, which can also be called 'teacher-oriented dashboards', and student-centred dashboards, which can be termed 'student-oriented dashboards'. This classification is based on the intended users of the dashboard.

The main goal of this chapter is to clarify the difference between student and teacher learning analytics dashboards. The chapter also aims to discuss the characteristics of an effective student-centred analytical dashboard considered in this research. Finally, it aims to show how students can provide their own analytical dashboard through answering the 'analytics at work' matrix questions.

This chapter is organized as follows. First, it builds a common understanding of what 'dashboard' really means and discusses the differences between a teacher-centred learning analytics dashboard and a student-centred learning analytics dashboard. Second, it presents the characteristics of an effective student-centred dashboard. Third, it explains how the 'Analytics at Work' matrix can be used to provide a student-centred analytical dashboard. Fourth, it discusses the significance of student-centred learning analytics dashboards.

Learning analytics dashboards

In order to discuss teacher and student dashboards it is important briefly to build a common understanding of what 'dashboard' really means. Dashboards have been implemented in many domains, such as business and health, therefore there are many different views about what a dashboard really is.

Few (2006) defined 'dashboard' generally as a 'visual display of the most information needed to achieve one or more objectives which fits entirely on a single computer screen so it can be monitored at a glance'. Eckerson (2010) defined 'performance dashboard' specifically as 'a multi-layered application built on a business intelligence and data integration infrastructure that enables organisations to measure, monitor, and manage business performance more effectively'.

The common ground of these two definitions is that the dashboard summarizes the results of the data of interest, with the focus being on the key performance indicators or key desired objectives. The results of the data analysis, which come from different sources, can be consolidated and presented in the dashboard in a way that helps the intended user to have a comprehensive understanding of the analysed data using different information visualization techniques (Card, Mackinlay et al., 1999).The focus here is on the learning analytics dashboard, which reports and presents the results of educational data analysis for different intended users such as teachers, managers and students (Verbert, Govaerts et al. 2013).

The dashboard concept has been used in many learning analytics systems for many purposes. These include to visualize and monitor students' online activities (Mazza and Dimitrova, 2007; Zhang, Almeroth et al., 2007; Dyckhoff, Zielke et al., 2012; Garc, a-Sol et al., 2012), to monitor student learning activities in face-to-face traditional learning environment (Pohl, Bry et al., 2012; Martinez-Maldonado, Clayphan et al., 2014), to visualize students' collaborative work in the online learning environment (Krčadinac, Jovanović et al., 2012), to monitor students who are working collaboratively using a multi-touch table (Martinez Maldonado, Kay et al., 2012) and to increase the awareness of both teachers and students of their time spent online and the resources used (Govaerts, Verbert et al., 2010; Govaerts, Verbert et al., 2011).

Teacher-centred dashboards

A teacher-centred learning analytics dashboard is intended to be used by teachers in such a way that they can use it to monitor the progress of their students. In addition, the analytics results are directed to the teacher to deal with students' detected learning problems using many methods of notification, such as computerized dispatch of emails to students with learning problems. For instance, the Course Signals system classifies students according to their efforts and provides information on their progress (Arnold and Pistilli, 2012). Teachers require to run the Course Signals system to start classifying students as red, yellow or green. This information is first delivered to the teachers; students will then be given feedback and notified by email. The analytics are directed towards and are intended to be seen by teachers, who will then notify their students about their progress; thus the dashboard provided by Course Signals is only a teacher-centred dashboard.

In addition, the LOCO-Analyst tool provides teachers with feedback about their students' activities in a web-based learning environment (Ali, Hatala et al., 2012). The tool provides teachers with different information about students such as time spent online, social interaction between students, contents viewed by students and quiz results. The LOCO-Analyst tool dashboard is a teacher-centred dashboard as it is intended to be used by teachers. Yet another example of an analytics application is the Academic Analytics Tool (AAT) tool, which aims to allow teachers to understand their students' behaviour during online courses. The tool can access and report on the data generated by any learning management systems such as Moodle (Kladich, Ives et al., 2013). The AAT tool dashboard is also classified as a teacher-centred dashboard, as the results are intended to be seen by teachers.

Student-centred learning analytics dashboard

A student-centred learning analytics dashboard directs and delivers the results to students to improve their awareness about their academic problems and self-evaluate their progress. There is no intervention from their teachers, which differentiates this type of dashboard from a teacher-centred analytical dashboard. In a higher education environment, directing the analytics results to students might serve to make them feel responsible for their work and for judging their own performances. In today's world of 'independent learning', students should be empowered with their own learning analytics dashboard to allow them to become better learners, not always under the university's scrutiny. This is especially true for adult learners who like to know how they are performing in courses so that they can improve themselves.

Kruse and Pongsajapan (2012) proposed directing the analytics only to teachers and stakeholders: 'This constant language of "intervention" perpetuates an institutional culture of students as passive subjects, the targets of a flow of information rather than as self-reflective learners given the cognitive tools to evaluate their own learning processes.' Slade and Prinsloo (2013) also support the need of directing the analytics results to the students, by mentioning 'When institutions emphasise analysis and use data primarily for reporting purposes, there is a danger of seeing students as passive producers of data resulting in learning analytics used as "intrusive advising".' Therefore, students should be empowered by a student-centred learning analytics dashboard to encourage them to be more responsible for monitoring their learning progress. They should not be marginalized as people only in receipt of decisions, with no knowledge of how decisions are made about their progress or how their results are calculated.

Characteristics of an effective student-centred learning analytics dashboard

A student-centred learning analytics dashboard should 'increase students' awareness' of their academic performance and should be in the hands of students instead of 'trapping' them when they have problems (Fritz, 2011; Govaerts, Verbert et al., 2011). The characteristics presented in this section are not intended to be comprehensive, but may be considered as aspects of an effective student-centred learning analytics dashboard.

Increasing personal awareness

A student-centred dashboard should provide students with information to help them to increase their awareness to understand their academic problems *and* self-evaluate their progress. Awareness is defined as 'understanding of the activities of others, which provides a context for your own activity' (Liccardi 2010). Even this definition is intended for a collaborative learning environment, yet may be considered here, as student-centred dashboards aim not only to help students evaluate their work or increase their personal awareness of their performance, but also to allow them to compare themselves with others in order to understand their academic problems comprehensively.

Allowing students to compare their performance with that of the class will help them to understand their position within the class, which may positively impact their performance. This is especially important in an online learning environment, where students may not know each other. However, most importantly, the comparison should be anonymized and not reveal students' identities. In this way, students will be able to judge their performance independently and without teacher intervention.

Avoiding information overload

Research reveals several different definitions for the basic concept of information overload (Eppler and Mengis 2004). For the purpose of this research, information overload is defined as 'the condition by which a person cannot process all communication and informational inputs, which results in ineffectiveness or terminated information processing' (Beaudoin 2008).

To avoid information overload issue, students' dashboard should provide concise and precise analytical results based on the requirement of each course. The data used in analytics should be goal-driven learning analytics, not simply data driven (Santos, Govaerts et al., 2012). With data-driven learning analytics, students may be overwhelmed with detailed analytics perhaps unrelated to the course. For instance, if the course does not require students to use a specific learning system, it is better to avoid analysing their activities in that system and reporting on to their dashboard.

Increasing student awareness of data being collected about them

Student data is the seed of learning analytics; originally, learning analytics research was developed to make sense of student data in order to identify learning problems at an early stage. To increase the effectiveness of the students dashboard, or to encourage students to use it to monitor their performance, the privacy of students' data as well as the concern related to profiling students based on their performance should be considered. Students should be informed of the tools (e.g. forum discussion, Wiki etc.) that they need to use in the course so they are more aware of the data being collected about them.

This might help them to use their dashboard as 'diagnostic tool' to monitor their performance independently. In addition, this will help them to focus more on using the learning tools than the fact that their interaction data is being collected and analysed. Most importantly, students should be clear about the goals of learning analytics dashboard tool and how analytics can impact them. Providing students with highly sophisticated and well-designed dashboards might be insufficient to help them understand their problems, and setting expectations is of great importance. This involves explaining to them how decisions are made about their progress, what they expect their dashboard to tell them, how they can use the information provided in their dashboard to monitor their progress and the meaning of each element of their dashboard.

Student-centred learning analytics dashboard and analytics at work matrix

This section aims to show how students can provide their own analytical dashboard through answering the 'analytics at work' matrix questions (Davenport, Harris et al., 2010), which we enhanced to facilitate providing more informative student dashboard. In the context of this research, we call the first the 'awareness' layer instead of the 'information' layer, as it is more relevant to the goal of providing students with their own dashboards. The matrix is used to organize the information that can be provided by a student-centred learning analytics dashboard as well as to classify the different types of student-centred learning analytics dashboards (see Figure 10.1).

The first question in the 'awareness layer' concerns what happened in the past. The student-centred dashboard should provide students with information about their past performance – for instance, if students use an LMS (e.g. Blackboard, Moodle, etc.), the number of threads added by students themselves to the discussion forum and how many learning activities the students completed in order to increase their awareness about their activities and help them to monitor their performance independently. It is better if these statistics are compared with those of students' peers to help them better understand their performance.

The second question in the awareness layer is about what is happening in the present. Past information usually leads to present information, so there is no difference between the two; the only difference is in the relativity of information provided at the time. This does not mean that the analytics from the present should be identical to the analytics from the past, but that they should have something in common to allow students to compare their past and their present. The dashboard information should be consistent, to help students to monitor their progress based on a specific group of indicators. For instance, if the dashboard provides students with information about the time that they spend on a task, it should allow students to compare the time that they spent in the past and their current times. The last question in this layer is 'What will happen?' Through the exploration of past patterns, it is possible to create assumptions about the future, or to clarify what students should do in the future. An example of this is PGRTracker dashboard,[1] not a learning analytics dashboard but one that aims to inform postgraduate students at the University of Southampton about the upcoming tasks that need to be performed, which can be based on their past or present work.

The first layer in the matrix aims to increase students' awareness of their work or performance compared to that of their peers. In addition, it provides informative reports about what is happening, rather than why something occurs or how it may recur in the future. For instance, the SAM (Software Asset Management) dashboard (Govaerts, Verbert et al., 2012) provides students with information about their online learning activities to increase their awareness of their work in comparison with the work of other students.

The second layer of the matrix is usually termed 'insight', but in this case we term it 'comprehension'. This layer requires advanced analytical techniques to carry out comprehensive investigations in order to gather new insights that can help students comprehend their learning progress. For instance, by using data-mining techniques such as predictive analysis, classification and clustering, it is possible to gain insight into the past and highlight any possible factors that caused

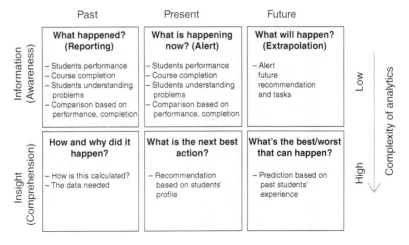

Figure 10.1 Student-centred dashboard based on an enhanced the 'Analytics at Work' matrix.

what happened in the past (Romero and Ventura, 2010). In addition, it is possible to gain real-time insights, which in turn help students better to understand what is happening at the present time and to assist in the formation of recommendations to ameliorate the situation. For instance, if students are classified as 'at risk' or underperforming, this layer not only reports to them this diagnostic news, but justifies to them why this happened, using available student data or by comparing with others with the same learning problems.

In addition, 'the present' in this layer is not only to report to students their present situation, but also guides them to different ways that might help in solving their problems or even how to enhance their performance. Finally, future insights can be achieved in many ways, such as using the data of the past from good students in the course and use it with the current students in order to provide them with different ways to be more successful. Having student-learning analytics dashboards that meet the requirements of this layer is confronted by many obstacles, such as the credibility of predation and the sophistication of the technical requirements, which many universities cannot afford (Fritz, 2011). An example of such dashboard, which is not student-centred, is a Signal dashboard, which provides teachers with information about students and helps them to identify the students who are underperforming or at risk (Arnold and Pistilli, 2012).

Discussion

When the analytics results presented in the dashboard are intended to be seen only by teachers, the dashboard is considered to be a teacher-centred dashboard, in contrast to the student-centred dashboard that directs the analytical results to students to understand their performance.

When a learning analytics dashboard is only teacher-centred, the big question to be asked is: 'Who needs to intervene when poor results are detected?' The answer to this question is not straightforward and may be complicated for three main reasons, as follows.

- Higher education lecturers have many academic responsibilities such as teaching and producing research papers, therefore intervening to solve their students learning problems might be to some extent difficult for them (Fritz, 2011).
- Students in a higher education environment are expected to be more independent learners, therefore any intervention from their lecturers might make them feel that they are being monitored. This might lead them to be more dependent learners who rely more on their lecturers to tell them about their learning problems.
- Students may also be concerned about the privacy of their data as well as the feeling of being monitored (Pardo and Siemens, 2014).

Directing the analytics to both teachers and students might serve to overcome this challenge, whilst directing the analytics to students might make them more responsible for seeking solutions for their detected learning problems. When a student is treated as an active object in the learning process, who does not need a lecturer to inform them about personal performance, he or she might become a more independent learner. In addition, when students are trusted to monitor their performance and to talk about learning problems, this may have a positive impact on progress. Learning analytics is a useful way to detect the students' learning problems in the early stages of their course. Therefore, universities are increasingly using learning analytics techniques to make scene of their educational data and uncover students' problems. Universities and teachers have the right to know about their students' performance and progress and make certain that they are on the right track to achieving the desired learning outcomes. However, students should be encouraged to be more responsible for monitoring their learning progress.

Conclusion

This chapter discussed the differences between teacher-centred learning analytics dashboards and student-centred learning analytics dashboards. In addition, it presented the characteristics of an effective student-centred learning analytics dashboard as developed in previous research. Furthermore, it clarified how our enhanced version of the 'Analytics at Work' matrix can be used to facilitate provision of a student-centred learning analytics dashboard, as well as to show how the information in the dashboard can be organized.

Finally, it discussed why learning analytics applications should provide both students with their own dashboards. Students should have their own learning analytics dashboard to encourage them to resolve their learning issues, whether independently or collaboratively with their friends, teachers or any university members. Students can share the results of the analytics with their teachers to work collaboratively towards solving any detected performance problems.

Note

1 www.gradschool.fpse.soton.ac.uk/PGRTracker

References

Ali, L., Hatala, M., Gašević, D. and Jovanović, J. (2012). A qualitative evaluation of evolution of a learning analytics tool. *Computers and Education* 58(1), 470–489. doi: http://dx.doi.org/10.1016/j.compedu.2011.08.030

Aljohani, N. and Davis, H. (2013). Learning analytics and formative assessment to provide immediate detailed feedback using a student centered mobile dashboard. Paper presented at the Seventh International Conference on Next Generation Mobile Apps, Services and Technologies (NGMAST).

Arnold, K.E. and Pistilli, M.D. (2012). Course signals at Purdue: using learning analytics to increase student success. Paper presented at the Proceedings of the 2nd International Conference on Learning Analytics and Knowledge.

Beaudoin, C.E. (2008). Explaining the relationship between internet use and interpersonal trust: taking into account motivation and information overload. *Journal of Computer-Mediated Communication* 13(3), 550–568. doi: 10.1111/j.1083-6101.2008.00410.x

Card, S.K., Mackinlay, J.D. and Shneiderman, B. (1999). *Readings in information visualization: using vision to think.* San Francisco: Morgan Kaufmann.

Ciampa, K. (2014). Learning in a mobile age: an investigation of student motivation. *Journal of Computer Assisted Learning* 30(1), 82–96. doi: 10.1111/jcal.12036

Crompton, H. (2014). A Diachronic overview of technology contributing to mobile learning: a shift towards student-centred pedagogies. *Increasing Access* 7.

Davenport, T., Harris, J. and Morison, R. (2010). *Analytics at work.* Boston MA: Harvard Business School Publishing Corporation.

Dyckhoff, A.L., Zielke, D., Bültmann, M., Chatti, M.A. and Schroeder, U. (2012). Design and implementation of a learning analytics toolkit for teachers. *Journal of Educational Technology and Society* 15(3), 58–76.

Eppler, M.J. and Mengis, J. (2004). The concept of information overload: a review of literature from organization science, accounting, marketing, MIS, and related disciplines. *The Information Society* 20(5), 325–344. doi: 10.1080/01972240490507974

Few, S. (2006). *Information dashboard design.* Sebastopol CA: O'Reilly.

France, L., Heraud, J.M., Marty, J.C., Carron, T. and Heili, J. (2006). Monitoring virtual classrooms: visualization techniques to observe student activities in an e-learning system. Paper presented at the Sixth International Conference on Advanced Learning Technologies, 5–7 July.

Fritz, J. (2011). Classroom walls that talk: using online course activity data of successful students to raise self-awareness of underperforming peers. *The Internet and Higher Education* 14(2), 89–97. doi: http://dx.doi.org/10.1016/j.iheduc.2010.07.007

García-Solórzano, D., Cobo G., Santamaría, E., Morán, J. A., Monzo, C. and Melenchón J. (2012). Educational monitoring tool based on faceted browsing and data portraits. Paper presented at the Proceedings of the 2nd International Conference on Learning Analytics and Knowledge. Vancouver, British Columbia, Canada.

Govaerts, S., Verbert, K. and Duval, E. (2011). Evaluating the student activity meter: two case studies. In H. Leung, E. Popescu, Y. Cao, R.H. Lau and W. Nejdl (eds), *Proceedings of the 10th international conference on Advances in Web-Based Learning (ICWL 2011)* (vol. 7048, pp. 188–197). Heidelberg, Berlin: Springer-Verlag.

Govaerts, S., Verbert, K., Duval, E. and Pardo, A. (2012). The student activity meter for awareness and self-reflection. Paper presented at the CHI '12 Extended Abstracts on Human Factors in Computing Systems. Austin TX, USA.

Govaerts, S., Verbert, K., Klerkx, J. and Duval, E. (2010). Visualizing activities for self-reflection and awareness. In *Advances in web-based learning (ICWL 2010)* (vol. 6483, pp. 91–100). Berlin, Heidelberg: Springer-Verlag.

Kladich, S., Ives, C., Parker, N. and Graf, S. (2013). Extending the AAT tool with a user-friendly and powerful mechanism to retrieve complex information from educational log data. In A. Holzinger and G. Pasi (eds), *Human–computer interaction and knowledge discovery in complex, unstructured, big data* (pp. 334–341). Berlin, Heidelberg: Springer.

Kosba, E., Dimitrova, V. and Boyle, R. (2005). Using student and group models to support teachers in web-based distance education. In L. Ardissono, P. Brna and A. Mitrovic (eds), *User modeling 2005* (vol. 3538, pp. 124–133). Berlin, Heidelberg: Springer,.

Krčadinac, U., Jovanović, J. and Devedžić, V. (2012). Visualizing the affective structure of students' interaction. In S. S. Cheung, J. Fong, L.-F. Kwok, K. Li and R. Kwan (eds), *Hybrid learning* (vol. 7411, pp. 23–34). Berlin, Heidelberg: Springer.

Kruse, A. and Pongsajapan, R. (2012). Student-centered learning analytics. CNDLS Thought Papers, 1–9.

Leony, D., Pardo, A., Valentin, L. de la Fuente, Castro, D.S. and Kloos, C.D. (2012). GLASS: a learning analytics visualization tool. Paper presented at the Proceedings of the 2nd International Conference on Learning Analytics and Knowledge, Vancouver, BC.

Liccardi, I. (2010). *Improving users' awareness interactions in the collaborative document authoring process: the CAWS approach*. PhD thesis, University of Southampton, UK.

Martinez-Maldonado, R., Clayphan, A., Yacef, K. and Kay, J. (2014). Towards providing notifications to enhance teacher's awareness in the classroom. In *Intelligent tutoring systems*, vol. 8474, pp. 510–515): Berlin, Heidelberg: Springer.

Martinez Maldonado, R., Kay, J., Yacef, K. and Schwendimann, B. (2012). An interactive teacher's dashboard for monitoring groups in a multi-tabletop learning environment. In *Intelligent tutoring systems* (vol. 7315, pp. 482–492). Berlin, Heidelberg: Springer.

Mazza, R. and Dimitrova, V. (2007). CourseVis: a graphical student monitoring tool for supporting instructors in web-based distance courses. *International Journal of Human–Computer Studies* 65(2), 125–139. doi: http://dx.doi.org/10.1016/j.ijhcs.2006.08.008

Pardo, A. and Siemens, G. (2014). Ethical and privacy principles for learning analytics. *British Journal of Educational Technology* 45(3), 438–450. doi: 10.1111/bjet.12152

Podgorelec, V. and Kuhar, S. (2011). Taking advantage of education data: advanced data analysis and reporting in virtual learning environments. *Electronics and Electrical Engineering* 114(8), 111–116.

Pohl, A., Bry, F., Schwarz, J. and Gottstein, M. (2012) Sensing the classroom: improving awareness and self-awareness of students in Backstage. Paper presented at the 15th International Conference on Interactive Collaborative Learning (ICL), 26–28 September.

Romero, C. and Ventura, S. (2010). Educational data mining: a review of the state of the art. *IEEE Transactions on Systems, Man, and Cybernetics, Part C: Applications and Reviews* 40(6), 601–618. doi: 10.1109/tsmcc.2010.2053532

Santos, J.L., Govaerts, S., Verbert, K. and Duval, E. (2012). Goal-oriented visualizations of activity tracking: a case study with engineering students. Paper presented at the Proceedings of the 2nd International Conference on Learning Analytics and Knowledge, Vancouver BC, Canada.

Shneiderman, B. and Ben, S. (2003). *Designing the user interface*. Taramani, Chennai: Pearson Education India.

Slade, S. and Prinsloo, P. (2013). Learning analytics: ethical issues and dilemmas. *American Behavioral Scientist* 57(10), 1510–1529. doi: 10.1177/0002764213479366

Verbert, K., Duval, E., Klerkx, J., Govaerts, S. and Santos, J.L. (2013). Learning analytics dashboard applications. *American Behavioral Scientist* 57(10), 1500–1509. doi: 10.1177/0002764213479363

Verbert, K., Govaerts, S., Duval, E., Santos, J., Assche, F., Parra, G. and Klerkx, J. (2013). Learning dashboards: an overview and future research opportunities. *Personal and Ubiquitous Computing* 1–16. doi: 10.1007/s00779-013-0751-2

Woodill, G. (2010). *The mobile learning edge: tools and technologies for developing your teams*. New York: McGraw Hill Professional.

Zhang, H., Almeroth, K., Knight, A., Bulger, M. and Mayer, R. (2007). Moodog: tracking students' online learning activities. Paper presented at the World Conference on Educational Multimedia, Hypermedia and Telecommunications, Vancouver BC, Canada. www.editlib.org/p/26016

11 Flipped classroom as a form of blended learning

Azizah Al Rowais

Introduction

This period is characterized by the rapid development in scientific and technological fields and the world is witnessing a huge technological revolution in information and communication. Since the function of education is to prepare individuals for life, education must keep pace with the nature and characteristics of the age.

Recent educational trends emphasize the importance of the development of educational systems to suit the requirements, needs and nature of the present as well as the future. As a result, current teaching methods focus on preparing the learner to be well qualified to deal with the modern age and its challenges and improve his or her ability to continue in lifelong learning. Developments in technology, especially the rapid growth in communications technology, have led to the spread of modern educational applications, including e-learning and blended learning.

There is general agreement in the literature that learner achievement grows, in part, out of the individual learner's acceptance of responsibility for his or her own learning. Learners must take at least some of the initiative to give shape and direction to the learning process and must share in monitoring progress and evaluating the extent to which learning targets are achieved. Blended learning supports these ideas through bringing together the best of technology-based online learning and face-to-face instruction, and flipped classroom, as a form of blended learning, demands the students' active engagement in the learning process. Findings of a number of studies support the potential of flipped learning in education and instruction.

The purpose of this chapter is to provide insight about blended learning and the flipped learning model, briefly note their historical foundations and address common misconceptions. It discusses learning theories that underlie the model and describes current, although limited, empirical research findings. It is also important to describe an example of implementation of a flipped classroom that focused on aspects that required more than students watching videos and completing worksheets, so the chapter describes concerns that have been raised and best practices centred around the flipped classroom in the Gulf region. These provide valuable insights about using lecture-capture technologies to flip the classroom.

In the section that follows we consider how blended learning combines the advantages of both e-learning and traditional learning and examine the four models of blended learning that will help you choose the appropriate 'blend' for your students.

Blended learning

With the expansion of e-learning patterns and the increasing demand to employ them in the learning process, some obstacles that may prevent their effectiveness have emerged, including the absence of direct social contact between the educational process elements, which negatively affects the learners' social communication skills. In addition, the application of e-learning patterns needs technological infrastructure and learning management platforms that are high cost and may not be available in many educational institutions. As a result of these obstacles, the need for a new pattern has emerged – a pattern that combines the advantages of e-learning and of traditional learning, and which is called blended learning.

Blended learning is a pattern of learning in which face-to-face classroom methods are combined with computer-mediated activities. It is a model of learning and teaching that uses the best aspects of computer-based learning and the power of face-to-face and small-group instruction to provide students with a challenging and individualized education.

Blended learning assumes the continued use of face-to face teaching as a basic building block of the learning experience, enriched and enhanced by the integration of the internet and other teaching and learning technologies into studies undertaken both in and out of the classroom. This integration should happen with the mediation and support of the teacher and, as with any materials used, should reflect and work toward the learning aims and needs of all learners (Marsh, 2012). It is a kind of effective integration that combines traditional classroom learning styles and methods of e-learning in a single framework, to achieve the desired goals while reducing time and effort.

According to the Clayton Christensen Institute for Disruptive Innovation (2015), a leader in the field of blended learning development, 'the majority of blended-learning programs resemble one of four models: Rotation, Flex, A La Carte, and Enriched Virtual. The Rotation model includes four sub-models: Station Rotation, Lab Rotation, Flipped Classroom, and Individual Rotation.'

Flipped classroom

A flipped (or inverted) classroom is a specific type of blended learning that moves lectures outside the classroom. It is a form of learning in which students learn new content online by watching video lectures, usually at home, and what used to be homework (assigned problems) is now done in class, with teachers offering more personalized guidance and interaction with students instead of lecturing. This is also known as backwards classroom (Barseghian, 2011).

In terms of Bloom's revised taxonomy (2001), this means that students are doing the lower levels of cognitive work (gaining knowledge and comprehension) outside of class, and focusing on the higher forms of cognitive work (application, analysis, synthesis, and/or evaluation) in class, where they have the support of their peers and instructor. This model contrasts from the traditional model, in which 'first exposure' occurs via lecture in class, with students assimilating knowledge through homework. Thus the term 'flipped classroom' (Anderson and Krathwohl, 2001).

To counter common misconceptions and bring clarity to discussions about 'flipped learning', the governing board and key leaders of the Flipped Learning Network (2014) announced a formal definition of the term:

> Flipped Learning is a pedagogical approach in which direct instruction moves from the group learning space to the individual learning space, and the resulting group space is transformed into a dynamic, interactive learning environment where the educator guides students as they apply concepts and engage creatively in the subject matter.

By providing an opportunity for students to use their new factual knowledge while they have access to immediate feedback from peers and the instructor, the flipped classroom helps students learn to correct misconceptions and organize their new knowledge such that it is more accessible for future use. Furthermore, the immediate feedback that occurs in the flipped classroom also helps students recognize and think about their own growing understanding.

Theoretical basis

The flipped classroom approach is rooted in socio-constructivist theories of education and active learning, but also includes and values educational media for delivery. Vygotsky (1978) posited the theory of the Zone of Proximal Development (ZPD), which is a theory of how students' learning is dependent on their prior knowledge in the area and how they fit new knowledge into their already existing mental schema. The theory of ZPD includes the assertion that students can reach some understanding of a topic area on their own through independent learning, but they need the assistance of a capable educator to reach their full potential specifically through educator and peer modelling, scaffolding and specific feedback.

The theory of ZPD informs the flipped class because instructional media can be assigned to introduce new knowledge, but without the guidance and feedback from a qualified educator, a student may not be able to make sense of the deeper meaning of the content. Collaborative learning and peer instruction during class time adds new knowledge and understanding to their prior knowledge in a topic area.

How People Learn, the seminal work from John Bransford, Ann Brown and Rodney Cocking, reports three key findings about the science of learning, two of which help explain the success of the flipped classroom. Bransford and colleagues (2000, p.16) assert that

> To develop competence in an area of inquiry, students must: a) have a deep foundation of factual knowledge, b) understand facts and ideas in the context of a conceptual framework, and c) organize knowledge in ways that facilitate retrieval and application.

The flipped classroom helps students learn to correct misconceptions and organize their new knowledge by providing an opportunity for them to *use* their new factual knowledge while they have access to immediate feedback from peers and the instructor.

The idea of a 'flipped classroom' is most often attributed to two high school science teachers, Jonathan Bergmann and Aaron Sams, who used online videos to provide instruction to their students so as to free up more time for lab work, and to Salman Khan, whose Khan Academy videos teaching people maths techniques were so popular that teachers began assigning them to students to watch outside of school time. In a recent interview, Jon Bergmann and Aaron Sams explained that a flipped classroom shifts the emphasis of teaching from the instructor to the learner (Noonoo, 2012).

Flipped learning has attracted research and practice-based attention for its potential to incorporate digital technologies in a new pedagogical method that is better aligned with current collaborative constructivist educational practice, also known as 'the flipped approach' or 'the inverted classroom'.

The essence of the flipped method is that content is delivered before class time and lectures themselves become forums for discussion, integration and application of that content. The pre-delivered content may take several formats, most typically a series of short videos recorded using simple video-capture software and uploaded to the internet. These videos may be supplemented by Web 2.0 resources or platforms such as wikis, blogs, discussion forums, social media sharing and social networking sites, which support active and social learning by acting as venues for collaborating, constructing and sharing information in support of active and social learning (Garrison and Akyol, 2009). In class time, the lecturer acts as facilitator, guiding students in discussion either individually or in groups.

Four pillars of flipped learning

The governing board and key leaders of the Flipped Learning Network (FLN) distinguish between a flipped classroom and flipped learning. Flipping a class can, but does not necessarily, lead to flipped learning.

To engage in flipped learning, teachers must incorporate the following four pillars into their practice (FLN, 2014). Figure 11.1 briefly describes the four pillars of flipping learning.

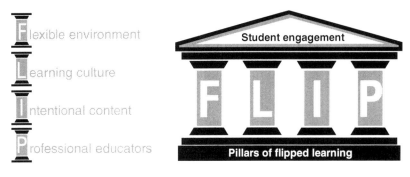

Figure 11.1 The four pillars of flipping learning (adapted from FLN, 2014).

First pillar

Flipped learning requires flexible environments. Flipped learning takes place everywhere, not only in the classroom. Learners are provided with a wide range of learning options to choose when and where they learn. Flipped learning offers students choices about their schedules, activities, performance and evaluation.

Second pillar

Flipped learning requires a shift in learning culture from the traditional teacher-centred model to a student-centred approach. Students move to the centre of learning, where they are actively involved in knowledge formation through opportunities to participate in and evaluate their learning.

Third pillar

Flipped learning requires intentional content. Educators use intentional content and evaluate what content they need to teach directly face to face and what materials students should be allowed to explore first outside classrooms. As a result, educators can have the chance to maximize classroom time in order to adopt various methods of instruction.

Fourth pillar

Flipped learning requires professional educators who should be knowledgeable about practising different roles as a teacher on learning process. Educators should be skilled in developing and applying knowledge of curriculum, instruction, principles of learning and evaluation needed to implement and monitor effective and evolving programmes for all learners.

Technology and social media

Technology and social media work hand in hand in the flipped classroom. To compile learning materials, teachers create video using various technologies that is then uploaded to social media sites like YouTube. The use of video to deliver content has become increasingly attractive for educators in Math, Science and Engineering courses. Franciszkowics (2008) argues that visual media is critical in courses where there are multiple steps that go into problem solving. Videos can be used to provide scaffolding for students through problems by modelling expert problem-solving strategies.

In addition to the videos, technology and social media have given teachers greater opportunities to meet the needs of their learners.

Personalization

In the flipped classroom students have increased flexibility to pace the sequencing and delivery of their lessons. Students can pause, rewind, replay and even fast forward the video lessons provided for the course. Technology also gives students flexibility in the way they access their learning. Students can view screencasts across virtually any personal electronic device in an asynchronous environment (Yee and Hargis, 2009).

Communication

Flipped classroom where technology is leveraged can increase the amount of time to do meaningful classroom activities and allow for a greater focus on communication. Additionally, the flipped classroom can provide increased opportunities for interactive discussions and activities between students as well as between students and teachers. These enhanced opportunities for communication are important in instruction as evidenced in the researches that consider communication between students and faculty in and out of the classroom to be critical in ensuring strong student motivation and involvement (Dunlap and Lowenthal, 2009).

Flipped learning in higher education

In higher education, teaching faculty have a history of moving course content to outside the class. Think of the science class where students read about the theory and then use lab time to practice the techniques, or the English course in which the professor gave instant feedback on writing exercises during class time. It is not surprising to see that a growing number of teaching faculty are leveraging new technologies and embracing the flipped model.

A growing number of higher education individual faculty have begun using the flipped model in their courses. At Algonquin College, a video production class has been using this model to explain the workings of editing software, a procedure that is notoriously difficult to explain in a standard lecture. Short tutorial video lectures let students move at their own pace, rewind to review portions and skip through sections they already understand, meaning students come to class able to use the software and prepared to do creative projects with their peers. A particularly successful example of a blended and flipped class in accounting at Penn State accommodates 1,300 students. In-class time is used for open discussion, a featured guest speaker or hands-on problem solving, where instructor support is supplemented by student assistants. At Harvard University, one physics professor not only employs the flipped model, but has also developed a correlative site, Learning Catalytics, which provides instructors with free interactive software enabling students to discuss, apply and get feedback from what they hear in lecture (EDUCAUSE, 2012).

Flipped learning is particularly well suited to higher education for a variety of reasons.

- The model can be especially useful in large lecture courses where student engagement and interaction is usually minimal.
- It improves students' critical thinking, creative problem solving, higher-order thinking and twenty-first-century professional skills.
- It improves faculty-to-student interaction and compensates for limited classroom space.
- It makes students the centre of learning and encourages student ownership of learning.

The benefits of this inverted model are many. Students pace and direct their own learning, exploring pre-delivered materials in their own time, repeatedly if they wish. The approach demands their active engagement in the learning process. The lecture room becomes an interactive space where students collaboratively construct their own knowledge in ways that are meaningful to them, receiving personalized guidance and becoming a part of a community of enquiry (Garrison and Vaughan, 2008).

Studies have indicated support for the appropriate use of flipped learning strategies. The goal of such studies is to allow students to choose the learning methodology that best fits them as individuals, so students can receive multiple methods of learning major concepts outside the classroom. Students could read a textbook, view a PowerPoint presentation or watch a video lecture online (Lage and Platt, 2000; Marcey and Brint, 2011; Chips, 2012).

Some studies also have indicated that open-ended problem-solving experiences can be learning-style conducted within the classroom environment to allow for more engaged pedagogies (Kellogg, 2009).

Findings of a number of studies support the potential of flipped learning in education and instruction (Papadapoulos and Roman, 2010; Baker, 2012; Johnson and Renner, 2012).

Flipped Learning Experiments in the Gulf Region

Recently, we started to hear about flipped learning in some of Arabic educational articles. Some described it as the future of education, combining face-to-face instruction with computer-mediated activities and instructional technology.

To my knowledge, few studies have been conducted about flipped learning in the Arab Gulf countries. However, I noticed that many new graduate students currently tend to conduct comprehensive studies about the flipped learning.

Al Thuwaikh (2012) conducted her experiment of flipped classrooms to investigate the effect of the independent variable (flipped classroom) on the dependent variable (self-learning skills) of female students on a computer course in a secondary school at Jubail Industrial City in the Eastern Region of Saudi Arabia during the first semester of the academic year 2012–2013. The researcher employed the quasi-experimental method with 26 secondary school students who were learning new computer skills lessons at home through the application of the concept of flipped classroom. Afterwards, the students discussed these lessons at Edmodo. Then they performed electronic tests, and the next day reviewed what had been learned at home and practiced a variety of activities. The application of a questionnaire before and after the experiment showed the increase in self-learning skills of these experimental group students.

Al Fheed (2012) conducted a study that aimed to find out the impact of flipped classroom strategy within the usage of podcasting through mobile devices on the achievement levels of female Saudi students who were studying an English grammar course in the preparatory programmes at Imam Mohammad bin Saud University at Riyadh. The study also examined the relationship between students' achievement and attitude toward classroom environment. The study sample consisted of 42 students who were equally divided into a controlled and experimental group, and it utilized the following research tools:

- a translated version of the College and Universities Classroom Environment Inventory (CUCEI);
- an English grammar achievement test.

The results of the study showed the effectiveness of flipped classroom strategy in developing students' attitudes toward their classroom environment and enhancing their achievement on the English grammar course. Furthermore, the study suggested adopting flipped classroom strategy in Saudi universities, since it allows students to be more active learners and benefits from podcast technology as more flexible for individualized learning.

Amiri et al. (2013) conducted a study to distinguish between the learning preferences of the students in UAE classrooms by comparing study in traditional and flip classrooms. The findings of the study showed the students' preferences for effective utilization of technology in providing a better learning environment, i.e. by implementing the concept of the flipped class.

Shams (2013) applied smart digital flipped classroom techniques in teaching in different chemistry laboratories, on Blackboard and in different chemistry tutorial classes at Qatar University. Through building an educational website with the theme of chemistry flipped for teaching, the students showed an extraordinary passion to the subject. The findings showed that the technique of smart digital flipped classroom was more dynamic and motivational than traditional.

Syam (2014) discussed the possibility of using the flipped classroom method in mathematics classes in the foundation programme at Qatar University. This study found that applying this method to a pilot group of students in mathematics classes was more difficult than for Art, Education or Sharia classes, but with some restrictions and conditions on the method of designing the model was possible. It was also found that results of the pilot group in a quiz for which this method used is better than their results in quizzes where it was not.

Lane-Kelso (2015) discussed the pedagogy of flipped instruction and the experiences of the flipping method with graduate students from Sultan Qaboos University in Oman. The researcher aimed to understand the potential impact of flipped instruction with Omani educators as well as examining what this may mean to the wider educational community. Flipped instruction appears to the researcher an appropriate bridge to integrate new technologies into a traditional educational system, and the participants seemed motivated to adapt the flipped instruction to their own learning and that of their colleagues, given their own struggles to design flipped lessons, their expressed concerns with the wider Omani community. It may require extending the experiences of flipped instruction to undergraduate teacher preparation courses to expose larger numbers of Omani educators to flipping earlier in their university education.

Al-Zahrani (2015) conducted a study to investigate the impact of flipped classroom on students' academic achievement based on the sixth level of Bloom's Taxonomy. The study context was higher education students in the Faculty of Education at King Abdul Aziz University in Saudi Arabia. The study implemented a quasi-experimental design, and the results indicated that the flipped classroom had significant impact the students' high-order thinking skills – applying, analysing, evaluating and creating.

In the light of previous studies about flipped learning in the Gulf, it seemed that the dramatic increase in use of technology in higher education and all the available services led teachers to apply some new methods of teaching, like the flipping classroom method. Evidence suggests that students generally preferred the inverted classroom to a traditional lecture in the Gulf countries. The results of the research should be very beneficial for universities and colleges in considering the use of latest technologies in providing students with a blended learning experience. On basis of the findings of the research, academics could consider different options for using technology to provide a better learning environment for their students.

Case study of flipped learning in a Saudi university

There is a continuous need for improvement and innovation of teaching methods and learning types. The current study is linked to the developmental dimension especially embodied in teaching methods and related to the students' requirements and abilities, the requirements for innovation and going beyond the borders of traditional methods, concerning the methods relevant to all implications of psychological and mental characteristics which should be observed.

In the light of the above, I felt the need for the application of this study as a response to the calls of education scholars for the employment of various educational methods and techniques, concerning the characteristics of age stage and students' requirements to develop self-autonomy. This study – according to my best knowledge – is highly probably one of the pioneering studies in Saudi Arabia aiming at application of flipped learning and examining its effectiveness on Saudi students' achievement and attitude towards learning on university courses. The problem of the study was identified in the following main question: What is the effectiveness of flipped learning on higher education students' achievement and attitudes towards studying courses?

To answer the study question, the following hypotheses were tested:

1 There are no statistically significant differences at (0.05 level) between the mean scores of the experimental group and the control group in the post application of the achievement tests of university courses.
2 There are no statistically significant differences at (0.05 level) between the pre-and post-measurement of the experimental group attitudes towards studying university courses.

Study method

In order to test the hypotheses, the present study employed the descriptive method to determine the principles of flipped learning to prepare the flipped classroom courses, and the quasi-experimental method to measure the effectiveness of the independent variable (flipped learning) and its impact on the dependent variables (achievement and attitude). Sixty-four students in two classes who represent the sixth level of the college of education were selected randomly at Prince Sattam bin Abdul-Aziz University in Saudi Arabia.

The study was conducted during the second term of the year 2013–2014. The two classes were randomly assigned as the experimental and control groups of the study. The variables assumed relevant to the present study were controlled as follows: all the students were females of the same age (20–21 years old); both groups were taught by me as the researcher of the current study; students in the two groups were at the same level of proficiency as measured by the pre-tests. The study instruments included the achievement tests of the courses that were pre-/post-administered to measure the students' achievement of the experimental and control groups, and the scale of students' attitudes towards learning and studying courses, which was pre-post-administered to the students of the experimental group.

The achievement tests were designed by the researcher and each of them included 50 multiple-choice items to measure the students' achievement. Each question had one correct answer and three 'distracters'. The tests were based on the table of specification organized for three chapters of the courses. The scale of students' attitudes towards learning and studying courses was designed by the researcher and included 30 items.

To determine the validity of the instruments, they were submitted to ten specialists in methodology and psychology. In light of the experts' comments and recommendations, the necessary modifications were made. The researcher tried out the instruments by administering them on a sample of 10 university students (other than the sample participants). This piloting aimed to determine the instruments' reliability and timing for application. The reliability coefficients of the tests were 0.80–0.85, which proved to be statistically reliable. The reliability coefficient of the attitude scale was 0.90, which proved to be statistically reliable.

Study procedures

The study procedures included the pre-administration of the study instruments, the treatment and the post-administration of the instruments.

The pre-administration of the instruments

The researcher pre-administered the two achievement tests to measure the sixth-level students' achievement in the experimental and control groups and identify their level in the two courses, Teaching Methods and Communication Skills, before the experiment. Also, she administered the scale of students' attitudes towards learning and studying courses, which was pre-administered to the students of the experimental group before the introduction of the treatment. The pre-administration of the instruments was conducted at the beginning of January 2014. It was administered to 64 students before they were exposed to the treatment. Table 11.1 shows the results of the independent samples t-test for the differences between two groups on the pre-administration of achievement test of the Teaching Methods course.

Table 11.2 shows the results of the independent samples t-test for the differences between two groups on the pre-administration of achievement test for the Communication Skills course.

Table 11.1 Independent samples t-test

Group	No.	Mean	T-value	p-value
Control	32	10.15	−1.62	0.11
Experimental	32	11.13		

Table 11.2 Independent samples t-test

Group	No.	Mean	T- value	p-value
Control	32	15.92	−1.36	0.17
Experimental	32	18.00		

The treatment

The treatment, to investigate the effectiveness of flipped learning on the students' achievement and attitudes towards learning courses at Sattam bin Abdul-Aziz University, lasted 12 weeks. The researcher chose the content from the two courses – Teaching Methods and Communication Skills – and lessons plans were developed for the courses based on the applications of flipped learning model. The materials the researcher used in the treatment were textbooks, online video lectures, PowerPoint presentations and course management systems. The researcher was involved in teaching the two groups: the experimental group (taught through the flipped classroom applications) and the control group (taught through the traditional method). The subjects of the experimental group were taught by the researcher through the applications of the flipped classroom. Students received instruction at home from videos and PowerPoint presentations on the website, and in class worked in small learning communities to problem-solve.

The following steps were used for the experimental group through the treatment.

- **Before the class**, the instructor prepared learning opportunities through creating videos and PowerPoint presentations and using course management systems. Students gained necessary knowledge before class through reading textbooks, and watching the video lectures and PowerPoint presentations online at home. Students were guided through a learning module that asks and collects questions.
- **At the beginning of class**, students had specific questions in mind to guide their learning, and the instructor could anticipate where students need the most help.
- **During class**, students practised performing the skills they were expected to learn. The instructor guided the process with feedback and mini-lectures. During class, students were broken into small groups and engaged in active learning assignments such as problem solving, presentations and discussions.
- **After class**, students continued applying their knowledge skills after clarification and feedback. The instructor posted any additional explanations and resources as necessary and graded higher-quality work. Students were equipped to seek help where they knew they needed it.

The post-administration of the instruments

After implementing the treatment, its effectiveness was evaluated by post-administration of the instruments. The content of the pre-administration and the post-administration was the same. The achievement tests of the courses were post-administered to measure the students' achievement of the experimental and control groups, and the scale of students' attitudes towards learning courses was post-administered to the students of the experimental group. The statistical procedures were applied on the data obtained using the means and t-tests. Table 11.3 shows the results of the independent samples t-test for the differences between two groups on the post-administration of achievement test of the course Teaching Methods:

The results of the independent samples t-test for the differences between two groups on the post-administration of achievement test of the course Teaching Methods revealed that there were significant differences at 0.05 level between the students mean scores on the post-application of the test and these differences, were in favour of the experimental group. So the research hypothesis was rejected, because there was a marked improvement in the experimental group performance on the post-administration of the test. This improvement indicated the effectiveness of the flipped learning in improving the students' achievement in the course.

Table 11.4 shows the results of the independent samples t-test for the differences between two groups on the post-administration of achievement test of the course Communication Skills.

The results of the independent samples t-test for the differences between two groups on the post-administration of achievement test of the course Communication Skills revealed that there were significant differences at 0.05 level between the students mean scores on the post-application of the test and these differences were in favour of the experimental group. So the research hypothesis was rejected because there was a marked improvement in the experimental group performance on the post-administration of the test. This improvement indicated the effectiveness of the flipped learning in improving the students' achievement in the course.

Table 11.5 shows the results of the paired samples t- test for the differences between the pre–post administrations of scale of students' attitudes towards learning on the two courses.

Table 11.3 Independent samples t-test

Group	No.	Mean	T- value	p-value
Control	32	10.65	−10.36	0.00
Experimental	32	18.68		

Table 11.4 Independent samples t-test

Group	No.	Mean	T- value	p-value
Control	32	23.37	− 5.00	0.01
Experimental	32	35.63		

Table 11.5 Paired samples t-test for the differences between the pre–post administrations of the scale of students' attitudes

post administration	No.	Mean	T- value	p-value
Pre-admin.	32	2.58	−13.18	0.00
Post-admin.	32	3.84		

The results of the paired samples t-test for the differences between the pre-post administrations of the scale of students' attitudes towards learning the two courses revealed that there were significant differences at 0.05 level between the students mean scores on the pre–post administrations of scale of students' attitudes and these differences were in favour of the post administration. So the research hypothesis was rejected because there was a marked improvement in the experimental group performance on the post-administration of the attitude scale. This improvement indicated the effectiveness of the flipped learning in improving the students' attitudes towards learning.

Conclusions and recommendations

In the light of the findings of this study, the main conclusions were:

1   There were statistically significant differences at (0.05 level) between the mean scores of the experimental group (taught through the flipped learning strategies) and the control group (taught through the usual method) in the post-application of the achievement tests, in favour of the experimental group.
2   There were statistically significant differences at (0.05 level) between the pre- and post-measurement of the experimental group's attitudes towards learning the university courses, in favour of post-measurement.
3   The results of the present study are in line with other researchers, (such as Lage and Platt, 2000; Marcey and Brint, 2011; Chips, 2012; Baker, 2012; Johnson and Renner, 2012).
4   The advantages of flipped learning affected the attitudes of students towards learning. It promotes peer interaction and collaboration skills, encourages higher student engagement, and makes learning central, rather than teaching. This result is in line with Garrison and Vaughan (2008).

Based on the results of the study, it was recommended that:

1   The faculty members be advised to adopt applications of flipped learning and the use of e-learning tools and educational software in teaching because of its effectiveness in the development of the knowledge and skills of students, and of their attitudes.
2   More attention should be paid to the preparation of workshops and training courses for the training of faculty members at universities on the use of

flipped learning strategies and employing e-learning tools and making use of these in the design of courses.
3 There was a need to provide to universities the necessary capabilities and material support required for teaching through management systems and using e-courses, and provision of the necessary equipment to activate technology's role in improving the level of student performance.
4 Course designers were advised to include the four pillars of flipped learning in their practices in order to cater for different types of learning styles and to shift the focus from teacher to learner in instruction.

Conclusion

As illustrated throughout this chapter, more qualitative and quantitative research needs to be done to identify how the potential of the flipped learning model can be maximized. But the existing research clearly demonstrates that the model can be one way in which to create popular instructional strategy as a consequence of the widely accepted trend to shift the focus from teacher to learner in instruction, and as a type of blended learning that combines face-to-face instruction with computer-mediated activities. Flipped classroom where technology is leveraged can increase the amount of time for meaningful classroom activities and allow for a greater focus on communication. Additionally, the flipped classroom can provide increased opportunities for interactive discussions and activities between students and student and teacher.

In the Arab Gulf countries, many researchers currently tend to conduct comprehensive studies about the flipped learning. At the same time, more attention should be paid to the preparation of workshops and training courses for the training of faculty members at universities and teachers on the use of flipped learning strategies and employing e-learning tools, and making use of them in the design of courses. Also, there is a need to provide the necessary capabilities and material support required for teaching through Learning Management Systems and e-courses to universities and schools, and to provide the necessary equipment to activate technology's role in improving the level of students' performance.

References

Al-Fheed, M. (2012). 'The effectiveness of flipped classroom strategy with mobile devices on students' attitude toward classroom environment and achievement in English language grammar course of preparatory programs in Imam Muhammad bin Saud University.' Unpublished Master's thesis, Riyadh, Imam Muhammad bin Saud University, Saudi Arabia.
Al-Thuwaikh, N. (2012). 'The impact of the application of flipped classroom on the growth of self-learning skills of the third level students in computer course.' Published article in *AlMarefh* 2014: www.almarefh.net/show_content_sub.php?C UV=428&Model=M&SubModel=216&ID=2295&ShowAll=On
Al-Zahrani, A. (2015). The impact of flipped classroom on cognitive achievement in e-learning course among students from the Faculty of Education at King

Abdul-Aziz University [Arabic]. *The Journal of the Faculty of Education at the University of Al-Azhar* 162(1).

Amiri, A., Ahrari, H., Saffar, Z. and Akre, V. (2013). The effects of classroom flip on the student learning experience: an investigative study in UAE classrooms. *Current Trends in Information Technology* 71–76.

Anderson, L.W. and Krathwohl, D. (eds) (2001). *A taxonomy for learning, teaching and assessing: a revision of Bloom's taxonomy of educational objectives.* Longman: New York.

Baker, C. (2012). Flipped classrooms: turning learning upside down – trend of 'flipping classrooms' helps teachers to personalize education. *Deseret News.* Retrieved from http://www.deseretnews.com/article/765616415/Flipped-classrooms-Turning-learning-upside-down.html?pg=all

Barseghian, T. (2011). Three trends that define the future of teaching and learning. Retrieved from http://ww2.kqed.org/mindshift/2011/02/04/three-trends-that-will-shape-the-future-of-curriculum/

Bransford J., Brown A. and Cocking R. (2000). *How people learn: brain, mind, experience, and school.* Washington DC: National Academy Press.

Chips, J. (2012). The effectiveness of using online instructional videos with group problem-solving to flip the calculus classroom. California State University, Northridge CA, USA.

Christensen Institute (2015). 'Blended Learning model definitions.' Accessed 12 May 2015. www.christenseninstitute.org/blended-learning-definitions-and-models/

Dunlap, J. and Lowenthal, P. (2009). Tweeting the night away: using twitter to enhance social presence. *Journal of Information Systems Education* 20(2), 129–135.

Educause (2012). Things you should know about flipped classrooms. http://creativecommons.org/licenses/by-ncnd/3.0/ Educause.edu/eli

Flipped Learning Network (2014). What is flipped learning? Retrieved from http://fln.schoolwires.net/cms/ lib07/VA01923112/Centricity/Domain/46/FLIP_handout_FNL_Web.pdf

Franciszkowicz, M. (2008). Video-based additional instruction. *Journal of the Research Center for Educational Technology* 4(2) 5–14.

Garrison, D. and Akyol, Z. (2009). Role of instructional technology in the transformation of higher education. *Journal of Computing in Higher Education* 21, 19–30. doi: 10.1007/s12528-009-9014-7

Garrison, D. and Vaughan, H. (2008). *Blended learning in higher education: framework, principles and guidelines.* San Francisco: Jossey-Bass

Johnson, L. and Renner, J. (2012). Effect of the flipped classroom model on secondary computer applications course: student and teacher perceptions, questions and student achievement. Doctoral dissertation, University of Louisville, KY, USA.

Kellogg, S. (2009). Developing online materials to facilitate an inverted classroom approach (pp. 1–6). IEEE. doi:10.1109/FIE.2009.5350621

Lage, M. and Platt, G. (2000). The internet and the inverted classroom. *The Journal of Economic Education* 31(1), 11–11.doi:10. 1080/002204800009 56756

Lane-Kelso, M. (2015). The pedagogy of flipped instruction in Oman. *Turkish Online Journal of Educational Technology* 14(1), 143–150.

Marcey, D. and Brint, M. (2011). Transforming an undergraduate introductory biology course through cinematic lectures and inverted classes: an assessment of the CLIC model of the flipped classroom. California Lutheran University, Thousand Oaks CA, USA.

Marsh, D. (2012). *Blended learning: creating learning opportunities for language learners.* New York: Cambridge University Press.

Noonoo, S. (2012). Flipped learning founders set the record straight. Retrieved from http://thejournal.com/articles/2012/06/20/flipped-learning-founders-q-and a.aspx#TTs2AhWil2zYaZjZ.99

Papadapoulos, C. and Roman, A. (2010). Implementing an inverted classroom model in engineering statistics: initial results. *American Society for Engineering Statistics.* Proceedings of the 40th ASEE/IEEE Frontiers in Education Conference, Washington DC, October. Retrieved from: http://jchipps.com/docs/thesis.pdf

Shams, E. (2013). My method in teaching chemistry and its application using modern technology. Qatar Foundation Annual Research Conference, 2013. doi: 10.5335/qfarf.2013.ICTP-042.

Syam, M. (2014). Possibility of applying flipped classroom method in mathematics classes in Foundation program at Qatar University. SOCIOINT14 – International Conference on Social Sciences and Humanities, 180–187.

Vygotsky, L. (1978). *Mind in society.* Cambridge MA: Harvard University Press.

Yee, K. and Hargis, J. (2009). iPhones and smart phones. *Turkish Online Journal Of Distance Education* 10(4), 9–11.

12 Managing the change during e-learning integration in higher education
A case study from Saudi Arabia[1]

Khalid Alshahrani and Len Cairns

Introduction

Information and Communication Technologies (ICTs) that are already familiar components in business environments are finding their way into education at all levels in many parts of the world. Such technologies, however, disrupt education (Christensen, Horn and Johnson, 2008; Bonk, Lee, Kim and Lin, 2010) as they require changes in the teaching approaches and structure of institutions (McPherson and Nunes, 2008). People, on the other hand, can resist change because it challenges them and drives them out of their comfort zone (Latchem and Jung, 2010). Therefore, managing the change during the transition phase is crucial (Kotter, 1996) and a challenging task for any leader (Tibi and McLeod, 2010). Universities experience such challenges during the transition from a traditional way of teaching to more e-learning-based teaching and learning, and this chapter has taken one Saudi Arabian university as a case study.

Despite the importance of e-learning leadership, it is not an issue that features a great deal in the literature of e-learning (Jameson, 2011; Satyanarayana and Meduri, 2007). However, the impact and necessary elements of any change facilitation in an organization depend, to a large extent, on leadership support and management. This chapter examines the role of leadership in the change process surrounding the implementation of e-learning at one Saudi Arabian university as a change from previous practices forms the site and context.

Recent developments of e-learning in Saudi Arabia

The higher education sector in Saudi Arabia has undergone tremendous development in the last 10 years. The number of universities has jumped from 8 in 2005 to 24 public and 10 private in 2012, including the Saudi e-University (SEU). Established in 2011, SEU is government funded and approved by the Saudi Ministry of Higher Education to provide graduate and undergraduate degree programmes along with lifelong education based on e-learning and distance-education technologies (SEU, 2013). SEU came about as the result of the development of e-learning initiatives in Saudi higher education, which included the establishment of the National Centre for eLearning and Distance

Learning (NCeL) and e-learning Deanships in almost all Saudi universities. This development was parallel with the rolling out of traditional distance-learning programmes, which had been operating in a number of local universities for the last decade. The National Commission for Academic Accreditation and Assessment (NCAAA) established Quality Standards for Distance Education Courses (NCAA, 2012) as a guide for universities in this relatively new endeavour. The concept of establishing an organizational unit (the e-learning Deanship) with a Dean as leader emerged as a particular Saudi government approach within this set of e-learning developments.

E-learning management and leadership in the transition phase

Leadership is critical in managing successful institutions in any domain. E-learning in higher education is no exception. Mapuva (2009) stated that 'institutional leaders are a determinant factor, given their decision-making which could either make-or-break the e-learning projects by either facilitating or impeding its implementation within their institutions' (p. 103). He continued that the direction and thrust of institutions towards learning programmes were mainly determined by the leadership of that institution, which largely determines the extent to which e-learning is implemented in learning and teaching. Implementation is mainly based upon the leadership's commitment to, and realization of, e-learning goals in their institutions.

Another main task that institutional leaders need to deal with is management of change (McPherson and Nunes, 2006; Tibi and Mcleod, 2010). Managing resistance effectively throughout the change phase has been reported in the literature as the cornerstone for any change to be successful (Kotter, 1996; Bridges, 2010). Such resistance is inevitable in the transition phase when traditional universities move toward more online/virtual learning, which requires a fundamental change in the structure of the institution as well as teaching approaches (O'Neill, Singh and O'Donoghue, 2004; McPherson and Nunes, 2006). There is a need for a leadership that deals with any resistance that may accompany such change in a cautious and assuring manner, given the growing number of universities that are migrating to increasingly digitalized learning environments. As universities endeavour to make this move, academics and e-learning leaders need to take into account the difficulties associated with these fundamental changes to the structure of their institutions and the changing landscape of higher education at large (O'Neill et al., 2004; Tibi and Mcleod, 2010). This process of change is particularly difficult and requires strong and supportive leadership as well as changes to the organizational culture (McPherson and Nunes, 2006). It involves changing faculty's attitudes, values and conceptions of teaching (O'Neill et al., 2004; Tibi and Mcleod, 2010). This may be best achieved when all stakeholders of institutions are involved in the process of change over considerable time (McPherson and Nunes, 2006). Other factors that contribute to leading successful change include clear and frequent communication and professional development opportunities. This is likely to lead to a better management of resistance as well as forming the basis of further successful change (Tibi and McLeod, 2010).

Leadership styles might be different in Middle Eastern, Asian and Western countries. Latchem and Jung (2010) believed that leadership in open and distance learning (ODL) in Asia sometimes comes from governments. This is probably true, as most universities in Asia and the Middle East are still dependent upon government support and therefore are excessively influenced and regulated by government policies (Latchem and Jung, 2010). Such government-driven initiatives can be both supportive and controlling or even frustrating for innovation, depending on the issues and areas of concern. E-learning has, in many nations, been an area where the scope and need for infrastructure developments on large scales has necessarily involved significant government intervention and drive. Dhanarajan (2002) supports this claim and attributed most of the advancement of ODL in India to the commitment and farsighted policies of the Indian government. E-learning in Saudi public universities has been supported and regulated through the Ministry of Higher Education (MoHE) and its affiliated NCeL. However, despite the importance of top-level support for e-learning developments, this alone is not sufficient to make all the necessary changes within organizations charged with the development and implementation of the desired outcomes and programmes (Cook, Holley and Andrew, 2007). Collegial support and learning communities are significant factors in encouraging faculty to reflect on their practices and possibly adopt new technologies (Palloff and Pratt, 1999). In all cases, there is a need for e-learning leadership that maintains a balanced approach, one that is not highly centralized and provides diverse and flexible professional development opportunities for all faculty members who are expected to adopt e-learning approaches in their university teaching.

Methodology

This chapter draws on a PhD study that was conducted between 2009 and 2013 in an Australian university. The data presented in this chapter were collected from a Saudi Arabian university, which will be referred to as SAU. Data were elicited mainly from interviews with four e-learning staff members and four faculty members. The faculty-member participants came from different faculties, including science, languages, education and medicine. The e-learning staff participants included the e-learning Dean, the e-learning manager and two e-learning specialists, who were all involved in the e-learning Deanship entity. Interviews were conducted individually in a face-to-face setting on the SAU campus and lasted for approximately 30 minutes each. Data were transcribed and imported into Nvivo®, software developed in Australia for analysing qualitative research. The study adopted a multisteps analysis process using two approaches. That is, 1. it adopted Miles and Huberman's (1994) principles of analysing qualitative data, and 2. it used the Activity Theory (AT) model (Engestrom, 1987) to identify the unit of analysis of the study, which acted as a lens through which the Activity system was discussed and interpreted.

E-learning evolution at SAU

One of the main goals of the e-learning Deanship at SAU according to its Strategic Plan for E-learning is to 'establish e-learning for everyone'. Among the steps outlined in the plan to achieve this goal is to 'furnish continuous support, training, incentives, rewards, and encouragement for faculty in the valuable integration of technology into the teaching and learning activities'. However, the focus of the Deanship during its earlier stages (between 2006 and 2008) was on the technical aspects of e-learning. 'In the first phase we were asking questions like what LMS should be used and similar technical questions about the hardware and soft- ware' (e-learning Dean). SAU faculty might require the technical training at the early stages of e-learning implementation, which can be seen as a prerequisite for pedagogical-driven different and new teaching practices. Lareki, de Morentin and Amenabar (2010) asserted that e-learning training for university teachers need to be adjusted to respond to teachers' needs at their different stages of development.

The e-learning Deanship at SAU appeared to have recognized faculty's needs beyond the early technical aspects. Therefore, as the basic e-learning infrastructure developed, the Deanship started to provide, during later stages, training that included some pedagogically specific instruction including an on-campus 'full week course in this notion of learner-centred learning ... provided by an academic from another local university last year' (Teacher-4). It also provided SAU faculty, via first-hand experience, a chance to be online learners, as explained by Teacher-2:

> I am enrolled in a distance online-learning course in the USA paid for by [SAU] along with another 50 teachers from the university, and I'm very glad for that. This course is about the effective use of e-learning and maintaining the quality for teaching online. I think there are plenty of training chances at [SAU], but I think it should be made compulsory. You know, it is still voluntary; not everyone will come.
>
> (Teacher-2)

The e-learning staff showed a reasonable pedagogical awareness of the importance of not focusing on the technology per se but rather encouraging faculty to use e-learning as the means for different, yet effective, teaching. 'I think the technology itself is not the main issue in using e-learning in teaching; it is what you do with it is the most important issue' (e-learning Dean). The e-learning manager explained the Deanship's view about e-learning:

> We [e-learning staff] tried to make technology and education meet at the right level and that was also mentioned clearly at least to the e-learning staff that technology should be in the background. This means we do not use technology for its own sake, this is an educational project. Technology is not our first concern; it should be used just as a tool.
>
> (e-learning Manager)

It can be said that the role of the Deanship has evolved from focusing on the technicality of e-learning to a more pedagogical-informed approach. The SAU appeared to have invested in developing teachers' and students' skills through extensive support and training. Teachers' experience of being online learners themselves can also change their conceptions of teaching (Al Mahmood and McLoughlin, 2004). Such studentship experience allows teachers to be reflective on their own beliefs and practices. Recently, Kukulska-Hulme emphasized that teachers need space and opportunities where they can be involved in concrete experiences that generate 'personal conviction' about any particular technology they use (Kukulska-Hulme, 2012, p. 247). In this manner, the opportunity provided by SAU to teachers to experience being online learners in the American university, as mentioned by Teacher-2, can be a concrete experience that might lead to personal conviction.

E-learning Deanship activity system

The Activity Theory (AT) model (Engestrom, 1987), which is also referred to as Activity System, has six aspects: subject, object, tools, community, rules and division of labour. The model was adopted to depict the activity structure of e-learning Deanship at SAU in order to examine the dynamics within and between the elements of the activity system (see Figure 12.1). It is not the individual aspects of the model that constitute the subject of analysis; it is the relations between them and the contradictions within and between activity systems as a whole (Engestrom, 1987). Contradictions is a term used in AT to describe misfits within elements of one activity and between different activities (e.g., technology) and rules or change and local culture. However, AT does not see such contradictions as problems, but rather as potential development spots in the activity (Engestrom, 2001). Therefore, the aim of the analysis is to find contradictions within the e-learning Deanship activity system and whether or not they have been dealt with.

Emerging challenges

Taking the e-learning Deanship as the unit of analysis, the activity system model revealed three contradictions among the different aspects of the activity. The first contradiction was between some of the activity tools (e.g. internet connection) and the object of the activity. That is, the internet connection interrupted e-learning implementation, especially at the earlier stages, which the Deanship tried to overcome by providing alternative options as well as reporting any faults to the internet provider. The second contradiction occurred between the community of the activity and its object – that is, the slow uptake of e-learning by faculty and students at the earlier stage of e-learning implementation. This has been overcome through local and international training for faculty and students. The e-learning staff also provided extensive technical support: 'We were accepting support requests till 12 a.m. midnight' (e-learning Manager). The e-learning

Tools

eLearning artifacts	eLearning training	Psychological tools
Laptops, *iPads*, data-show projectors Internet eLearning labs Web-based applications e.g. Blackboard, *Elluminate Live, Tegrity* etc.	On-campus training by local and international academics Online courses provided by international universities Training by SAU staff Online technical support from eLearning Deanship	Teaching conceptions Perceptions of the role of eLearning in teaching and learning

eLearning awards

SAU eLearning prize ($3000, Laptops)
Appreciation certificates
Highlighting teachers' success stories

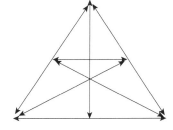

Subjects

Teachers

Object
Integrate eLearning in teaching and learning

Outcome
More effective and flexible learning

Rules	Community	Division of labour
SAU eLearning strategic plan SAU E-government strategic plan Course guidelines SAU norms and culture	eLearning staff Colleagues Faculties incl. deans and admins University admins Students	Teachers' roles eLearning specialists; roles Students' roles

Figure 12.1 E-learning Deanship Activity. Adapted and used with permission from Yrjö Engeström.

specialists also provided immediate help to faculty and visited them in their offices when needed. Figure 12.2 shows a help page that was added to all courses, for both teachers and students, in Arabic and English.

The third contradiction arose within the community of the activity – between the e-learning staff and some academic staff across some faculties. Resistance to adopting e-learning occurred across faculties. In fact, the Deanship itself was, at times, conceived as a threat: 'We posed as competitors' (e-learning Manager). This may have resulted from the different change of pace between the e-learning Deanship and some other faculties. 'Some faculties thought we did what we were doing to make them in a difficult position' (e-learning Manager). Coates, James

Figure 12.2 Blackboard screen-shot showing e-learning support page for faculty and students.

and Baldwin (2005) believe that introducing technology into university teaching creates new relationships, especially between teachers and other university staff. This often results in an overlap of responsibilities of teaching. It is this overlap of responsibilities that has been perceived differently within the community of the Deanship activity (e.g. e-learning staff and faculty deans). Knoster (1991), as cited in Latchem and Jung (2010), stressed the importance of maintaining a balance between the pace and the extent of change to avoid creating incoherence and disintegration within the target environment.

Managing the change

According to the SAU website, the e-learning Deanship is the body that manages e-learning at SAU and develops the skills and abilities of university faculty and staff that are required for e-learning integration in teaching and learning. At the heart of this mission is managing the change that e-learning brings to the overall culture of teaching and learning at SAU. When asked about the main challenges in integrating e-learning at SAU, the e-learning Dean stated clearly:

> Well, the biggest barrier we faced and are still facing is the human factor in the change management process. Honestly, the change is a very difficult issue we are facing. How can we deal with the opposition that we sometime have? How can we deal with some of the very enthusiastic staff? How can we deal with people who might have different goals from using e-learning? How can we deal with the negative people?
>
> (e-learning Dean)

Integrating e-learning in teaching often results in new and complex divisions of labour between faculty, e-learning staff and students. Faculty may no longer be the sole organizers of the learning materials of their courses. They need the technical expertise of instructional designers and other e-learning staff to prepare for teaching on e-learning environments (Coates et al., 2005). However, this change challenges teachers' status quo, which may result in teacher resistance. This makes managing change during the transition phase crucial (Kotter, 1996) and a challenging task for any leader (Tibi and Mcleod, 2010). SAU is no exception in experiencing this challenge during its transition from a traditional way of teaching to a more e-learning-based teaching and learning.

McPherson and Nunes (2006) believed such resistance from university teachers was expected and possibly unavoidable. It was a result, they contend, of the fact that teaching in e-learning enhanced environments requires fundamental changes in the teaching approaches and the structure of the institutions. Some of the changes referred to by McPherson and Nunes seemed to be happening at SAU. The Dean of e-learning gave a relevant example: those who had good positions in the university, but not necessarily the desire to change, started to think of the new players (who integrated e-learning in their teaching) who can attract the attention of the university community' (e-learning Dean). Therefore, such resistance might have some cultural interpretations. E-learning Specialist-2 observed that 'some of the university teachers, especially the professors, regard themselves as the elite in their society and therefore might find it difficult to be taught by others'. To respond to this contradiction in the SAU activity, the Deanship adopted strategies, such as targeted training for senior groups: 'It happened few times that we did specific training for certain groups such as Deans and Department Heads. That training is also different from the training we offer faculty as it focused more on the value and benefits of e-learning' (e-learning Manager).

Another change management strategy was 'to do some public relations across university and continue to give assurance to all parties involved of the main goals of the e-learning Deanship' (e-learning Manager). The Deanship also chose a faculty member from each faculty as an e-learning coordinator and provided him or her with additional training. Their designated role was to liaise between the Deanship and each faculty and to be a first point of contact for their colleagues in relation to integrating e-learning into teaching.

In addition to the abovementioned support, the Deanship adopted different approaches to motivate SAU faculty and students to be more creative in integrating e-learning in their teaching and learning. An e-learning award was one of the Deanship initiatives toward that aim. This included incentives for faculty and students, comprising an amount of cash, laptop computers and certificates of appreciation as well as highlighting success stories on the university website. The strategy of highlighting faculty success stories served two purposes. First, it worked as recognition of teachers' efforts. Second, it showed other teachers some examples for e-learning use from their own context. The e-learning specialist at the Faculty of Medicine (e-learning Specialist-1) explained how the Deanship highlighted the experience of one professor from the faculty:

One of our professors who used e-learning in teaching Surgery in the previous semester gave an introductory session for medicine staff about his experience, titled Is E-learning Suitable for Clinical Use? So, that was another story from one of their colleagues that encouraged them further to be more active with e-learning in their teaching.

(e-learning Specialist-1)

Students were also included in the e-learning prize: 'I have two postgraduate female students who won SR5000 [approx. $1,300] for each of them' (Teacher-3). Faculty, on the other hand, expressed their gratitude towards the Deanship and university: 'Look, every one of us needs appreciation, regardless of our age' (Teacher-1). However, there might have been other motives driving teachers' use of e-learning that were not made explicit during interviews for any reason (e.g. motivation to win the e-learning prize, to be recognized nationally or internationally, and/or gaining the sense of accomplishment after being recognized). Indeed, they could be influenced by any one of these factors, or all of them.

Professional development opportunities for teachers, as well as other university staff, coupled with accessible and multiple support channels seemed to be the main factors managing the change rather effectively (Tibi and Mcleod, 2010). Change is not an easy process and relies on both the e-learning leadership and socio-cultural context of the organisation (McPherson and Nunes, 2006), especially in a context where e-learning is not yet fully established. The change itself within the organization is a dialectical process, as it involves changing teachers' conceptions and practices (O'Neill et al., 2004), while at the same time the teachers' beliefs are affected by the perceptions of the institutional support. Therefore, there is a pressing need for e-learning leadership that ensures the alignment of e-learning policies and organizational cultures with the objective of e-learning implementation in educational organizations. Whilst acknowledging the role of individual teachers in making effective use of e-learning, teachers need leadership that facilitates their efforts in all stages of e-learning implementation.

Conclusion: the future of e-learning Deanships in Saudi Arabia

By 2015, e-learning Deanships initiatives would have almost completed a decade of managing e-learning in Saudi universities. Therefore, studies that review the nationwide initiative and the future of such Deanships are invaluable. However, we believe that there is an ultimate need for within-faculties leadership of e-learning. In other words, leadership and management for e-learning need to emerge organically from within faculties. Ultimately, the role of e-learning Deanships will need to change as faculties and departments build the e-learning capacities of their teachers and students. Teachers and students are also changing, as part of a rapidly changing society, both locally and across the increasingly globalized world. Therefore, e-learning Deanships in Saudi Arabia need to be restructured so that the focus shifts gradually to excellence and innovation in teaching. It is helpful to think of e-learning Deanships as an evolving activity system with its tools, community and object. This also means that it must set new object(s) that are of a more challenging and innovative nature. As the expertise of the community (in this case faculties and teachers) develops and their requirements change, the object of the activity needs to be revised and developed so it continues to meet the community's demands and aspirations.

Note

1 This chapter was originally published as Alshahrani, K. and Cairns, L. (2015). Managing the change during e-learning integration in higher education: a case study from Saudi Arabia. In M. Ally and B. Khan (eds), *The international handbook of e-learning: case studies and implementation*. New York, London: Routledge.

References

Al-Mahmood, R. and McLoughlin, C. (2004). Re-learning through e-learning: changing conceptions of teaching through online experience. Paper presented at the 21st ASCILITE Conference, Perth, Australia. Retrieved from www.ascilite.org.au/conferences/perth04/procs/al-mahmood.html

Bonk, C., Lee, M., Kim, N. and Lin, M. (2010). Wikibook transformations and disruptions: looking back twenty years to today. In S.C.Y. Yuen and H.H. Yang (eds), *Collective intelligence and e-learning 2.0: implications of web-based communities and networking*, (vol. 2, pp. 127–146). New York: Information Science Reference.

Bridges, P.W. (2010). *Managing transitions: making the most of change*. Philadelphia: Da Capo Press.

Christensen, C., Horn, M. and Johnson, C. (2008). *Disrupting class: how disruptive innovation will change the way the world learns*. New York: McGraw-Hill.

Coates, H., James, R. and Baldwin, G. (2005). A critical examination of the effects of learning management systems on university teaching and learning. *Tertiary Education and Management* 11(1), 19–36.

Cook, J., Holley, D. and Andrew, D. (2007). A stakeholder approach to implementing e-learning in a university. *British Journal of Educational Technology* 38(5), 784–794.

Dhanarajan, G. (2002). Open and distance learning in developing economies. Paper presented at the UNESCO Conference of Ministers of Education of African Member States (MINEDAF VIII), Dar Es Salaam, Tanzania, 6 December.

Engestrom, Y. (1987). *Learning by expanding: an activity-theoretical approach to developmental research*. Helsinki, Finland: Orienta-Konsultit Oy.

Engestrom, Y. (2001). Expansive learning at work: toward an activity theoretical reconceptualization. *Journal of Education and Work* 14(1), 133–156.

Jameson, J. (2011). Distributed leadership and the visibility paradox in on-line communities. *An Interdisciplinary Journal on Humans in ICT Environments* 7(1), 49–71.

Kotter, J.P. (1996). *Leading change*. Boston MA: Harvard Business School Press.

Kukulska-Hulme, A. (2012). How should the higher education workforce adapt to advancements in technology for teaching and learning? *The Internet and Higher Education* 15(4), 247–254. doi:10.1016/j. iheduc.2011.12.002

Lareki, A., de Morentin, J.I.M. and Amenabar, N. (2010). Towards an efficient training of university faculty on ICTs. *Computers and Education* 54(2), 491–497. doi:http://dx.doi.org/10.1016/j.compedu.2009.08.032

Latchem, C. and Jung, I. (2010). Distance and blended learning in Asia. London: Routledge.

Mapuva, J. (2009). Confronting challenges to e-learning in higher education institutions. *International Journal of Education and Development Using ICT* 5(3), 101–114.

McPherson, M. and Nunes, M. (2006). Organisational issues for e-learning: critical success factors as identified by HE practitioners. *International Journal of Educational Management* 20(7), 542–558.

McPherson, M. and Nunes, M. (2008). Critical issues for e-learning delivery: what may seem obvious is not always put into practice. *Journal of Computer Assisted Learning* 24(5) 433–445.

Miles, M. and Huberman, A. (1994). Qualitative data analysis: an expanded sourcebook. Los Angeles CA: SAGE.

NCAAA (2012). Standards for quality assurance and accreditation of higher education programs offered by distance education. Retrieved from www.ncaaa.org.sa/ siteimages/ProductFiles/40_Product.pdf

O'Neill, K., Singh, G. and O'Donoghue, J. (2004). Implementing e-learning programmes for higher education: a review of the literature. *Journal of Information Technology Education* 3(2), 313–322.

Palloff, R. and Pratt, K. (1999). Building learning communities in cyberspace. San Francisco CA: Jossey-Bass.

Satyanarayana, P. and Meduri, E. (2007). The qualities of leadership required in distance education. *Asian Journal of Distance Education* 5(1), 4–7.

SEU. (2013). Saudi e-University: Vision and mission. Retrieved from www.seu.edu. sa/sites/en/AboutSEU/ Pages/VMG.aspx

Tibi, S. and McLeod, L. (2010). Faculty members' perceptions about the management of organizational change. *Learning and Teaching in Higher Education: Gulf Perspectives* 8(1), 1–16.

13 MOOC in the Arab world
A case study

Khalid Alshahrani and Mohamed Ally

Introduction

Massive Open Online Courses (MOOCs) have been spreading and receiving attention worldwide in the last few years. Universities mainly in the USA led the trend in distributing online courses to interested students across the globe. The Middle East is no exception. Recently, the MOOC movement started to gain some popularity in this region. The end of year 2013 witnessed the beginning of the first Arabic MOOC in the Arab World, namely *Rwaq*. What makes this initiative unique is that the course content is in Arabic, and presented by Arab lecturers to Arabic-speaking students.

Purpose of the study

'In contrast to the burgeoning number of MOOCs and press articles, there is a striking lack of formal published research; (Boyat, Joy, Rocks and Sinclair, 2014, p. 141). Moreover, the authors are not aware of any published work that discusses use of MOOC in the Arab region and/or by Arabic lecturers and students. Hence, the current paper aims to introduce *Rwaq*, this being one of the earliest MOOC initiatives wholly in Arabic and in the Middle East in particular. It also aims to examine the e-readiness for eLearning and MOOCs in particular in this region.

What is Rwaq?

Rwaq, 'riwaq' رواق, is an Arabic word that means 'Pavilion of an exposition; dormitories and workrooms of the students of Al Azhar University in Cairo, divided according to provinces and nationalities' (Hans Wehr Dictionary); 'Any tent-like building' (Mawrid Dictionary). According to its website (www.rwaq.org), *Rwaq* is an educational electronic platform that presents free academic courses in Arabic. It started in September 2013 with four subjects in three areas – Computer Science, Giftedness and Religion Studies. By January 2016, there were 97 courses spanning a number of categories, as shown in Figure 13.1.

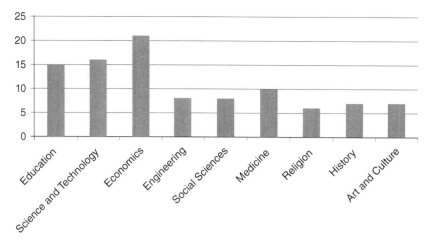

Figure 13.1 Number and fields of *Rwaq* courses.

The website generates certificates of completion for students who watch lectures videos and do all required assignment and tests. None of the courses delivered through *Rwaq* is accredited by any institutions locally or internationally. In fact, initial communication between *Rwaq* and Saudi universities showed Saudi universities do not grant credits for MOOC courses. However, by the time of writing this paper, three faculty members from local Saudi universities had started uncredited courses through the platform. Some organizations and MOOC providers in other countries will grant course credits to students who complete MOOC, but only if they pass the university's course requirements.

Lecturers record their video lectures in advance, with technical support from *Rwaq* to ensure high-quality videos and for any required editing. The weekly lectures are 30–60 minutes long, and are then divided into smaller videos of 7–15 minutes, depending on the number of elements in each lecture. Each lecture is followed by an assignment, with a deadline announced through emails and on the discussion board for each course.

Literature review

What is a MOOC?

A MOOC is a course delivered free on the web with open enrollment available to anyone, from anywhere, and the learners decide on the outcome (Ally, 2014). The concept was originally invented in Canada in 2008 but started to be more popular when adopted by some American universities a few years later. The term MOOC was first coined as a result of the 'Connectivism and Connective Knowledge' (CCK08) course facilitated by Stephen Downes and George Siemens in 2008 (McAuley, Stewart, Siemens and Cormier, 2010). However, open education was known before MOOC, e.g. David Wiley's Open Education course, but it is the idea of 'distribution' that marked the beginning of MOOC and gave it the popularity that made it 'massive' in terms of the number of students enrolled (Downes, 2014). MOOC has been seen as a disruptive concept for current teaching and learning practices in higher education as well as an opportunity for better access to education (Porter, 2014). The year 2012 witnessed the expansion of MOOC use by universities associated with platforms such as Coursera and Udacity. These platforms allowed universities either to adapt some of their current courses or create new ones that could be made available for learners from different parts of the world.

Types of MOOC

It can be said that a common goal for a MOOC is to bring a large number of students into one online environment to take a particular course. However, course delivery differs across MOOCs in terms of the degree of students' engagement and its learning platform. xMOOC such as Coursera and Udacity tend to adopt traditional lecture format in addition to discussion boards and automated exercises. This type of MOOC is normally delivered through MOOC custom-designed platforms. cMOOC is another type that adopts more of constructivist approach by encouraging learners to construct their learning through social interaction with the help of MOOC teachers. It often relies on Open Educational Resources (OER) rather than MOOC-specific platforms. The latter is the model that Stephen Downes and George Siemens adopted in delivering CCK08, as mentioned in the previous section. There is also a hybrid model of MOOC, e.g. Edx, that adopts open source platforms and traditional lecture format. Bates (2012) argued that xMOOC better fit domain knowledge subjects whereas cMOOC are ideal for subjects where learners need to gain high-order skills. In the case of this study, *Rwaq* seems to fall within the xMOOC model due to its delivery format and limited learners' engagement.

Benefits of MOOC

One of the main benefits of MOOC to learners is the 'openness' that has been facilitated by the advancement of technology. This has created major changes in knowledge sharing and exchange amongst people of different resources and education levels (Rizzardini, Gutl, Chang and Morales, 2014). This allowed a high level of flexibility for learners to access learning resources in a time and place convenient to them. MOOC is a cost-effective and flexible solution for educators. Some institutions adopted MOOC to reach out to greater number of learners while others were motivated by the low cost of delivery (Romiszowski, 2013).

MOOC is appealing for educational institutions in Saudi Arabia for a variety of reasons. It is a cost-effective mode of training and development in a country of around 2 million km^2 with a population of around 30 million scattered in vast and dispersed cities. Furthermore, the 'openness' of MOOC can improve female learners' access to education in the Saudi context (Mayan, Ismael and Alshahrani, 2014).

MOOC initiatives in other countries

The Commonwealth of Learning (COL) collaborated with the Indian Institute of Technology (IIT) Kanpur in delivering a MOOC on the topic of 'Mobiles for Development' (Porter, 2014). For six weeks, beginning October 2013, the course was delivered through the open source software platform Sakai. It attracted 2,282 learners from 116 countries. The majority of learners were located in five countries – India, Nepal, Mauritius, Grenada and South Africa. A main goal for M4D MOOC course was to examine the best ways of using MOOC in needs development specifically in communities with poor resources. Of the highlighted issues in the M4D report are: 1. Teaching and content quality as well as the high availability of online services are critical to keeping students in MOOC; 2. MOOC instructors need to have sufficient preparation in online moderating [for e-moderating, see Salmon, 2011]; 3. MOOC can be offered in less popular platforms e.g. Sakai (and in case of our study *Rwaq*), and not necessarily through 'branded' platforms e.g. Coursera and Udacity.

Rizzardini, Gütl, Chang and Morales (2014) examined MOOC learning experience with cloud-based tools use in learning activities, considering emotional, motivational and usability aspects. The MOOC course 'e-Learning Introduction' was offered by the Galileo University in Guatemala in October 2012 to 1,680 learners from 30 countries. The course limits the learning tools to a set number of cloud-based tools rather than allowing the students to choose from a variety of tools. The majority of participants were located in Guatemala, Spain, USA, Honduras and Mexico. The course reported a high dropout rate (only 143 participants, 8.5 per cent, of the enrolled users completed the course). However, learners showed positive learning outcomes, and their attitudes toward motivational and emotional aspects were high. The overall performance of learners who completed the course was very good.

The Friday Institute for Educational Innovation at North Carolina State University in partnership with the Alliance for Excellent Education developed and implemented MOOC-Ed project in 2013. The project was specifically designed to provide K12 educators with self-directed and flexible online professional development to meet district and school goals. The Digital Learning Transition MOOC-Ed had seven (week-long) units delivered through a cloud-based platform for course management, discussion and collaborative tools, e.g. Google applications. The MOOC-Ed participants came from more than 80 countries and had different education roles and experiences. Based on the final survey, more than 90 per cent made progress in their personal goals, and would recommend future course to colleagues.

In a 2014 article, 'Educational Paradigm Shift: Are We Ready to Adopt MOOC?', Sadhasivam questions the readiness of universities to adopt MOOC. He conducted an empirical study to analyse opinions of e-learning stakeholders, including faculty, students and systems administrators, in the higher education context in India. A survey was distributed to a total of 792 respondents out of 2,000. Sadhasivam found that e-learning was used for administration purposes more than for teaching and learning and that the use of MOOC is still debatable. Sadhasivam concluded that India need to 'make a balanced investment in distance education and MOOC programs and provide resources needed for effectively implement the use, integration and diffusion in distance learning rather than paying lip service' (p.54).

Research questions

- What does data tell us about the status of MOOC in Saudi Arabia? How this is compared to other countries?
- Does data tell us about any particular behaviour for Arab learners?
- Have there been particular courses or fields that are more popular than other? Why?

Methodology

Participants

In the *Rwaq* MOOC initiative a total of 97 courses were delivered between September 2013 and December 2015. The courses were delivered in Arabic. Students' data were collected from the *Rwaq* learning management system, which kept track of students' demographics and participation. A total of 330, 000 students from 10 different countries registered on these courses; 76 per cent of the students either worked in public organizations or attended public educational institutions, while 24 per cent either worked in private organizations or attended private educational institutions. There were 41 instructors involved in delivering the courses, with 9 moderators to assist the instructors in the delivery. The MOOC courses covered a variety of disciplines, with the largest number from economics (21) followed by science and technology (16).

Procedure

Rwaq is open for anyone to enroll in courses at no cost. Each learner needs internet connection and a computing device to enroll and access courses. The courses were delivered using video lectures, which were between 7 and 15 minutes in length. The total length of videos learners had to view in one week ranged between 30 to 60 minutes, depending on the length of the course. In addition to the video lectures, each course had assignments that learners could complete. Each course also had a discussion board that allowed learners to interact with the instructor and with other students. The discussion board was also used to post information such as assignments and their due dates and updates to learners.

Results and discussion

Location of participants

Participants in *Rwaq* were from 10 different countries, with the largest number (37 per cent) from Saudi Arabia, followed by Egypt (22 per cent) (Figure 13.2). The main reason these two countries had the highest percentages of delegates was because the courses were delivered in Arabic, the primary language in Saudi Arabia and Egypt. Other reasons could be because these two countries are more populated than the other countries and they are more connected to the internet, which allowed the learners to access the courses.

Language setting of participants devices

Although the courses are delivered in Arabic, data retrieved from *Rwaq* platform showed participants' used other languages as system language for their devices. Fifty-four percent of the learners used English as default language, 34 per cent was Arabic, and 12 per cent was French (Figure 13.3). The percentage of devices using English as a default language is high compared to Arabic. This implies a high percentage of learners in *Rwaq* with reasonable English language skills. It could also mean some of learners who participated in the MOOC were foreign workers in Arab countries.

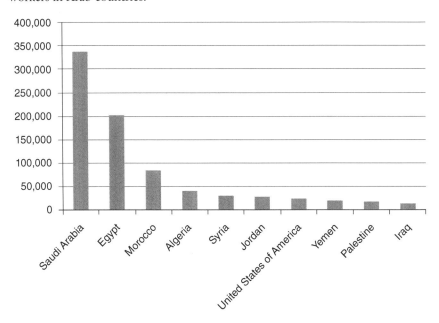

Figure 13.2 Location of learners and number of sessions accessed.

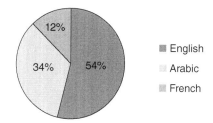

Figure 13.3 Language setting of participants' devices.

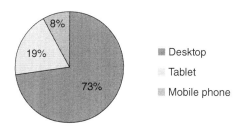

Figure 13.4 Computing device used to access MOOC.

Computing devices used to access MOOC

Since the MOOC were delivered online, learners needed to have a computing device with internet connectivity to access the courses. The *Rwaq* system allowed learners to use a variety of devices to access the MOOC. Of these learners, 73 per cent used a desktop computer to participate in the MOOC, 19 per cent used a tablet, while 8 per cent used a mobile phone (Figure 13.4). The learners who used mobile devices to participate in the MOOC used both the Apple and Samsung mobile devices. It is important for MOOCs to be delivered on a variety of technology and platforms to make sure there is flexibility for access and to reach as many learners as possible, especially in developing countries where only mobile devices are available and there is limited connectivity (Porter, 2014). Future MOOC developers must design the MOOC for delivery on any device to maximize the reach of the MOOC.

Number of sessions and page views

Over all of the courses there were 920,109 sessions with 5,047.267 page views. Since there were 92,242 learners enrolled in all of the courses, the average number of sessions a learner accessed was 10 sessions and the average number of pages a learner accessed was 55. The average number of pages accessed in a session was 5.49 and the average session duration was 9 minutes, 12 seconds. This shorter-than-traditional session duration is good, since people who participate in MOOC may be busy working full time or may have other life responsibilities and only limited time to participate in MOOC. In addition, the current and upcoming generations of learners prefer shorter learning segments, which reflect how they interact in social media and when communicating with their peers. Also, to deliver MOOC on mobile devices, it is important to deliver the learning materials in short segments.

The month of February 2014 had the highest frequency for numbers of sessions accessed. This is an indication that for the Arab countries February is the most convenient time for learners to access online courses. February also marks the beginning of Spring Semester in most of universities in the region. This might mean that some *Rwaq* learners are university students and teachers eager to learn about their field of study. The month of December 2013 had the lowest number of sessions accessed. Perhaps during this month learners were getting started with the courses and as a result did not access the courses on a frequent basis. MOOC should be recorded so that learners who want to review the course at a convenient time can access the course at any time.

Enrolment pattern

The course with the highest enrolment was 'Introduction to Web Development', with 11,270. This was followed by 'Searching for the Natural Religion', with an enrolment of 6,480. It seems that MOOC with emerging content and MOOC of general interest attract the most learners. When developing MOOC, organizations should give priority to courses that will be of interest to many learners.

Conclusion

The MOOC organized and delivered by *Rwaq* was the first attempt to implement MOOC in the Arab world. This was a large-scale implementation with thousands of learners from many countries. It is encouraging to see so many learners participate in the MOOC. This is an indication that MOOC will have a major impact in the Arab region if implemented properly. MOOC initiatives similar to *Rwaq* need to be encouraged to fill the gap caused by the severe lack of educational Arabic content on the internet. The Arab region has one of the highest rates of young population who need further education and development to gain global-level competencies and skills. MOOC is a tool that can participate in developing the region's intellectual capital.

It is important to know that learners participate in MOOC for many reasons. Some will participate in a MOOC for professional development and to update their knowledge and skills, some will participate to interact with others with similar interests, some would like to meet the expert instructors who are facilitating the MOOC, some learners participate because they want to get current information from the expert MOOC facilitators, and some will participate because they would like to get credit in a course. However, to get this, learners will have to pass a certificated exam. Because of the variety of reasons why people participate in MOOC, drop-out rate is not a relevant measure of the success of MOOC. More research is needed to measure success of MOOC and to develop KPIs for

MOOC. To be effective, MOOC must be developed at a high quality to meet the needs of a variety of diverse learners and to facilitate the development of high-level knowledge and skills. Research is needed on how to develop quality MOOC and how to measure the quality of MOOC.

Because of the extensive reach of MOOC there are many benefits to organizations. MOOC is a good marketing tool for potential students, since an organization's brand is attached to the MOOC. Global marketing could increase enrolment, which could increase revenue. MOOC delivery requires use of innovative technologies, hence the organization will be seen as being innovative in its approach to reach out to learners to provide flexible education. Also, by delivering MOOC that are free to learners, the organizations will be seen as contributing to society to improve people's quality of life.

The following are recommended for future MOOC in the Arab region.

- A survey should be administered to learners to get their feedback on satisfaction with the MOOC. This is especially important for the first implementation of any MOOC. Feedback from the learners will provide suggestions on how to improve the MOOC for future implementations.
- Instructors and moderators should be interviewed to determine their experience with the MOOC and to get feedback on improvements required.
- A team approach should be used to develop MOOCs to make sure they are of high quality. A team should consist of subject matter expert, instructional designer, multimedia expert and IT specialist.
- Interactivity should be included in MOOC for high-level learning. This can be achieved by including learning activities such as problem-based learning, simulation and games.
- Pedagogical models must be developed to successfully integrate MOOC in distance education, blended learning and flipped classroom.
- Government and private sectors including universities should encourage MOOC initiatives in the region to supplement the current formal education and to extend education opportunities for all.

References

Ally, M. (2014). Mobile learning for MOOCs. Presentation at the KMOOC (Korea MOOC) for Knowledge Sharing Symposium, Seoul, South Korea, September.

Bates, T. (2012). What's right and what's wrong about Coursera-style MOOCs? Retrieved from www.tonybates.ca/2012/08/05/whats-right-and-whats-wrong-about-Coursera-style-moocs/

Boyatt, R., Joy, M., Rocks, C. and Sinclair, J. (2014). What (use) is a MOOC? In L. Uden et al. (eds), *Proceedings of the 2nd International Workshop on Learning Technology for Education in Cloud* (pp. 147–158). Rotterdam: Springer.

Downes, S. (2014). Free learning from a development perspective. Retrieved from www.downes.ca/presentation/345

Kleiman, G., Wolf, M.A. and Frye, D. (2013). *The digital learning transition MOOC for educators: exploring a scalable approach to professional development*. Retrieved

from http://all4ed.org/reports-factsheets/the-digital-learning-transition-mooc-for-educators-exploring-a-scalable-approach-to-professional-development/
Mayan, Ismael and Alshahrani, K. (2014). E-learning as a mediating tool for equity education in Saudi Arabia and Zanzibar. In H. Zhang et al. (eds). *Equality in education: fairness and inclusion* (pp. 133–145). Rotterdam: Sense Publishers.
McAulay, A., Stewart, B. and Siemens, G. (2010). The MOOC model for digital practice. University of Prince Edward Island. Retrieved from https://oerknowledgecloud.org/sites/oerknowledgecloud.org/files/MOOC_Final_0.pdf
Porter, D. (2014). Mobiles for Development (M4D) report. Commonwealth of Learning, Vancouver, Canada. Retrieved from http://hdl.handle.net/123456789/519
Rizzardini, R.H., Gütl, C., Chang, V. and Morales, M. (2014). MOOC in Latin America: implementation and lessons learned. *Proceedings of the 2nd International Workshop on Learning Technology for Education in Cloud* (pp. 147–158). Rotterdam: Springer.
Romiszowski, A. (2013). Topics for debate: what's really new about MOOCs? *Educational Technology* 53(4), 48–51.
Sadhasivam, J. (2014). Educational paradigm shift: are we ready to adopt MOOC? *International Journal of Emerging Technologies in Learning* 9(4), 50–55.
Salmon, G. (2011). *E-moderating: the key to teaching and learning online* (3rd ed.). New York: Routledge.

14 Smart classrooms in the context of technology-enhanced learning (TEL) environments
A holistic approach

Salah Al-Sharhan

Introduction

The main objective of technology-enhanced learning (TEL) implementation is to provide an interactive learning environment based on the tools of ICT. In this environment, a wide range of collaboration tools, technologies and internet and computer applications are utilized in the learning process (Arora and Chhabra, 2014). Hence, conventional classrooms are dramatically changed into TEL-based or smart classrooms, where students/learners can access learning resources at any time and from any location, and where the e-learning system provides the necessary tools to monitor and track learners' performance. However, educational technologies are changing rapidly and will continue to do so, faster and faster every day. In such a rapid revolution, teachers must pay attention to their teaching methodologies, which must adapt and reflect this technological development (Simonson, Smaldino, Albright and Zvacek, 2014). Traditional classroom learning was limited to the knowledge the teacher had and could access. Today, students are able to find and then to evaluate information and construct new knowledge thanks to the accessibility of the world outside the classroom. This has opened up new possibilities, allowing them to build new nodes of knowledge depending on their needs and learning styles (Tomlinson, 2014).

The core idea of smart classrooms/schools is revolutionizing the educational system through a holistic approach to TEL, with an emphasis on the students, and where education and knowledge are rights granted to anyone, anytime and anywhere. In today's complex educational environment, an efficient model and integrated implementation framework are a necessity to achieve the vision and mission of smart classrooms/schools in TEL environments. This vision brings together the vital components required to exploit technology to improve the educational system and the delivery medium. Furthermore, it helps in achieving the objectives related to the development of a technology-literate workforce and to the students' physical, mental and emotional development, in addition to the broad goal of building modern and democratic education systems (Lubis, Ariffin, Muhamad, Ibrahim and Wekke, 2009).

Accordingly, the requirements of developing an integrated TEL environment are identified, namely, the integration of e-learning technologies in a conventional classroom to teach in a blended manner. Such integration, if well implemented, can help in improving the operation of e-learning integration in the educational institutions of any country (Kituyi and Tusubira, 2013). Therefore, smart classrooms should be associated with organized and set learning space in schools in a way that the best conditions for learning, physical and methodological, are generated, and in the most efficient and satisfactory way possible for all agents involved in the process. Pedagogical design should consider and maximize learning space in order to utilize it efficiently. In addition, teachers should also contribute to making a learning space a perceivable one in the same way as methodology, resources and learning activities are (King and Boyatt, 2014).

The smart classrooms strategy, as a cornerstone in the integrated e-learning framework, is a transformative one that focuses on connecting the digital generation, improving individualized learning opportunities, sparking innovation in learning, enhancing teachers' digital pedagogy and getting the best from schools' ICT investment (Al Sharhan, Al Hunaiyyan and Gueaieb, 2006; Al-Sharhan and Al-Hunaiyyan, 2012a). It's mainly about re-designing schools' structures around the students according to their learning needs and achieving a successful transition from traditional ways and learning practices to innovative ones based on a digital working environment that is meaningful, engaging and connected. However, the challenge lies in shifting from conventional teaching and learning to teaching and learning with and through ICT. The technology to do old things should be eliminated, as the trend is using new ways – using modern technology to enter a new era of smart classrooms in the context of a TEL environment (Vasilescu, Epure and Florea, 2013).

The rest of this chapter is organized as follows. Section 1 introduces concepts related to e-learning and blended learning. Section 2 presents an integrated model for an efficient e-learning environment that considers several successful factors related to educational systems and society, whilst section 3 depicts an implementation framework based on the integrated model. The features of the smart classroom in the context of the smart school are described in section 4, while section 5 presents a smart classroom model in that context. A new quality assurance model in the TEL environment and smart classroom environment is presented in section 6. Section 7 presents a new instructional competency level that enables instructors to be an efficient factor in TEL smart classroom environments. A case study is presented in section 8 and section 9 presents the conclusion and future directions.

1. E-learning and blended learning

E-learning is an efficient method that can enhance traditional learning space and create an interactive learning environment. In the literature, there are several definitions of e-learning, depending on the background that triggers the definition, such as education, IT or psychology (Al-Sharhan et al., 2006). A common definition of e-learning is the utilization of a computer's applications and ICT in the learning process and the delivery of content via an all-electronic medium. These technologies may include, but not be limited to, computer applications, internet, intranet, satellite communication, broadcast, video, interactive TV, CBT applications and learning management systems (LMS). Using these technologies, the face-to-face learning space can be extended to blended learning and virtual learning spaces that provide efficient collaborative tools and enrich learning activities; hence, e-learning encompasses all the learning that people undertake, whether formal or informal, through electronic delivery (OECD, 2007; Horton, 2011).

Today, e-learning comes in different types and formats, such as standalone courses, virtual-classroom courses, learning simulations, embedded e-learning, blended learning, mobile learning (Horton, 2011) and virtual reality-based learning. The latest technology holds great promise for creating efficient learning spaces (Fowler, 2015). However, there are three main modes of learning that can be identified, namely:

- **Full-fledged online, or distance, learning:** here, the learning content is provided fully online, using LMS, as e-courses. The LMS forms the heart of the learning environment and space and provides collaborative tools to facilitate communication between teachers/instructors and learners.
- **Standalone electronic courses:** courses are taken by learners at self-pace without any control from instructors. This type of e-learning is offered in parallel to classroom learning as supplemental learning materials or activities in order to enhance education quality and effectiveness.
- **Blended learning:** this type is based on the integration of the education technologies and e-learning tools within the conventional classroom. Here, online courses and learning can be accessed within classroom sessions as teaching aids inside computer laboratories or smart classrooms technologies. Students and faculty can access courses anytime, anywhere, using the LMS and the internet. Bonk and Graham (2012) define blended learning as follows:

A blended learning approach can combine face-to-face instruction with computer-mediated instruction. It also applies science or IT activities with the assistance of educational technologies using computer, cellular, Satellite television channels, videoconferencing and other emerging electronic media. Learners and teachers work together to improve the quality of learning and teaching, the ultimate aim of blended learning being to provide realistic practical opportunities for learners and teachers to make learning independent, useful, sustainable and ever growing.

2. An integrated e-learning model

The fact that e-learning systems incorporate a wide range of different fields and components, such as technological components related to computer engineering and sciences, pedagogical aspects, cultural and social components and psychological and learning aspects, poses a real challenge to building a successful e-learning system. Hence, a successful e-learning system must orchestrate all these different components. Examples of these components are an efficient infrastructure based on computer networks and communication technologies, smart classroom technologies such as interactive smartboards and multimedia elements, providing an efficient LMS, designing and developing online digital content that requires software experts, and training and society awareness that requires experts in public relations and mass media. In addition, any e-learning adoption must match learners' expectations in terms of quality and tools in order to keep them motivated and attracted to the system. Learners and instructors also must have efficient tools for knowledge presentations, searching for information and retaining information (Abramovici and Stekolschik, 2004; Bedri and Al-Nais, 2005; Pei-Chen, Ray, Glenn, Yueh-Yang and Dowming, 2006). Another challenge is to implement and deploy the integrated platform at a certain level of quality, and with a practical quality of assurance framework. This is due to the fact that quality assurance (QA) in the education sector is a growing need, not only to improve the standard and quality of education, but also to remain competitive in the education market (Hanushek and Wmann, 2007). In addition, QA is an external review and audit on the whole educational environment and should be based on clear and well-established standards (Stronach, 1993). However, implementing such standards in an e-learning environment is not an easy task and requires an efficient QA framework that incorporates all the success factors of e-learning system.

Al-Sharhan et al. introduced a delivery model for the new e-learning environment, as explained in Al-Sharhan, Al-Hunaiyan and Gueaieb (2006). The delivery environment defines the main components for creating the learning space in an e-learning environment and include, but are not limited to, LMS, smart classrooms and the internet. In other words, the main components required to create an e-learning learning space are the LMS, multimedia-equipped classrooms and communication network. This blended model was enhanced after the perusal of several foregoing cases of studies related to the implementation of e-learning in order to deliver the environment required for achieving learning activities. The new proposed model extends the previous delivery model and addresses all the factors related to both internal and external environments of implementing an efficient e-learning. By the internal environment we mean the school environment, whilst the external environment means the society environment. Figure 14.1 depicts the new model.

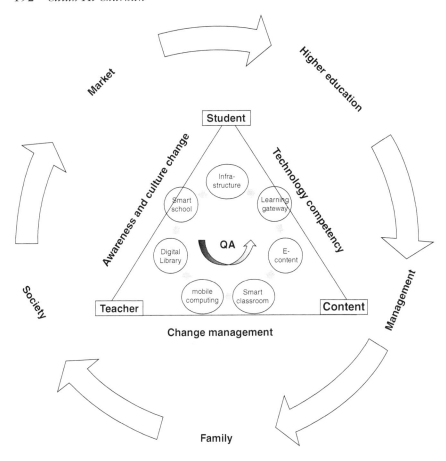

Figure 14.1 An integrated e-learning model.

3. Integrated implementation framework

For the above model, an efficient integrated implementation framework is required to guarantee synchronized implementation of the different components and the effective e-learning system. For example, and since the internet is a vital component, especially as it is usually the medium of e-learning course delivery, an infrastructure component should be efficiently and professionally engineered so that it can serve numerous students as well as the entire educational society. However, success is conditional in factors related to the smart school, bandwidth, application architecture and network security incorporating the data centre, network efficiency and the dynamic and scalable physical infrastructure environment. This means that sufficient bandwidth plays a key role in ensuring smooth delivery. It also guarantees good wireless coverage and up-to-date tools and protocols in smart classrooms. Moreover, every student will have his or her mobile device, which requires direct access to content via the wireless network inside the classroom. It is evident that the faster the network is, the better the learning experience is in avoiding boredom and hurdles caused by slow content download. It is worth mentioning here that these issues should be tackled in the delivery framework as high-level factors and not from the perspective of technical and low-level design. The framework above comprises several factors towards an efficient, blended e-learning implementation in K12. Specifically, the frameworks that form the blended e-learning programme in K12 are as follows (Figure 14.2):

1 **Infrastructure component at both the central and distributed levels:** this component aims to provide a high-performance central data centre in the head office and the required computing devices in the schools. It also provides the network facilities entirely in the schools as well as the head office to work in both centralized and decentralized manners. This component forms the core to create the private e-learning cloud to serve all the schools at the national level. Another alternative for the private is the public cloud, which is considered to reduce the cost of the designing and building the data

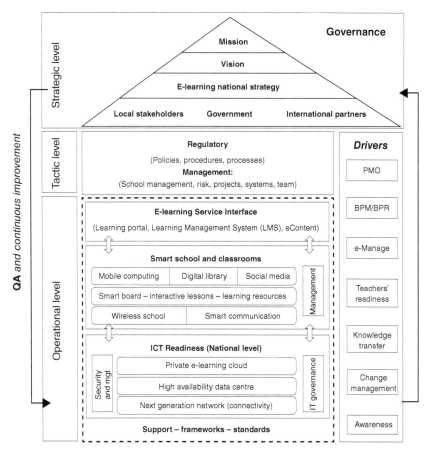

Figure 14.2 The integrated implementation framework.

centres in addition to the operational cost. For more information about these options, the reader may refer to Cheng, Xiong and Zhang (2015).

2   **The LMS:** this provides a single sign on the portal from where students, teachers, management and parents will have an access point to the bundle of efficient tools and features available during the modern learning process. The LMS is the core system in creating technology-enhanced learning, as it is the system responsible for the administration of online courses, tracking students' activities, delivering electronic learning material and reporting the learning process and students' performance. It also provides a complete hierarchy of public websites for the different stakeholders in the e-learning initiative.

3   **Interactive multimedia based content (e-content):** the main objective of e-content in the e-learning environment is to digitize the conventional curricula and transferring the curricula into interactive online courses that are hosted on the Learning Gateway and tracked by the LMS. On the other hand, the digitized courses can be utilized offline by provision on CDs, laptops or desktop computers. It is worth mentioning here that the digital content must be developed based on international standards, such as SCORM, and based on a scientific development methodology using an a very well-defined structure.

4   **The smart classroom component:** the main objective of this component is to acquire and implement smart technologies in the conventional classroom and transform it into a twenty-first-century smart classroom. This component bridges the gap between modern technology-based and traditional classroom activities in terms of the teacher's and students' experiences. More specifically, the components of the smart classroom enable the teacher to utilize modern educational technologies to create an effective learning space. All the learning activities can be recorded and hosted on the learning gateway for future consideration. In addition, the smart classrooms component will provide the teacher with efficient tools to manage the class and provide the students with an exceptional teaching and learning experience. Teachers in the smart classroom can utilize different smart components inside the class or freely using conventional teaching methods to instruct students in a blended methodology. The rest of this chapter presents an effective model for designing and building effective smart classrooms.

5   **The mobile computing component:** this component aims at providing each student and teacher with a mobile computing device. The optimal goal here is that mobile computing will be a major tool that students will need in and outside school, where they can access interactive digital content of the curricula from their devices, using the internet.

6   **Smart schools:** within the e-learning era, schools must be smart in terms of providing full wireless accessibility, IP (Internet Protocol) telephony and video conferencing. The students may access the portal from their mobile devices via the wireless network while school management, for example, can have a video conference with others from their own desks, and may invite other educators.

7   **The e-library component:** this component is a crucial one in enrichment of the learning process and space and in supporting student-centric learning. The e-library, or digital library, avails huge scientific and international research databases, e-books and other online resources that are required during the learning process. The e-library can be accessed anytime and anywhere.
8   **Teachers' readiness component:** one of the most critical challenges that faces successful e-learning adoption is the technical skills of the teachers. Naturally, when introducing new technology in a conventional environment, one should assess the knowledge and skills of the users prior to them dealing with the new technologies and to evaluate teachers' as well as management's training needs to ensure and affirm the success of the e-learning components' implementation.
9   **Media and awareness campaign:** it goes without saying that awareness is a crucial factor for any project to be a success. Awareness has a vital role in e-learning projects to the fact that these projects target different levels in the society and deal with behaviour change. E-learning works directly to introduce new educational models, skills and attitudes at the level of the schools, managements and society (Naveh and Pliskin, 2004).

Figure 14.2 depicts the e-learning components incorporated in full-fledged e-learning implementation in K12. It is worth mentioning here that all these components are highly interconnected – failure in one chain may cause serious problems in the whole implementation. The model is efficient as it takes into consideration all the success factors needed for effective implementation of national e-learning initiatives. It is based on the national e-learning strategy, with a clear vision and mission, in addition to the engagement of all the stakeholders, locally and internationally. Furthermore, the framework incorporates a robust governance structure, various drivers such as Program Management Office (PMO) (Hamilton, 2014), Business Process Management and Re-engineering (BPM/BPR) (Rosemann and Vom Brocke, 2015), teacher readiness programmes, knowledge transfer, change management and clearly delineated stakeholder needs and roles. For more information about the implementation model and framework, the reader may refer to Al-Sharhan, Al-Hunaiyyan and Al-Sharah (2010).

4. Smart school and classrooms

The main objective of launching and implementation of different e-learning initiatives in many countries around the world was providing an interactive learning environment. This environment relies on mobile computing, internet applications and the collaboration between them. In such an interactive, combined learning environment, students access learning resources anytime and from anywhere. Moreover, e-learning offers up-to-date learning methods using the most modern communication tools such as computers, networks and multimedia, whether audio, video, graphics, search mechanisms and e-libraries. A LMS that is remote or in the classroom contributes to and promotes the transition towards the twenty-first-century learning. However, an efficient engineering process is the key to an efficient e-learning system that integrates all the elements and components as well as comprising modern communication technologies, infrastructure, education, social networks, awareness and teacher/instructor readiness. Implementing such a system requires an efficient engineering methodology that incorporates all the essential components of a proper e-learning implementation.

Smart schools and classrooms utilize various smart technologies to implement more efficient educational environment for both the instructors and the students and to convert the conventional classroom into one of modern technology and an enhanced teaching experience. Amid the technologies used in smart classrooms, the smart/interactive board and data projector, class management station, digital library, mobile computing and wireless school are commonly used. The different components implemented in smart schools and classrooms are presented in Figure 14.3.

Mainly, smart schools aim to promote a student's learning performance as well as create a distinguished environment that assists the excellence of the active learning of each student. The most notable benefits offered by the smart schools are listed below (Zandvliet and Bin Man, 2003; Trinidad and Pearson, 2004):

- offering effective and modern pedagogical practice in a dynamic, interactive educational environment;
- developing the students' skills and promoting their methodical thinking;
- enabling the teacher to utilize new studies and activities, which assist with advancing the students' learning performance;
- promoting the teacher's performance as well as qualifying him or her to diversify methods of pedagogy and teaching practice in order to make study more in line with the different capabilities of the students;

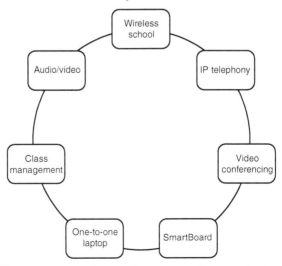

Figure 14.3 The components of smart classrooms and smart schools.

- developing and integrating the thinking and learning skills of the students; physically and emotionally;
- fortifying twenty-first-century teaching skills amongst teachers.

Wireless schools

Full wireless accessibility is considered critical in smart schools and classrooms. The students and instructors expect high-speed wireless connectivity in order to access the portal of the e-learning system, online repositories and resources from any place inside the school, using their laptops. In addition, and due to the increased demand on personal and public security requirements, managers and administrators must ensure adoption and implementation of the necessary security elements and the counter measures in order to meet and satisfy those requirements. This can be achieved by providing a wireless network accessible in every smart classroom in the smart school, using high-performance 802.11n wireless connection and up-to-date tools and protocols, in addition to a network management server and a security server through which the smart school is connected to the central management server in the head office (Al-Sharhan and Al-Hunaiyyan, 2012b). This will provide the required secure delivery medium for data inside the walls of the smart classrooms, between the buildings and any elsewhere inside the smart school campus, all seamlessly integrated with a robust wired campus network infrastructure.

IP telephony and video conferencing

Due to the continuous increase in the number of schools and the need for faster and easier ways of communication between the management in schools and in the head office, IP telephony and video conferencing can be used to provide extended communication services and replace face-to-face meetings with online meetings, without staff having to leave the workspace. In IP telephony, voice communications are transmitted over the data network using open, standards-based Internet Protocol; in video conferencing, interactive video is transferred instead of voice only.

5. Smart classroom model

Smart classrooms aim at offering a distinguished educational environment capable of enhancing students' learning performance and providing diverse sources of knowledge as well as all necessary interactive tools. In the literature, the concept of a smart classroom has evolved from a broader concept of distance education systems that had utilized the internet as a medium or the transferring of the conventional classroom into an intelligent environment equipped with several hardware and software components (Xie, Shi, Xu and Xie, 2001).

Over the years, the internet has dramatically evolved from a 'network of computer networks' into a network that seamlessly connects all kinds of digital devices, i.e. the Internet of Things. These connected 'things' are also smart digital objects with different levels of collaboration. The internet of things will enable connectivity for anyone and anything from anywhere at any time (Reports, 2005). This rapid development of the internet and communication has a direct effect on educational technologies and the smart classrooms concept.

It should be emphasized here that the concept of a smart classroom should not be associated with a conventional classroom that is equipped with certain education technologies, such as the projectors and overheads of the early days (Bautista and Borges, 2013). Rather, it is a learning space that now has several dimensions, namely the face-to-face learning space and the virtual learning space. In these multidimensional spaces, pedagogical change management and innovation become necessities to present a real twenty-first-century smart classroom – an interactive environment with more benefits for teachers as well students via educational technology, the teaching–learning practice and active learning.

A smart classroom consists of several components to form an interactive and interesting learning environment that enriches teaching methods, develop students' skills, raises their academic levels and allows them increased participation in the learning process. Overall, the smart classroom consists of the following components, from an educational technology perspective. The innovation and pedagogical change management will add the dimensions of real 'smartness':

- interactive smartboard;
- classroom and multimedia control centre;
- computers and mobile computing that serve the students inside or outside the classroom;
- audio/video elements such as data show, projectors and recording systems;
- a classroom management system that uses highly efficient software and allows the teacher to have full control of the smart classroom components and students' equipment.

These smart classroom components interact with the other components of the e-learning system to form a unique learning environment that will effect a quantum leap in educational systems and will contribute effectively to the move towards twenty-first-century education. The proposed smart model in this work incorporates all the essential components of a smart classroom, including multidimensional learning space, integrated levels, technologies, innovation and change management. Figure 14.4 depicts this model.

Interactive smartboard

A smartboard is an interactive whiteboard that works as a computer monitor, which enables the user to use a keyboard, a special stylus pen or even a finger to interact with the screen (Jelyani, Janfaza and Soori, 2014; Nichols, 2015). This component is very useful, since it enables students' engagement and allows recording of whatever is written on the board in video/flash format, so that the

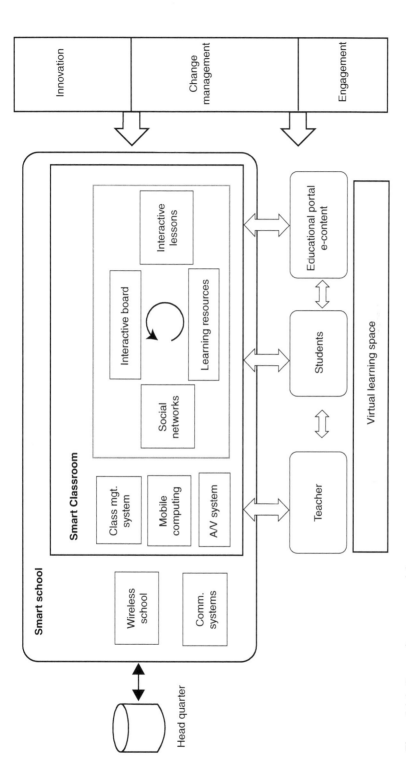

Figure 14.4 Smart classroom model.

instructor can later post this on the learning gateway as a reference for the students. Such videos can be used to form a complete online course that enhances the e-learning process and helps the students gain a better learning experience. Smartboards are very important component in student engagement, whole-class teaching, constructivism and active learning. In short, student engagement is crucial to learning. Using smartboards as a part of smart classrooms has been proven to increase students' engagement (Allen, 2010; Bacon, 2011). In addition, smartboards increase interactions between the students, the teacher and lesson content. Thus, smartboards promote collaboration and interaction in the classroom and increase students' learning. They are powerful tools that also allow the integration of media content into the class and support collaborative learning. When used innovatively, smartboards creates a wide range of learning opportunities. The main features of this tool in the smart classroom are:

- providing the required tools to explain scientific definitions in a simple and interactive way;
- containing a library rich in applications that suit various educational stages and can be constantly updated and upgraded;
- the ability to add annotations;
- the ability to highlight texts;
- the ability to add notes and drawings and then saving them to be printed out and shared, or added to a VLE;
- the ability to show pictures and educational videos to a whole lecture theatre and allow the labelling/highlighting of elements of an image;
- demonstrating the content available on a website in a teacher-directed activity;
- control of the library by touch in a way that facilitates writing by the usual way with the ability to merge it with the applications needed to clarify the different concepts;
- explained material can be saved on the interactive whiteboard and stored on the computer or portal so that the students can always refer to the teacher's explanation;
- using the interactive board as a screen to display different applications (data show);
- using the interactive board for sound recording and saving this in order to refer to the teacher explanation;
- presenting lessons in an interesting way and with full control.

The smart interactive board is designed to achieve many educational objectives, including creating interactive, interesting and unique learning environments. Also, it develops teachers' and students' skills and improves the pedagogical methods and tools that positively reflect on the entire educational process. In addition, a smartboard provides an excellent medium for interaction between families and teachers as it can be displayed on the learning gateway (educational portal) and referred to in the educational process.

Mobile Computing project

In a smart classroom, students will be able to access digital content available online using the wireless network. Therefore, it is necessary that every user (teacher/student) gets a laptop, to be used as the only tool needed to access the interactive digital content (Al-Sharhan and Al-Hunaiyyan, 2012b).

Teachers, students and educational supervisors are the keystones of advancement in the educational process. Teachers' skills and capabilities should be developed in the e-learning environment through provision of better education regarding technical and electronic means of preparation of lessons that will deliver target information and curriculum material. To achieve this, providing portable and mobile devices (e.g. tablets, laptops or pads) for them is important in allowing teachers to prepare lessons and teach in a better way, as well as facilitating information access for students. The Mobile Computing project reflects how e-learning environments are enabled through the provision of the interactive education model. The teacher should be enabled to provide efficient lessons with the assistance of a learning management system and classroom management system that can easily monitor the performance of students.

The vision of Mobile Computing implementation is to ensure the development of learning and educational environment that supports interactive learning and contributes to the creation of a learning generation that is capable of keeping pace with technological developments and global knowledge revolution. Hence, we can summarize the overall objectives of Mobile Computing implementation as follows:

- help the students and the teachers to acquire twenty-first-century learning skills;
- improve and develop scientific research skills among students to facilitate a continued access to knowledge sources using portable devices;
- encourage students towards critical thinking, problem solving and self-learning skills;
- create and maintain a continuous interaction between the teacher and the students and among the students themselves;
- improve the students' performance and achievements by providing access to e-content and learning sources.

Class management system

This component will be used by the instructor to manage learning activities, which can be recorded and hosted on the learning gateway as a reference for future use. It will also help the instructor in controlling the different smart technologies/components in the smart classroom to guide the teaching process efficiently and provide the students with an outstanding learning experience (Al-Sharhan and Al-Hunaiyyan, 2012b).

Learning systems and platforms

This level mainly consists of three components: the learning gateway, leaning management system (LMS) and e-content management system. These represent the translator between the top level (smart classrooms and schools) and the bottom level (infrastructure) through which the different components of these two levels interact. According to Ellis, a LMS can be defined in many ways, but, basically, it is a software application that is used for the purpose of automating administration, tracking and reporting of educational courses. In addition, although many LMS exist, standard functions have to be available, including centralizing and automating the management process, providing the digitized educational content to the user quickly and easily, supporting usability of the digitized educational contents, using a web-based platform to deliver the educational course, supporting common standards, and enabling the users to personalize courses and contents according to their needs.

Learning gateway

The learning gateway is considered to be the access point of any user, whether a student, parent, instructor, administrator or even manager, to the LMS and e-content management system. It provides a single sign-on portal with collaboration tools for the educational learning process, on the top of a complete hierarchy of public websites for the various stakeholders in the e-learning enterprise. The main features of the learning gateway include managing the e-learning systems, hosting the digital interactive e-content, providing the integration mechanism with the administrative and education systems, and acting as a platform for collaboration between educational system stakeholders, represented by students, parents, instructors, administrators and managers (Torres Maldonado, Feroz Khan, Moon and Jeung Rho, 2011).

E-Content management systems

A content management system (CMS) can be defined as

> a system facilitating the creation, retrieval and editing of information/ knowledge in digital fashion including raw, semi processed or fully processed content handling text, images/graphics/animation, audio/video etc., in real time or otherwise as needed.
>
> (Subramaniam, Nordin and Krishnan, 2013)

This system is used to convert the conventional curricula such as the textbooks and handouts into digitized interactive e-content that can be used in online courses being hosted on the learning gateway and tracked by the LMS. In addition, offline utilization of the digitized interactive e-content can be achieved using CDs, DVDs or any other recording medium. Also, the use of e-learning gained the attention of curriculum development in education to increase the knowledge and skills and ICT is the ruler of the teaching and learning process (Subramaniam et al., 2013; Adeoye and Anyikwa, 2014; Eren, Yurtseven Avci and Seckin-Kapucu, 2014).

Innovation in classrooms

Innovative pedagogy of the twenty-first century is based on increasing the individualization of teaching and the personalization of learning – in other words, promoting the brainstorming of the students, sharing ideas back and forth until the class members agree on the topic they want to tackle. Creative classrooms embed ICT entirely in an innovative learning environment in order to innovate learning and teaching practices in all forms and settings, whether formal or informal, in order to ensure promotion of investigation, data collection and analysis, interviews, looking at the issues from environmental, social and economic perspectives, formulating strategies and developing innovations for positive change. This will result in a generation aware of the powerful relationship between collaborative planning and sustainable change. Accordingly, the students will truly understand sustainability works, and how human behaviour, economic activity and environmental capacity are related (Bocconi, Kampylis and Punie, 2012).

Emotional intelligence is the key factor for creative learning and classrooms. A variety of activities help learners to manage emotions and form positive relationships. Furthermore, this enables the use of learning resources that foster learners' emotional knowledge skills (e.g. self-awareness, empathy for others) (Domitrovich, Cortes and Greenberg, 2007). Also, teachers should encourage learners to develop their talents and creative potential to the fullest extent in all possible areas (Kaufman, Beghetto, Baer and Ivcevic, 2010). ICT applications offer unprecedented opportunities for exploratory learning and creativity. On the other hand, creative classroom (CCR) teachers should build on learners' strengths, potentials and preferences (i.e. understanding their backgrounds, interests, skills) as crucial resources and drivers for motivation to learn, and this approach does offer multiple ways in which to express learners' interests (e.g. through social networks) and can facilitate the development of their creativity (Rogers, 2013; Bracey, Lee, Huang, Beriswill and Sherman-Morris, 2015).

Change management

Generally speaking, change in most organizations is considered to be a critical challenge. One of the most crucial challenges facing educational institutions fostering an e-learning system is managing change within the institution, since this affects all processes, activities and components as well as the managers, administrators, content designers and developers, decision makers, employees, students and instructors within it. In order for the change process to succeed, the principles of change management have to be applied properly, starting with extensive and in-advance planning. According to Dublin, 'Change Management is the combination of processes, activities, and approaches that manage the people of the organization through the transition from the old way of doing things to the new way, from the old way of training to e-learning' (Dublin, 2007). The goal of change management is to change the attitudes and behaviours in the educational sector at different levels, including different organizational and individual layers such as the schools, educational management, teachers, students, families and employees. Such adaptation is usually hard, and adopting a new e-learning strategy is a major change. Naturally, people resist it. Therefore, using change management techniques will support moving towards a new era with confidence.

It is noteworthy that change management, in general, implies adopting the new ideas, approaches and even systems, causing change in financial and different resources, which have to be managed and coordinated by a powerful representative governance unit in order to balance an institution's needs for adopting the culture of change through exploring new innovations over controlling the real implementation of such innovations. The representative governance unit must have a high level of understanding to be able to support the persons going through the change process's adaptation to it, keeping in mind that the effectiveness of adapting any technological innovation is measured by the ability of its weakest user to use/handle it. Definitely, an adequate technology that is well accepted will be more effective than a good technology that is not (Davis, Little and Stewart, 2004). Unfortunately, change management is sometimes neglected by many institutions going through a change process, although it is very important and critical to ensure the success of the change. It goes without saying that any change management process, especially in the education field, must have a clear strategy in addition to a well-defined implementation framework. Change management strategy must be developed with specific consideration of the following issues:

- The identification of the magnitude and nature of the expected change with the implementation of re-engineered processes and the assessment of educational sector readiness for change.
- The identification of key members of the change management team and the team capabilities requirement. The recommended change management team structure under the team model will be specified, along with their role descriptions and capability/skill requirements, in order to successfully lead the change-enablement process.
- The preparation of pedagogy and training material requirements. The training plan and materials will be developed on the basis of the communication strategy.
- Planning for the resistance management, including a resistance management plan that contains a study of the impact of the change on different stakeholders. It should also highlight their readiness for the change, and interaction with stakeholder groups will reveal the type and magnitude of resistance expected from each.
- Change management implementation plan. A detailed implementation plan for change management must be prepared to deal with the different layers of

stakeholders to be considered when implementing e-learning components and smart classrooms.

One efficient solution for change management is to develop a roadmap to guide stakeholders gradually during the change process. For example, El-Naga and Abdulla (2015) presented comprehensive analysis of online challenges related to students, faculties and management, and then constructed a generalized roadmap outlining key activities that can be undertaken by educational institutions to ensure a successful change process and a smooth transition to blended learning environment.

6. An education quality assurance (EQA) model

Quality assurance (QA) in educational environments aims at ensuring that educational infrastructure and its components lay the foundation of quality of the institution. Hence, the quality assurance of an educational system is a crucial success factor in creating an effective educational system enabled to achieve the goals of education. Worldwide, there is a vast number of initiatives to implement and enforce QA standards in order to provide an excellent education environment. However, these QA systems can be a burden and adversity if not implemented correctly, which may lead to failure. A major reason of quality assurance systems' failure is omission of a complete EQA model and framework for adopting a new system. In K12 schools, the challenge of implementing an efficient QA system is even greater and more complex due to the fact that it touches the foundation of the education system. It is now evident that the proper selection of the QA model is the key of a successful QA implementation. In the literature there are many models of quality in e-learning environments. For example, Kidney, Cummings and Boehm (2014) introduced a set of QA strategies in an effort to define the quality of online courses and establish course standards. They constructed a matrix of quality attributes related to different stakeholders in the e-learning environment.

In the context of the integrated e-learning environment, a new educational quality assurance model and framework is introduced. The proposed model takes into consideration the factors related to the foundation of an education system, or what we call the internal factors, in addition to external factors.

Quality assurance in the TEL environment: an integrated model

E-learning QA and control is a great challenge. The size of a project, the different layers of implementation and the vast segments of audience as introduced in the e-learning model and framework (section 3) add a new dimension of complexity to the quality control. Hence, a clear QA model and a total quality management (TQM) of online content as well as the teaching in the smart classroom environment are required. Parents, students, management, teachers, staff and the market – in the other words, all of the stakeholders – have to be involved and be given input regarding the system and feedback resulting from the learning and teaching process. This feedback should be analysed and evaluated by the TQM system and based on the output of output, the learning and teaching process is enhanced. Finally, the e-learning system will be fed with improved content, allowing any loopholes to be closed and resulting in a desired and efficient integration system. Based on the proposed QA model shown in Figure 14.5, the e-learning quality implementation framework is introduced based on eight quality dimensions to ensure the targeted quality of education. These dimensions depict the different areas educational management should consider. These areas are:

- teacher/staff competency;
- student/teacher interaction and behaviour;
- conventional/digital content;
- infrastructure;
- support services;
- sustainability/reliability;
- measurement and assessment tools.

The proposed QA model for K12/higher education educational systems addresses all the quality-related factors in both the internal and external environments for an efficient implementation of quality assurance. By internal environment we mean the school environment, whilst external environment means the society environment. The previously listed eight QA dimensions deal with the internal educational environment, whilst external quality-related factors are:

- educational management;
- market requirements and needs;
- higher education;
- competency level of the educators;

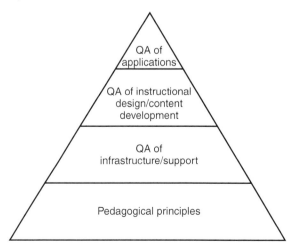

Figure 14.5 The quality assurance integrated model.

- the society;
- the family.

The reader may refer to Al-Hajraf and Al-Sharhan (2012) for more information about the quality of the e-learning environment.

7. An instructional competency model

E-learning systems implementation propels a modern technological environment in schools. Such technology confronts the instructor/teacher with many hurdles and various challenges. This new era requires him or her to cope with modern developments educationally, technologically and behaviourally. The modern environment, educational-wise, means applying and investing technology in the educational process and ensuring the improvement of the role of the teacher as a cornerstone to the success of education and a smooth transition into the educational world of the twenty-first century.

In such an environment, the teacher becomes creative, capable, aware and dependable while conducting, directing, interacting and managing the learning process. Such an environment motivates and leads the learners to become themselves researchers of information, not just passive recipients. Regarding the key role of the teacher, it becomes vital to develop his or her skills in a unique way, enabling the chance to perform and manage his or her role efficiently, not overlooking the fact that this new technological environment will influence the teacher's character in several important ways, summarized follows:

Knowledge and cultural competencies

It is evident that knowledge and culture have a direct impact on the instructor's/teacher's personality in the e-learning environment. These aspects include knowledge based on the different learning resources. Internet, curricula and knowledge databases are some examples. The teacher facilitates, leads, guides, supervises, monitors and evaluates the educational process in the e-learning environment. He or she should possess the knowledge, insight and intelligence to understand the cultural background of his or her students and determine the proper method to handle each.

Technical and technological competencies

In the e-learning environment, the role of the teacher/instructor is to explain the curriculum using all technological tools. Therefore it is crucial that he or she possesses the required competencies and skills to enable him or her to master and improvise these intelligently and creatively and in a way that will teach the students to use them.

Practical competencies

The practical and hands-on aspects of the educational field have multiple forms and require many skills and abilities. The teacher should have the skills and competencies required in his or her interactions with the students and the curriculum inside and outside the classroom.

Behavioural and social competencies

As the instructor/teacher role in the e-learning environment is to facilitate the learning process, and he or she should play multiple roles when interacting with the learners to promote the positive behaviours, he or she should possess certain behavioural and social competencies. These competencies are crucial to a positive and healthy learning space. Furthermore, the teacher has to achieve his her pedagogical goals and objectives by understanding the learners' needs, behaviours and abilities. Generally speaking, behavioural and social competencies include but are not limited to promotion of the ethical use of social networking tools between the learners and encouraging interaction between learners and colleagues in scientific competition atmosphere. In addition, the teacher should ensure respecting others rights among learners in addition to respecting intellectual property rights and to raise the awareness about technology and safe internet use.

Supervision and planning competencies

Here, the teacher must be prepared to possess certain capabilities in planning and designing the learning process and its required tools to improve the capabilities and abilities of the students. Planning and supervision competencies may include determining the overall objectives of the e-curriculum, identifying the requirements of the curriculum and how to deliver it, planning the lessons for certain groups of learners with different characteristics and identifying various tools used in the e-curriculum and the feedback methods.

Teaching methods and instructional design competencies

Based on a highly interactive and integrated e-learning environment, the role of the teacher is to play an effective role in contributing to the instructional design process and identifying learning objectives and learning reality for learners, as well as the best teaching methods and tools.

Figure 14.6 depicts the instructional competency model. It is worth mentioning here that the proposed model is a capability maturity model where the teacher can gradually achieve all these competencies. For further information, the reader may refer to Al-Hunaiyyan, Al-Sharhan and Al-Sharrah (2012).

Figure 14.6 The instructional competency model.

8. Case study

The proposed integrated e-learning model has been utilized to implement the national e-learning strategy in the Ministry of Education (MoE) of Kuwait. In Kuwait there are 850 public schools spread across six educational districts. The MoE caters to around 500,000+ students spread across kindergarten, primary, intermediate and secondary schools. Table 14.1 depicts the situation at the MoE Kuwait.

The MoE has launched a national e-learning project based on the Kuwaiti e-learning strategy that was developed in 2008. The implementation plan of this e-learning project was divided into three phases, as follows:

1 **Phase I:** high schools (years 10–12)
2 **Phase II:** intermediate schools (years 6–9)
3 **Phase III:** primary schools (years 1–5)

Phase I was launched in 2010 and all the projects incorporated in the implementation framework (Figure 14.2) are either completed or in progress. Phase I caters for 80,500 students and teachers. In this phase, the infrastructure

Table 14.1 Public schools in Kuwait

Stage	Schools		Classrooms		Teachers		Students	
	M	F	M	F	M	F	M	F
Kindergarten KG1 – KG2	199		1,807 6,332		43,120	0 6,332	20,930	22,190
Primary Education Year 1 – Year 5	133 259	126	2,912 5,941	3,029	1,366 22,742	21,376	68,848 143,773	74,925
Intermediate Education Year 6 – Year 9	100 206	106	2,172 4460	2,288	8,331 18,554	10,223	51,419 106,663	55,244
Secondary Education Year 10 – Year 12	65 139	74	1,307 2,966	1,659	5,859 13,274	7,415	28,712 67,289	38,577

project, the learning gateway portal and LMS, the smart classrooms and schools (≈3,000 classrooms) and the teacher readiness and awareness projects were completed and implemented to serve students in years 9 to 12 at 139 secondary schools spread across the 6 educational districts. The proposed model for smart classrooms has been implemented. Currently, the teacher readiness programme is being executed to prepare teachers for the new era. This programme is designed by the e-learning team at MoE and international vendors. In addition, an assessment programme will be launched in 2015–2016.

The challenges and lessons learned

The challenges and difficulties that may impede this e-learning project at the national level and hamper the achievement of its goals are diversified and should be thoroughly studied in the context of the different environments. The most efficient ways in which to handle problems should be specified. Different work teams should be formed to continuously support the e-learning project in its different aspects and levels. It is worth mentioning here that the author has summarized the challenges and difficulties as lessons learned during the execution of the Kuwait e-learning project at the MoE. In addition, guidelines are set to address the challenges that confront the project. The challenges may be limited to the following:

- educational;
- human resources;
- cultural and social;
- technical;
- physical resources.

One of the biggest challenges related to the educational category is changing educational thought and practices to match new mechanisms and techniques that will be present in the new environment. The new TEL environment requires a new educational ways of thinking and continuous work to prepare teachers and to design new teaching methodologies and manage the educational process according to the latest scientific methods. Challenges related to human resources can be summarized by preparing teachers to use the interactive smart classroom and interactive systems by using e-learning technologies. This is a major challenge, as most teachers are used to traditional teaching methodologies and tools. In addition, there is a shortage of teachers who are familiar with e-learning concepts and techniques; this is not the fault of the teachers, as such concepts were not sufficiently introduced to them during university education or while training at the MoE. Such a challenge requires effective cooperation between higher education institutions and the MoE. Furthermore, teachers should be encouraged towards innovation and creativity in order to be able to create an interactive teaching environment away from the exhausting effort in preparing lessons the traditional evaluation processes. A national e-learning project is a great opportunity to encourage societies to think differently in terms of educational activities and flow of information. Hence, society should be prepared for this , and cultural and social movement should be directed towards adopting the project for it to be as beneficial as possible within the school and society in general. Therefore, an extensive media awareness campaign is required, and is considered as an important component of the implementation model. In addition, designing e-content and learning resources must take cultural factors into consideration. For more information about cultural issues and other challenges in the blended learning environment, the reader may refer to Al-Hunaiyyan and Al-Sharhan (2008).

9. Conclusions and future work

This work presented a new model for smart classrooms as part of an efficient integrated e-learning model and framework for K12 schools and higher education. The presented integrated model is a crucial factor in successful implantation of e-learning systems. This is due to the fact that contemporary learning environments are complex, incorporate several systems and require certain expertise and competencies in order to provide high-quality education. However, several future directives are required to extend the research toward a fruitful and efficient e-learning system. These can be categorized into three main areas. The first is studying e-learning's impact on educational system performance and the challenges facing it in order to achieve the necessary transformation toward twenty-first-century learning. The second direction for the future extension and exploration is behavioural change. Changing stakeholders' behaviour is one of the main challenges in implementing successful e-learning and spans multiple levels, such as the students', teachers' and society's behaviour. The third direction in which to extend this work is in evaluation of the e-learning system and experience. Evaluation and assessment is crucial in guiding e-learning adopters' directions and future impact.

References

Abramovici, K.B.M. and Stekolschik, A. (2004). The changing face of design education. In P. Lloyd, N. Roozenburg, C. McMahon and L. Brodhurst (eds), *Proceedings of the 2nd international engineering and product design education conference*. 2–3 September, Delft University of Technology, Delft, The Netherlands.
Adeoye, B.F. and Anyikwa, E. (2014). The era of digital technology in teaching and learning in African universities. In Blessing F. Adeoye and Lawrence Tomei (eds), *Effects of information capitalism and globalization on teaching and learning* (pp. 36–47). Hershey PA: Idea Group.
Al-Hajraf, H. and Al-Sharhan, S. (2012). Total quality management (TQM) of blended e-learning systems: a new integrated model and framework. *The Literacy Information and Computer Education Journal (LICEJ)* 3(1), 591–598.
Al-Hunaiyyan, A. and Al-Sharhan, S. (2008). Blended learning design: discussion of cultural issues. *International Journal of Cyber Society and Education* 10, 17–33.

Al-Hunaiyyan, A., Al-Sharhan, S. and Al-Sharrah, H. (2012). A new instructional competency model: towards an effective e-learning system and environment. *International Journal of Information Technology and Computer Science* 5, 94–103.

Allen, A. (2010). *Interactive whiteboard evaluation*. Retrieved 23 March 2011.

Al-Sharhan, S., Al-Hunaiyyan, A. and Gueaieb, W. (2006). Success factors for an efficient blended learning. In Proceedings of the 10th IASTED International Conference on Internet and Multimedia Systems and Applications (pp.77–82).

Al-Sharhan, S. and Al-Hunaiyyan, A. (2012a). Towards an effective integrated e-learning system: implementation, quality assurance and competency models. In Tang, R., Fong, S., Yang, X.-S and Deb, S. (eds), *Proceedings of the seventh international conference on digital information management* (pp.274–279). ICDIM.

Al-Sharhan, S., Al-Hunaiyyan, A. and Al-Sharrah, H. (2010). A new efficient blended e-learning model and framework for K12 and higher education: design and implementation success factors. In *Proceedings of the fifth international conference on digital information management* (pp.465–471). ICDIM.

Al-Sharhan, S., Al-Hunaiyyan, A. and Gueaieb, W. (2006). Success factors for an efficient blended e-learning. In *Proceedings of the 10th IASTED international conference on internet and multimedia systems and applications* (pp.77–82). IMSA.

Arora, R. and Chhabra, I. (2014). Extracting components and factors for quality evaluation of e-learning applications. In *Recent advances in engineering and computational sciences* (pp.1–5). RAECS.

Bacon, D. (2011). The interactive whiteboard as a force for pedagogic change. *Information Technology in Education Journal*, 15–18.

Bautista, G. and Borges, F. (2013). Smart classrooms: innovation in formal learning spaces to transform learning experiences. *Bulletin of the IEEE Technical Committee on Learning Technology* 15(3), 18–21.

Bedri, R. and Al-Nais, A. (2005). Blended learning approach: a strategy to address the issue of declining enrollment in mechanical programs. In Reggie Kwan and F. Joseph (eds), *Web-based learning* (pp. 57–66). New York: CRC Press.

Bocconi, S., Kampylis, P. and Punie, Y. (2012). Innovating teaching and learning practices: key elements for developing creative classrooms in Europe. *E-learning Papers* 30, 1–13.

Bonk, C.J. and Graham, C.R. (2012). *The handbook of blended learning: global perspectives, local designs*. San Francisco: John Wiley & Sons.

Bracey, P., Lee, S.J., Huang, K., Beriswill, J. and Sherman-Morris, K. (2015). Enhancing technology integration in Mississippi foreign language and social studies classrooms. In D. Slykhuis and G. Marks (eds), *Proceedings of Society for Information Technology and Teacher Education international conference 2015* (pp.2894–2895). Chesapeake VA: AACE.

Cheng, S., Xiong, Z. and Zhang, X. (2015). An e-learning system based on cloud computing. In *Network security and communication engineering: proceedings of the 2014 international conference on network security and communication engineering* (p.141). Hong Kong, 25–26 December. NSCE 2014.

Davis, A., Little, P. and Stewart, B. (2004). Developing an infrastructure for online learning. In T. Anderson and F. Elloumi (eds), *Theory and practice of online learning* (pp. 97–114). (Athabasca AL: Athabasca University Press).

Domitrovich, C.E., Cortes, R.C. and Greenberg, M.T. (2007). Improving young children's social and emotional competence: a randomized trial of the preschool paths curriculum. *The Journal of Primary Prevention* 28(2), 67–91.

Dublin, L. (2007). Marketing and change management for e-learning: strategies for engaging learning, motivating managers and energizing organizations. In W. Brandon (ed.), *Handbook of e-learning strategy* (pp. 45–49). Santa Rosa: The eLearning Guild.

El-Naga, N.A. and Abdulla, D. (2015). A roadmap to transform learning from face-to-face to online. *Journal of Education and Training* 2(1), 168–183.

Eren, E., Yurtseven Avci, Z., Seckin-Kapucu, M. (2014). Developing a scale for competencies and perceptions of necessity about using practical tools for content development. *Journal of Theory and Practice in Education (JTPE)* 10(5).

Fowler, C. (2015). Virtual reality and learning: where is the pedagogy? *British Journal of Educational Technology* 46(2), 412–422.

Hamilton, G. (2014). *The essential program management office (Best practices and advances in program management* series). Boca Raton FL: Auerbach

Hanushek, E. and Wmann, L. (2007). The role of education quality in economic growth. World Bank Policy Research Working Paper 4122.

Horton, W. (2011). *E-learning by design.* San Francisco: John Wiley & Sons.

Jelyani, S.J., Janfaza, A. and Soori, A. (2014). Integration of smart boards in classrooms. *International Journal of Education and Literacy Studies* 2(2), 20–23.

Kaufman, J.C., Beghetto, R.A., Baer, J. and Ivcevic, Z. (2010). Creativity polymathy: what Benjamin Franklin can teach your kindergartener. *Learning and Individual Differences* 20(4), 380–387.

Kidney, G., Cummings, L. and Boehm, A. (2014). Toward a quality assurance approach to e-learning courses. *International Journal on ELearning* 6(1), 17–31.

King, E. and Boyatt, R. (2014). Exploring factors that influence adoption of e-learning within higher education. *British Journal of Educational Technology.*

Kituyi, G. and Tusubira, I. (2013). A framework for the integration of e-learning in higher education institutions in developing countries. *International Journal of Education and Development using Information and Communication Technology* 9(2), 19.

Lubis, M.A., Ariffin, S.R., Muhamad, T.A., Ibrahim, M.S. and Wekke, I.S. (2009). The integration of ICT in the teaching and learning processes: a study on smart school of Malaysia. In *Proceedings of the 5th WSEAS/IASME international conference on education technology* (pp. 189–197).

Naveh, G., Tubin, D. and Pliskin, N. (2004). Critical success factors of e-learning implementation at a university. In *1st European conference on e-learning and IS education* (pp.204–209).

Nichols, B.E. (2015). The interactive classroom an overview of smart notebook software. *General Music Today* 28(3), 28–32.

OECD (2007). *The UK perspective – e-learning in post-secondary education, UK country note. Seventh OECD/Japan seminar, e-learning in post-secondary education. Trends, issues and policy challenges ahead, Tokyo* (available at www.oecd.org).

Torres Maldonado, U.P., Feroz Khan, G., Moon, J. and Jeung Rho, J. (2011). E-learning motivation and educational portal acceptance in developing countries. *Online Information Review* 35(1), 66–85.

Pei-Chen, S., Ray, J., Glenn, F., Yueh-Yang, C. and Downing, Y. (2008). What drives a successful e-learning? An empirical investigation of the critical factors influencing learner satisfaction. *Computers and Education* 50, 1183–1202.

Reports, I. T.U.-I.I. (2005). The Internet of Things. (www.itu.int/osg/spu/publications/internetofthings/InternetofThings summary.pdf)

Rogers, M. (2013). Virtual classrooms: teaching and learning online. *ICERI2013 Proceedings, 6th International Conference of Education, Research and Innovation* (p. 3300). 18–20 November, Seville.

Rosemann, M. and Vom Brocke, J. (2015). The six core elements of business process management. In *Handbook on business process management 1* (pp. 105–122). Berlin, Heidelberg: Springer.

Simonson, M., Smaldino, S., Albright, M.J. and Zvacek, S. (eds) (2014). *Teaching and learning at a distance*. Charlotte NC: Information Age.

Stronach, I. (1993). Quality assurance in education: plans, targets and performance indicators. Current issues. HM Inspectors of Schools, Audit Unit, United Kingdom, 1–19.

Subramaniam, S.T.S., Nordin, N. and Krishnan, M. (2013). E-content development in engineering courses: students' needs and readiness. *International Journal of Business and Social Science* 4(6), 282–288.

Tomlinson, C.A. (2014). *Differentiated classroom: responding to the needs of all learners*. Alexandria VA, ASCD.

Trinidad, S. and Pearson, J. (2004). Implementing and evaluating e-learning environments. Australian society for computers in learning in tertiary education 2004 conference, Perth, Australia.

Vasilescu, R., Epure, M. and Florea, N. (2013). Digital literacy for effective communication in the new academic environment: the educational blogs. B. Patrut, M. Patrut and C. Cmeciu, *Social media and the new academic environment: pedagogical challenges* (pp.368–390). Hershey PA: Information Science Reference.

Xie, W., Shi, Y., Xu, G. and Xie, D. (2001). Smart classroom-an intelligent environment for tele-education. In H.-Y. Shum, H.-Y. M. Liao and S.-F. Chang (eds), *Advances in multimedia information processing PCM 2001: second IEEE Pacific Rim Conference on multimedia, Beijing, China, 24–26 October 2001 – Proceedings* (pp.662–668). Berlin, Heidelberg: Springer.

Zandvliet, D. and bin Man, U. (2003). Learning environments in Malaysian 'smart school' classrooms. Annual Meeting of the American Educational Research Association, April, Chicago.

Part III
The future

15 Towards teaching and learning mathematics using mobile technology

Fatima M. Azmi and Aqil M. Azmi

Introduction

The higher education model of lecturing and examination has hardly changed for centuries. Now, three disruptive waves are threatening to change established ways of teaching and learning. On one front, there is a funding crisis. Institutions' costs are rising, owing to pricey investments in technology, teachers' salaries and hefty administrative fees. This comes as governments conclude that they can no longer afford to subsidize universities as generously as they used to. At the same time, a technological revolution is challenging higher education's business model. An explosion in online learning, much of it free, means that the knowledge once imparted to a lucky few has been released to anyone with a smartphone or laptop. These financial and technological disruptions coincide with a third great change: whereas universities used to educate a tiny elite, they are now responsible for training and retraining workers throughout their careers.

During the past quarter of a century, university-level mathematics teaching has encountered new challenges, and this is contributing to changes in teaching practices in higher education. On one hand, we have an increase in the university enrolment of those students interested in STEM (Science, Technology, Engineering and Mathematics), and on the other hand college entry-level students who are inherently weak in mathematics. The latter group is a consequence of a poor high-school maths upbringing. This resulted in a decline in mathematical preparedness of newly enrolled students in universities. Then the emergence of new technologies that are available for teaching created a fresh outlook and increased the demand for changes in teaching practices. The perceived weaknesses in students' mathematical readiness and the ever-growing availability of technology encouraged many mathematicians to experiment with these tools. In doing so, a number of mathematicians turned their attention to pedagogical issues. In many cases, the integration of technology into undergraduate teaching is seen as a way to invigorate teaching and assist students to raise their level of mathematical understanding. Although university-level mathematics teaching is undergoing considerable changes and is in need of assistance, little attention has been paid to teaching issues at this level by the educational research community. In particular, little is known about the current extent of technology use and mathematicians' practices in university teaching (Lavicza, 2007; Stols and Kriek, 2011; Ozen and Kose, 2013).

Most of the studies regarding educational use of technology have been conducted at school level (Pierce and Ball, 2009; Cavanagh and Mitchelmore, 2011). It is possible that some of these studies may be applicable at universities; however, there are considerable differences between the characteristics of both teaching levels. Studies that deal exclusively with issues at university level are needed. There are studies reporting on technology use at universities, but the bulk of research describes innovative practices, application of software packages and case studies of student learning. Some studies outline results of experimental studies, comparing technology-enhanced environments with control groups of traditional teaching methods (Lavicza, 2006). Though these studies are valuable, they provide a limited overview of the state of technology use at the university level. Compare this to large-scale research projects that are periodically carried at school level to review the scope of technology integration (OECD, 2004; Ofsted, 2004; Cavanagh and Mitchelmore, 2011).

It is important that both teachers and students have regular access to technologies that support and advance mathematical sense making, reasoning, problem solving and communication. Given that the Gulf Cooperation Council (GCC) countries occupy a vast land, which is sparsely populated, and a population that is young (average age under 30), this puts a lot of pressure on governments to construct physical colleges everywhere. We now live in an era of smart mobile devices, and people in the educational field are keen to look into how mobile technologies can be used in local and global contexts. The prices of smart mobiles are coming down, while at the same time these devices have powerful processors that – just a decade ago – were in the realm of premium desktop computing. This translates to a vision of tiny mobiles as perfect teaching devices. So our goal should be to operate e-universities serving remote locales through technology.

In a blog, Wiseman (n.d.) claims that education systems in the Arabian Gulf are routinely criticized because of their comparatively low mean student performance on internationally comparative assessments of mathematics and science achievement. In particular, the participation of several GCC countries in the 2007 Trends in International Mathematics and Science Study highlights the low levels of student performance in each Gulf country compared to the international mean. This lack of competent teachers may be compensated by proper employment of technology to serve the students.

In this work, we reason that educational researchers ought to pay more attention to technology-related teaching practices of mathematicians to understand better and enhance innovations in mathematics teaching at all levels.

We explore the integration of technology in teaching mathematics; for example, Dynamic Geometry Software (DGS), for example a Geometrics sketch pad, helps in teaching and learning geometry at different levels of education. Moreover, we explore technology-enhanced algebra and investigate how much help students obtain using it.

Technology's role in teaching and learning mathematics

The National Council of Teachers of Mathematics (NCTM, 2000) stated: 'Technology is essential in teaching and learning mathematics; it influences what is taught and enhances students' learning' (p.24). Whether technology will enhance or hinder students' learning depends on teachers' decisions when using technology tools, decisions that are often based on knowledge gained during a teacher preparation programme.

Teacher education and research on teachers has been greatly influenced by Shulman's (1986) idea of teachers' Pedagogical Content Knowledge (PCK).

We need to look at ways that are appropriate to teaching mathematics using technologies. Koehler and Mishra (2005) and Mishra and Koehler (2008) described Technology, Pedagogy and Content Knowledge (TPACK) as a type of teachers' knowledge needed for teachers to understand how to use technology effectively to teach specific subject matter (Figure 15.1).

Niess (2005) described the four different aspects that comprise teachers' TPACK: 1. an overarching concept of what it means to teach a particular subject, integrating technology in the learning process; 2. knowledge of instructional strategies and representation for teaching particular topics with technology; 3. knowledge of students' understanding, thinking and learning with technology; and 4. knowledge of curriculum and curriculum material that integrates technology with learning.

The next natural question is how teachers can integrate technology into their teaching. An approach is needed that treats teaching as an interaction between what teachers know and how they apply what they know in the unique circumstances or contexts within their classroom. There is no best way to integrate technology into a curriculum. There have been some studies that have examined the role of technology in mathematics literacy and curricula and explored the factors influencing technology integration into mathematics teaching and learning at universities.

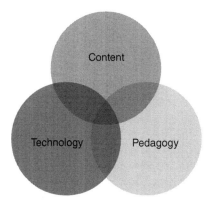

Figure 15.1 Components of technological pedagogical content knowledge.

For mathematics education, we have tools that are both content specific and content neutral. Content-specific technologies include Computer Algebra Systems (CAS), Dynamic Geometry Environment (DGE), interactive java applets (geometric animation generator), handheld computation, data collection and analysis devices, and computer-based applications. These technologies support students in exploring and identifying mathematical concepts and relationships.

Lavicza's (2008) study indicated that mathematicians use technology for teaching more extensively than school teachers. Many mathematicians have a great deal of knowledge about mathematical software packages through their own research. This knowledge, along with their own skill in mathematics and the freedom of developing their own curriculum materials, provides a great opportunity for innovations in technology-assisted teaching. Surprisingly, mathematicians view positively the role of technology in mathematical literacy and curricula. We claim so since mathematicians are often conserved and are slow at adopting technology; they rather like to do things by hand. Consequently, it is likely that there are already remarkable innovations and successful teaching practices that already exist at the university level. And so it is worth paying close attention to mathematicians' technology-assisted teaching. Documenting and researching these practices and innovations could significantly contribute to not only advancement in research and practice at universities, but also at the school level.

Content-neutral technologies include communication and collaboration tools and web-based digital media. These technologies increase students' access to information, ideas and interactions that can support and enhance sense making.

Therefore, strategic use of technological tools can support both the learning of mathematical procedures and skills as well as the development of advanced mathematical proficiencies.

For learners, mathematical knowledge is not fixed but fluid, constantly being created as the learner interacts with ideas, people and environment. When technology is part of this environment, it becomes more than a substitute for mathematical work done with pencil and paper. Consider, for example, the way in which dynamic geometry software allows students to transform a geometric object, by 'dragging' any of its constituent parts to investigate its invariant properties. Through this experimental approach, students learn to make predictions and test conjecture in the process of generating mathematical knowledge that is new for them.

Then the next important question comes – are we really helping students to learn and understand mathematics by using DGS, or are we killing students' ability to think and produce proofs for mathematics problems? Is proof ability endangered by the use of DGS? This is a very important question, addressed by Laborde (2000) and many others. Laborde (2000) attempted to develop a global discussion about the roles of DGS by addressing four papers that dealt with these points:

- the variety of possible contexts for proof in a DGS;
- the dual nature of proof (cognitive and social) as reflected in the 'milieu' constructed around the use of a DGS;

- the transformation from observing to proving;
- overcoming of the opposition between doing and proving.

He started by saying:

> Not surprisingly, proof has given rise to many debates among researchers in mathematics education since it is the essence of mathematics and the teaching of proof in mathematics is a key issue which has been investigated over more than 30 years.

Theoretical frameworks have been developed and numerous empirical data have been gathered in experiment setting inside or outside the mathematics classroom. The four papers (whose contents are mentioned above) that Laborde addressed claimed that the opportunity offered by DGS to 'see' mathematical properties so easily might reduce or even kill any need for proof and thus any learning on how to develop a proof. Laborde ended his paper by mentioning the role of Dynamic Geometry Environment:

> without doubt the dynamic geometry environment fostered the interaction between construction and proof, between doing on the computer and justifying by means of theoretical arguments as claimed by Hoyles (1998): Some commentators may question whether the presence of the computer was necessary, it was to make construction methods explicit, to allow reflection on properties, to check things out and obtain immediate feedback but most crucially to foster an experimental atmosphere that the teacher could exploit to introduce formal proofs in ways which matched rather than supplemented students construction.
>
> (Laborde, 2000, p. 160)

A study carried out by Souter (2002) compared the effect of technology-enhanced algebra instruction and traditional algebra instruction in terms of students' academic achievement, students' motivation and students' attitude towards algebra. She mentioned that a number of different technologies are being used in today's mathematics classrooms, for example graphing calculators allow students to explore more difficult problems than educators would have dared to assign years ago. Graphing calculators allow investigation of functions through tables, graphs and equations in ways that were not then possible. Furthermore, graphing calculators allow the focus to be on understanding and setting up and interpreting results (Dick, 1992).

The positive effects of mathematics and technology instruction such as Computer-Mediated Learning are becoming more prevalent in mathematics courses. The researchers in one study that used the mediated learning approach in introductory and intermediate college algebra found that students who took two mediated learning courses received a higher proportion of grade C or better than those who took two courses in the traditional form. Recent research indicates that the purposeful use of computers in classroom instruction can indeed enhance students' outcomes (Archer, 1998).

Conclusion

Integrating technology into the mathematics classroom can increase students' achievement, increase students' motivation and foster students' positive attitude. Moreover, it can enhance students' outcomes. We need to decide for which purpose we are using technology while teaching mathematics. Is it to help students visualize the graph and understand the properties of different geometric shapes, or to help them simplify algebra problems, or to solve mathematics problems using formative assessment guidance? Teaching and learning has to be interactive. Teachers need to know about their students' progress and difficulties with learning so that they can adapt their work to meet their needs, which vary from student to student. Teachers can find out what is needed in variety of ways – through observation, discussion in the classroom and from a student's method of solving maths problems. Azmi and Kankarej researched the use of technology in solving mathematics problems in several mathematics courses at Zayed University (Azmi and Kankarej, 2015). The result showed that in the Basic Algebra course level only 50 per cent of students benefited from and were satisfied by learning basic algebra using technology, while in a more advanced-level maths course the result of benefit and satisfaction was 83 per cent.

This wide range of difference indicates that students still prefer the traditional way, and it takes times for them to adopt new technology in learning mathematics. Mathematicians themselves are slow in adopting new technology and tend to forget the struggle they went through while studying mathematics before mastering it. In this, they would like their students to go over the same struggle, hopping that this will sharpen their skill. Mathematicians should keep in mind that many of the students are not studying mathematics for its own sake, but rather as a tool to be used in some other field. We are optimistic that the use of technology will help students to learn and enjoy solving mathematics problems.

References

Archer, J. (1998). The link to higher test scores. *Education Week* 18(5), 10–21.
Azmi, F. and Kankerj, M. (2015). The role of formative assessment in teaching mathematics. Proceedings of the 4th International Conference for e-learning and Distance Education, Riyadh, Saudi Arabia.
Cavanagh, M. and Mitchelmore, M. (2011). Learning to teach secondary mathematics using an online Leaning system. *Math Education Research* 23, 417–435
Dick, T. (1992). Super calculators: implication for calculus curriculum, instruction, and assessment. In J.T. Fey and C.R. Hirsch (eds), *Calculators in mathematics education: 1992 yearbook* (pp. 145–157). Reston VA: National Council of Teachers of Mathematics.

Hoyles, C. (1998). A culture of proving in school mathematics. In D. Tinsley and D.C. Johnson (eds), *Information and communication Technologies in School Mathematics*. London: Chapman & Hall, pp. 169–181.

Koehler, M. and Mishra, P. (2005). What happens when teachers design educational technology? The development of technological pedagogical content knowledge. *Journal of Educational Computing Research* 32(2), 131–152.

Laborde, C. (2000). Dynamic geometry environments as a source of rich learning contexts for the complex activity of proving. *Educational Studies in Mathematics* 44, 151–161.

Lavicza, Z. (2006).The examination of Computer Algebra Systems integration into university-level mathematics teaching. In L.H. Son, N. Sinclair, J.B. Lagrange and C. Hoyles (eds), *Proceedings of the ICMI 17 study conference: background papers for the ICMI 17 study* (pp. 37–44). Hanoi University of Technology, Hanoi, Vietnam.

Lavicza, Z. (2007). Factors influencing the integration of Computer Algebra Systems into university-level mathematics education. *International Journal of Technology in Mathematics Education*.

Lavicza, Z. (2008). The examination of technology use in university-level mathematics teaching. Proceedings of the Symposium on the Occasion of the 100th Anniversary of International Commission on Mathematical Instruction. Rome, Italy.

Mishra, P. and Koehler, M. (2008). Introducing technological pedagogical content knowledge. Paper presented at the annual meeting of the American Educational Research Association, New York.

Niess, M.L. (2005). Preparing teachers to teach science and mathematics with technology: developing a technology pedagogical content knowledge. *Teaching and Teacher Education*, 21, 509–523.

National Council of Teachers of Mathematics (2000). *Principles and standards for school mathematics*. Reston VA: NTCM.

Ozen, D. and Kose, N. (2013). Investigating pre-service mathematics teachers' geometric problem solving process in dynamic geometry environment. *Turkish Online Journal of Qualitative Inquiry* 4(3).

OECD. (2004). Learning for tomorrow's world: first results from PISA 2003. OECD Programme for International Student Assessment. Retrieved from www.pisa.oecd.org/dataoecd/1/60/34002216.pdf

Ofsted (2004). ICT in schools: the impact of government initiatives five years on. Office for Standards in Education. Retrieved from www.ofsted.gov.uk

Pierce, R. and Ball, L. (2009). Perceptions that may affect teachers' intention to use technology in secondary mathematics classes. *Educational Studies in Mathematics* 71(3), 299–317.

Shulman, L. (1986). Those who understand: knowledge growth in teaching. *Educational Researchers* 15(2), 4–14.

Souter, M. (2002). Integrating technology into the mathematics classroom: an action research study. http://chiron.valdosta.edu/are/artmanscrpt/vol1no1/souter_am.pdf

Stols, G. and Kriek, J. (2011). Why don't all math teachers use dynamic geometry software in their classrooms? *Australasian Journal of Educational Technology* 27(1), 137–151.

Wiseman, A.W. (n.d.). Analysis: teacher quality eludes Arabic Gulf educational systems. Retrieved from www.comparative-education.com/teacher-quality-eludes-arabian-gulf-education-systems/

16 The future of mobile learning and implications for education and training[1]

David Parsons

The future is now

A few months ago, a student research assistant brought one of his home projects – a robotic vehicle controlled by the orientation of a mobile phone – to show to a class. His current project uses off-the-shelf hardware to control the robot with brain waves. In a world where amateur student projects involve the mind control of robots, it is hard to look ahead without finding that one's predictions are already part of everyday life. With this caveat in mind, the present chapter begins with a brief mobile learning (m-learning) scenario from a possible future.

Mobile learning as we approach the middle of the twenty-first century is just part of life. The old model of educational institutions has withered away, with learning now a lifelong, pervasive experience, delivered via the practically invisible devices that I have with me day and night, the personal network that delivers information to my eyes, ears and other senses, the e-glasses, the flexible smart-touch screen that folds into a small case but expands to poster size and will stick to or project on to any surface. These devices seamlessly connect and collaborate with ambient technologies in the environment. For example, in my informal learning activities related to photography, my camera will scan for nearby 3D printers to create models from my 3D photos. For my interest in literature, scenes from books play out in front of me if I happen to enter a location used by one of my favoured authors. For somewhat more formal learning, I attend immersive virtual reality classes whenever I want, mixing my avatar with those of other virtual students and both real and robot instructors. I learn when I need to, where I want to. When I am at work, I have professional learning support with me at all times, guiding me in new situations, online artificial intelligence systems reacting to my ever-changing contexts and giving me expert task and problem-solving support. I have all the knowledge ever gathered available in an instant, tailored to my own learning profiles and preferences, quality controlled by the world's best minds. Not that I am just bombarded with data. The mobile learning systems that I use are able to help me filter the huge amount of data in the computer cloud, assisting me in making meaning out of a mass of information, working with my own goals, learning styles and changing moods and activities to ensure that the material I am exposed to will help me learn rather than overwhelm me. As a mid-twenty-first-century learner, I am never lost, never alone, never unsupported, never not learning.

If there is one thing that can be said for trying to predict the future, it is that we are bound to be wrong, at least if we try to go beyond very broad assumptions such as 'the use of m-learning in education and training will increase'. We might therefore consider what the merits might be of attempting to look ahead to the future of m-learning, and the possible implications for education and training.

Perhaps in doing so we might reflect on the idea that writing that purports to look to the future is often instead recasting the present through another lens. A classic example of this would be George Orwell's *1984*, the title of which a number of commentators, including Burgess (1978), have suggested is a partial inversion of the year the book was written (1948). Much science fiction follows similar themes, projecting current concerns either near or far into the future. Those who look at 'near-future' fiction and dismiss its inaccurate predictions (think *The Shape of Things to Come, 2001: A Space Odyssey, Blade Runner* or even *Back to the Future*) miss the point that accurate prediction is not the purpose of such creative works. Rather, they hold a mirror up to the present that reflects the potential implications of our present actions.

Thus, this chapter does not propose to attempt accurate predictions of the future. Instead, it intends to reflect on the current technologies and affordances of m-learning, and consider which of these might continue to be useful to us in the future, as the worlds of work, learning, technology and society continue to evolve. In fact, the somewhat futuristic scenario above is based on the work of Golding (2008), who begins his book with a similar type of proposition based, as he makes clear, not on fantasy technology but by extrapolating from what we already have, here and now.

Top five mobile learning myths and misunderstandings

In an attempt to look ahead to the future of m-learning, one thing that may unnecessarily hold us back is making assumptions about what m-learning is, or what it could be, and so we could fail to appreciate its full set of potentials. This section lays out a 'top five' of m-learning myths and misunderstandings. In doing so, it should be noted that these are not necessarily wrong; rather, they provide excessively limiting definitions of m-learning that do not serve us well in truly knowing what it means to be a mobile learner. In fact, in the examples that follow, we might easily insert the word 'only' to make the point that these are all valid views of m-learning, but all are too restrictive to truly reflect what m-learning can be. In this section, we will take apart each of these myths and misunderstandings and explore how these definitions can limit our ideas about what can be achieved in m-learning.

Mobile learning is 'anytime, anyplace' learning

This is perhaps the most prevalent view of m-learning. The image is frequently used of commuters 'learning' from a mobile device on the bus, on the train, etc. The limitation of this definition is that it focuses on the pervasiveness of the learning, but perhaps neglects the concept of m-learning at this time, in this place –in other words, contextualized or situated learning (Seely Brown, Collins and Duguid, 1989). One of the major affordances of a mobile device is that it can be brought to use in a specific context, a concept not acknowledged by 'anywhere, anyplace'. To only follow this thread is to risk disconnected learning fragments, isolated from the reality around us.

Mobile learning is 'just-in-time' learning

There is nothing wrong with the concept of just-in-time learning. In fact, it is often used as the main justification for using m-learning in the workplace; the ability to get the information when and where you need it, at the point of delivery. The problem with just-in-time learning is that it potentially bypasses any concept of a curriculum or a developmental frame within which learning takes place. It raises rather deeper questions about what we mean by learning. Is looking something up on the fly learning? Does it matter if you remember it or not (given that you can always look it up again)? This type of learning is sometimes called 'performance support', and perhaps this is how we should define it: not as learning, but as a tool to be used in the performance of various duties and responsibilities. Learning, we must assume, should go deeper than this.

Mobile learning is learning while mobile

This is an interesting misunderstanding, as it challenges us to consider what we mean by 'mobile'. Is there an inherent expectation that the key to what we are doing is mobility? And what does mobility mean? Actually being in motion? Or being able to transition from place to place? We rarely learn while physically moving (leaving aside being in a moving vehicle) since the distractions are usually too problematic (Doolittle, 2009). What we tend to do is take our learning tools with us to the appropriate places. This raises the question: Do these learning tools need to be mobile devices? Or can we do m-learning with books, pens, paper, etc.? Indeed, in some experiments comparing m-learning solutions to paper-based solutions, it has been difficult to see the benefits of using the mobile device over the paper-based version (Fisher et al., 2012). Of course this will depend very much on the affordances that we require to deliver a particular type of learning. In some cases, traditional learning tools, in a learning context, will be able to deliver as much learning as any technology-based solution. In other cases, new technologies are essential to the activities.

Perhaps if there is confusion of perceptions here, it may be that some approaches to m-learning are seen as device centric whereas others are seen as learner centric.

Both approaches, of course, have merit, but a learner-centric approach might tend to consider types of learning where the mobile device plays a minor role, whereas device-centric approaches are often those that push the boundaries of current tools exploring the new potentials of emerging and disruptive technologies (e.g., Ogata and Yano, 2010). It is interesting to consider Amit Garg's 'Top 7 Myths of Mobile Learning' (2012) and note how many of these myths are about technology rather than learning, including perceived issues with screen size, costs of creating and distributing content, security, fragmented platforms and SCORM compliance. Garg's point is, perhaps, that we can easily get hung up on technological aspects of m-learning when these are not important barriers at all.

Mobile learning is an extension of e-learning

There is a common approach to m-learning that is based on the mobilization of existing eLearning systems, particularly learning management systems (LMS). An example of this would be mobile clients for the Moodle LMS. Many commercial eLearning providers have embraced the rush to HTML 5, keen to stress how the same content can be developed for desktop computers, tablets and smartphones. The problem with this approach is that the best that can be hoped for is content designed for eLearning adapted for a different form factor. It does not take into account any of the additional affordances of the mobile device, such as location awareness and both synchronous and asynchronous collaborative communication.

In reality, mlearning is different from elearning in terms of size of courses that can (or should) be delivered on mobiles; the context in which mlearning is accessed. Designers must consider the always on nature of phones which help capture the moment of creative learning and other such factors.

(Garg, 2012)

Mobile learning is an extension of distance learning

It is true that distance learners can benefit from m-learning. However, once again, to regard the mobile device as only for use at a distance is to miss its opportunities for use in the classroom, where mobile applications can support learning processes. Indeed, one of the major current movements in education worldwide is the integration of mobile devices, particularly tablets, into the daily life of the classroom. Some applications of mobile devices in the classroom have in fact seen them become embedded in the environment itself, thus becoming entirely static (e.g. Moher, 2006). Nevertheless, they still provide one form of m-learning, with mobile students using mobile devices that just happen to remain in one place.

To draw some ideas from these myths and misunderstandings about the future of m-learning in education and training, perhaps the main concern is that future m-learning tools may continue to use narrow definitions of what m-learning is (for example, just the mobilization of an existing e-learning system driven by the target markets of a particular vendor, or an emphasis on worker support tools by

228 David Parsons

employers). To ensure that future m-learning systems meet their full potential, it is necessary that our understanding of m-learning encompasses all of its unique characteristics, and that we recognize that any form of learning that takes place using a mobile device is m-learning, whether on the move or static, whether in formal or informal settings, whether working collaboratively or alone.

Top five mobile learning innovations

If the previous section took a somewhat negative viewpoint about myths and misunderstandings that might hold back the development of future m-learning, this section provides a more positive perspective of how m-learning is unique and powerful. In looking at the 'top five' innovations describing the ground-breaking features of m-learning, we can see why definitions saying that m-learning is just an extension of eLearning or distance learning do not do it justice. It is important to note that these are not just technical innovations, but examples of how technology and pedagogy have been used together. Most (though not all) of the ways of learning listed below have an intimate relationship with the concept of mobility, emphasising the unique role that a mobile device can play in learning. In all cases, there are significant differences between these activities and traditional eLearning. Even where these are also standard learning activities (e.g. contributing to shared learning resources), doing these things with mobile devices provides a much broader range of opportunities for gathering and exchanging knowledge with other learners and teachers.

Placing learning in a specific context

One of the main affordances of a mobile device is that you can take it with you wherever you go. Much has been written about the importance of context in learning, to support situated cognition (Seely Brown et al., 1989). This idea has been much explored in m-learning projects, where the museum, the woodland or the city become meaningful locations for learning to take place. The great thing about having a modern mobile device is that it is a compendium of tools, an electronic Swiss Army knife. As such, once you are in a given context, it can help you to measure and analyse, to capture and publish, to organize and communicate. This means, for example, that learners can apply mathematical or scientific enquiry in real-world problem-solving situations, using m-learning tools such as MobiMaths (Tangney et al., 2010).

Augmenting reality with virtual information

With a mobile device, you can overlay something virtual on to something real. This has proved a very popular theme in recent mobile applications. Augmented reality tools such as Google Goggles, Wikitude and Layar show the potential for using a mobile device to give you information about artefacts, locations, etc. in areas as diverse as architecture, history and geography. Beyond these common tools, which overlay factual information on to what is physically present, there have been a number of m-learning applications where a virtual reality has been superimposed on to a physical location in order to provide a new learning experience. These include Savannah (Facer et al., 2004) and Invisible Buildings (Winter and Pemberton, 2011).

Contributing to shared learning resources

One of the key themes of Web 2.0 is the concept that web-based resources no longer work in one direction only (from a server to a client), but that users become their own content creators. A valuable aspect of learning is the ability to create new material and share it with others, for peer review and collaborative learning. Being able to do this with the assistance of a mobile device, which you can have with you in many contexts, broadens the range of sharing opportunities. It also further enhances the concept of bricolage and diverse learning ecologies (Seely Brown, 2000), in this way making meaning out of the digital artefacts we create from the physical and conceptual learning moments that we constantly encounter. The ability to learn while communicating and contributing at a distance with other learners supports the concept of distributed cognition (Hutchins, 1995). While the initial work in this area found this distribution to be among groups physically co-located, the concept also includes communication with others at a distance. An early example of this type of m-learning can be seen in the distributed collaborative field work described in the Wireless Coyote project (Grant, 1993).

Having an adaptive learning toolkit in the palm of your hand

A mobile device is increasingly a toolkit. As well as the tool-like functions that are built in to the device hardware (camera, sound recorder, video recorder, multimedia messaging, etc.), there are also many applications that can take advantage of various combinations of functions and sensors to make the phone into all kinds of tool. Your mobile can be a distance-measuring device, a guitar tuner, a musical instrument, a compass, a speedometer, a spirit level and a whole range of other things. This allows the device to be adapted for use as a supporting tool in an almost infinite range of learning activities. In particular, the role of device as tool is well suited to supporting enquiry-based learning (Powell et al., 2011). Whether being used as a support tool to scaffold learning in the classroom or as a means to capture learning experiences in the field, there will be some kind of hardware and/or software feature that can be utilized in the learning process.

Taking ownership of learning

One of m-learning's most significant innovations has to do with the ownership of personal learning devices. The personal digital device gives learners the ability to appropriate and personalize their own learning experience, to autonomously acquire the learning material that they want, whenever and wherever they wish to do so. Equally, they have to ability to capture their own learning moments (take photos, videos, notes) and share their insights or questions with others using social media and LMS. Emphasizing the personalization of learning, Sergio (2012) notes that "'m" usually stands for "mobile" but also just as easily for "me"'. He further acknowledges the importance of accessibility, noting that m-learning opens access to all kinds of people who previously had limited access to learning, in particular in areas of the globe where some members of society have had no previous access to any technologies that could support learning.

To reflect on the innovations covered in this section, we can see that m-learning encompasses learning that is situated, collaborative and adaptive. In addition, it provides for augmented and virtual realities that provide learning opportunities that go beyond physical environments. Increasing accessibility also means that m-learning can be for the many, not just the few. In the future, we can look forward to these themes developing more broadly and becoming more pervasive. Future mobile learners will have devices that can act as all kinds of learning tools, simulating and supporting all kinds of learning environments, and providing access to m-learning for all, regardless of their location, culture or socio-economic status.

Top five future potentials for mobile learning

Perhaps the most important aspect of a chapter looking at the future of mLearning is to look forward to its main potentials. These are based primarily around the increasing power and pervasiveness of mobile devices, and their mass integration into the world of teaching and learning.

All students in a class can use their own device for learning

Perhaps the defining characteristic of m-learning in the second decade of the twenty-first century is that the Bring Your Own Device (BYOD) approach has suddenly become the norm rather than the exception. This opens up major new opportunities for digital learning in the classroom, since the old constraints of having to provide all learning technologies from central resources gradually fade away. Not that central resources are no longer required, since networks and cloud-based services become even more essential, but enabling a learner's own devices to be used for learning leads to greater efficiencies and digital inclusion.

We capture existing technology and best practice for learning

We should always be wary of reinventing the wheel. Educational research, including research into educational technology, has a long history and we would be foolish to embark on new technology-driven interventions in the classroom without taking full account of what we have learned in the past, and already understood about the processes of teaching and learning. The balance that needs to be struck is between embracing new ways of teaching and learning that are afforded by mobile devices,

The future of mobile learning   231

while holding to the underlying principles of good education. One very positive aspect of mobile technology is that it allows us to share the very best of existing practice using mobile technology. A good example of this would be the O2 Learn website (O2, 2012), which provides not only a video-sharing website for categorized educational content, but a tailored mobile app for easily capturing and uploading this content directly from the learning context.

Everything we want to teach can have a mobile app

To some extent this is probably true already. Indeed, in some cases there are more apps (and other learning resources) for a given topic than you could possibly absorb. How many applications and websites teach basic mathematics, for example? We have seen the rise of online initiatives such as iTunesU and the MOOC (massive open online course) phenomenon, all of which threaten to overwhelm us with quantity without necessarily giving us the means to select the right applications for our own teaching or learning purposes. However, we can assume that over time the wisdom of crowds will assist us in finding the most suitable apps for a particular learning content; that, over time, the best apps will go viral while the weaker offerings fall by the wayside.

We re-engage students by integrating mobile technologies into the classroom

Lecture attendance in non-compulsory education has never been 100 per cent, but gradually we have been eroding the reasons why students should come to class, particularly to large lectures (as opposed to smaller workshops, seminars, labs, etc.), by adopting LMS that often do no more that host a mass of uncontextualized material. The alternative to this is that we rethink our pedagogy by integrating mobile technologies so that face-to-face classes, even in large lecture halls, can become engaging and productive. We have already seen initiatives such as clickers and the 'flipped classroom'. However, there is huge potential to do much more in transforming our teaching philosophy to embrace mobile technologies in the classroom. The recent surge in BYOD initiatives suggests that many educators see the potential of m-learning as part of regular classroom delivery.

We teach things in a practical way that could previously only be taught theoretically

One of the major potentials of learning technologies is that they enable us to provide access to learning experiences that were previously too expensive, complex, dangerous or specialised to provide. We can now overcome these limitations by connecting learners to remote learning activities. It is already the case that distance students can perform engineering experiments remotely using remote data connections (Toole, 2011). Indeed, such virtual interactions need not take place only with physical contexts but also virtual contexts, performing experiments in virtual worlds (Vallance, Martin, Wiz and van Schaik, 2010). As mobile technologies become more pervasive and seamless, new opportunities will arise for us to create practical learning experiences, accessed remotely through mobile devices.

In general, the future potential for m-learning is to enhance learning both inside and outside the classroom and workplace. By bringing devices into the classroom, we have the opportunity to transform formal education into a more engaging, relevant, collaborative and outward-facing activity. By taking learning outside the classroom using mobile devices, we have the opportunity to transform informal education, by turning the whole world into a learning space.

Top five future risks for mobile learning

While we are looking ahead, it would be unwise to focus only on the potential positives. We also need to guard against possible negative impacts. Some of the most important of these are outlined in this section.

Entrenched digital divides

Any approach to learning that involves technology may have an impact on digital divides. These divides can be quite subtle. They relate not only to access to equipment and connectivity, but also to the skills to make use of that equipment, and other aspects of the learners' situation that may impact on their ability to make meaning, to appropriate and to contribute. Wei, Teo, Chan and Tan (2011) defined three levels of digital divide: the digital access divide, the digital capability divide and the digital outcome divide. Each influences the next and has an impact on learning. The message here is that we cannot address digital inequality just by providing access to technology. In addition, we need to address many aspects of digital literacy and digital citizenship.

Digital distractions and threats

Many schools have sought to ban mobile devices from the classroom on the grounds that they are purely distractions. For example, Greenwich Free school in London states in its public documents that 'Mobile phones are a huge distraction in lessons, with pupils thinking about text-messaging, Twitter or Facebook in class instead of their work' (Greenwich Free School, 2012). This school is by no means unusual in this policy. In addition, fears about theft of devices and cyber bullying exist too. A further dimension to distraction is the potential for information overload, distracting us from our learning objectives. We want to make meaning, not just accumulate data (Shum and Crick, 2012).

The opposite of a green manifesto

Already, there are more computers in landfill sites than on the desktop, and we continue to turn the planet to trash at a frightening rate. Every year, hundreds of

The future of mobile learning 233

millions of electronic items go to landfill in the United States and, globally, tens of millions of tons of e-waste go to landfill. To compound the problem, mobile phones have a particularly short lifespan. 'Cellular contracts are 2 years for a reason; it takes approximately 1 year to recoup the costs of marketing, manufacturing, activating, and maintaining a cell phone, and the average cell phone lasts only 2 years. Battery life spans average 18 to 30 months' (Walker, 2010).

Even where electronic material is recycled, the impacts on developing countries can be disastrous, with dangerous recycling practices poisoning individuals and the environment (Bosavage and Maselli, 2006). Although many aspects of this negative environmental impact may be out of our direct control, we should nevertheless attempt to make wise choices in the purchase and use of mobile devices for learning, preferring devices that have low power consumption and a long service lifetime (e.g., have maintainable components), and that can be safely recycled – even if these may be more expensive to purchase in the first instance.

Uncontrolled, misleading effects on outcomes

One of the issues facing us in evaluating the value or otherwise of m-learning is that we may find it hard to measure the real, as opposed to the perceived, impacts of new technologies. There are two well-known types of effect that can lead to false positives in assessing changes in practice or new forms of presentation.

Various proposed effects, such as the 'Hawthorne effect', suggest that it is hard to measure directly the real benefit of a change to a learning process because the context of the experiment itself may have effects that are separate from the actual intervention. The other effect that might be relevant is the 'Dr Fox effect', which is where people tend to give more value to something that is well presented regardless of the real value of the content being presented (Naftulin, Ware and Donnelly, 1973).

Whilst the original Dr Fox experiment, where an actor posing as an academic gave a highly engaging but meaningless lecture to a great reception, would now be hard to repeat without a considerable amount of fake material being posted on the Web, the same effect might be seen in the tendency for many student researchers to regard Wikipedia as the default first port of call for information and, further, to cite it with an uncritical eye. Thus, we should be careful not to allow the allure of new technologies and novel activities to suggest real teaching and learning benefits that may not really be present. We still have much to learn about instructional design, as new technologies present new challenges. In assessing new strategies, we must be mindful of drawing the right conclusions (Merrill, 2007).

Poor return on investment

Much literature (e.g. Brynjolfsson and Yang, 1996) has concerned itself with the 'IT productivity paradox', referring to the elusiveness of productivity returns from information technology (IT) investments. Remarkably, it seems to be very hard to see where the return on investment comes from with IT. Whilst that debate is complex and ongoing, we should at least acknowledge that return on investment in learning technologies (indeed, any form of educational investment) is very important. Investment in education should see a return in terms of learning taking place, whether in a public school system, a university or a corporate training environment. Large investments in educational technologies take funding away from alternative investments in education. It is therefore essential that the return on investment in any form of m-learning be at least as valuable as alternative forms of educational investment.

Researchers are failing in their duty if they do not consider what negative outcomes might flow from their work. Those of us who wish to promote m-learning need to be aware of its impacts on individuals, organizations and the environment that may be negative, and attempt to mitigate these. In addition, we need to ensure that our research methods are rigorous enough to avoid false positives, and ensure that any benefits we claim are in fact real.

Conclusion

Attempting to predict the future is an uncertain business, but an essential characteristic of the researcher is an interest in looking ahead to what we might be able to achieve. By addressing some major issues in m-learning as a series of 'top fives', this chapter has attempted to contextualize both current and future concerns from both positive and negative perspectives.

In addressing myths and misunderstandings, the chapter has outlined the areas where m-learning has been characterized in limited and unimaginative terms. By being aware of these assumptions, we may be able to more fully exploit m-learning in the future.

In addressing m-learning innovations, the chapter has explored the broad range of affordances that are now offered by the types of mobile devices that are widespread in the learner community.

In addressing future potentials, the chapter has shown how such technological progress, coupled with imaginative approaches to teaching, can bring true innovation to the classroom and to learning experiences in the wider world.

Finally, in addressing possible future risks for m-learning, the chapter has attempted to raise awareness of potential negative effects, to assist researchers and educators in avoiding possible pitfalls of m-learning innovation.

In this chapter, we have seen the past contributions of m-learning, its most innovative characteristics, and some of its potentials and risks for the future. Whatever developments may come in technology and pedagogy, it is certain that the concept of mobility will have an increasingly important role to play in lifelong learning, as our experiences as learners and with the supporting technologies become more fluid, adaptive, collaborative and exploratory.

Note

1 This chapter was originally published as D. Parsons (2014). The future of mobile learning and implications for education and training. In M. Ally and A. Tsinakos (eds), *Increasing access through mobile learning* (pp. 217–229). Vancouver: Commonwealth of Learning Press.

References

Bosavage, J. and Maselli, J. (2006). Are computers destroying the earth? Retrieved 22 October 2012 from www.drdobbs.com/special-report-are- computers-destroying/186100362

Brynjolfsson, E. and Yang, S. (1996). Information technology and productivity: a review of the literature. *Advances in Computers* 43, 179–214.

Burgess, A. (1978). *1985*. London: Hutchinson.

Doolittle, P. (2009). iPods as mobile multimedia learning environments. In H. Ryu and D. Parsons (eds), *Innovative mobile learning: techniques and technologies*. Hershey PA: IGI Global.

Facer, K., Joiner, R., Stanton, D., Reidz, J., Hullz, R. and Kirk, D. (2004). Savannah: mobile gaming and learning? *Journal of Computer-Assisted Learning* 20, 399–409.

Fisher, F., Sharples, M., Pemberton, R., Ogata, H., Uosaki, N., Edmonds, P., Hull, A. and Tschorn, P. (2012). Incidental second-language vocabulary learning from reading novels: a comparison of three mobile modes. *International Journal of Mobile and Blended Learning* 4(4), 47–61.

Garg, A. (2012). Top 7 myths of mobile learning. Retrieved 22 October 2012 from www.upsidelearning.com/blog/index.php/2012/07/05/top-7-myths-of-mobile-learning/

Golding, A. (2008). *Next generation wireless applications: creating mobile applications in a Web 2.0 and mobile 2.0 world*, 2nd ed. Chichester: Wiley.

Grant, W. (1993). Wireless Coyote: a computer-supported field trip. *Communications of the ACM* 36(5), 57–59.

Greenwich Free School (2012). Mobile phones Q&A for parents. Retrieved 22 October 2012, from www.greenwichfreeschool.co.uk/documents/GFS_Q_As_mobile_phones.pdf.

Hutchins, E. (1995). Cognition in the wild. Cambridge MA: MIT Press.

Merrill, M. (2007). The proper study of instructional design. In R. Reiser and J. Dempsey (eds), *Trends and issues in instructional design and technology*, 2nd ed. (pp. 336–341). Plcae: Pearson Prentice Hall.

Moher, T. (2006). Embedded phenomena: supporting science learning with classroom-sized distributed simulations. In *Proceedings of CHI 2006* (pp. 691–700). Place: ACM Press.

Naftulin, D., Ware, J. and Donnelly, F. (1973). The Doctor Fox lecture: a paradigm of educational seduction. *Journal of Medical Education* 48, 630–635.

O2 (2012). O2 learn. Retrieved 22 October 2012, from https://www.o2learn.co.uk/

Ogata, H. and Yano, Y. (2010). Supporting awareness in ubiquitous learning. *International Journal of Mobile and Blended Learning* 1(4), 1–11.

Powell, C., Perkins, S., Hamm, S., Hatherill, R., Nicholson, L. and Harapnuik, D. (2011). Mobile-enhanced inquiry-based learning: a collaborative study. Educause Review. Retrieved 22 October 2012, from www.educause.edu/ero/article/mobile-enhanced-inquiry-based-learning-collaborative-study

Rogers, Y., Price, S., Randell, C., Fraser, D., Weal, M. and Fitzpatrick, G. (2005). Ubi- learning integrates indoor and outdoor experiences. *Communications of the ACM* 48(1), 55–59.

Shum, S. and Crick, R. (2012). Learning dispositions and transferable competencies: pedagogy, modelling and learning analytics. In Proceedings of LAK'12 (pp. 92–101). Vancouver, BC: ACM Press.

Seely Brown, J. (2000). Growing up digital: how the web changes work, education, and the ways people learn. *Change*, March/April 2000.

Seely Brown, J., Collins, A. and Duguid, P. (1989). Situated cognition and the culture of learning. *Educational Researcher* 18(1), 32–42.

Sergio, F. (2012). 10 ways that mobile learning will revolutionize education. Retrieved 22 October 2012, from www.fastcodesign.com/1669896/10-ways-that-mobile-learning-will-revolutionize-education

Tangney, B., Weber, S., O'Hanlon, P., Knowles, D., Munnelly, J., Salkham, A., Watson, R. and Jennings, K. (2010). MobiMaths: an approach to utilising smartphones in teaching mathematics. In M. Montebello, V. Camilleri and A. Dingli (eds), MLearn 2010 Mobile Learning, Proceedings of 9th World Conference on Mobile and Contextual Learning (pp. 9–15). University of Malta.

Toole, T. (2011). Social media: key tools for the future of work-based learning. *Development and Learning in Organizations* 25(5), 31– 34.

Vallance, M., Martin, S. Wiz, C. and van Schaik, P. (2010). Designing effective spaces, tasks and metrics for communication in Second Life within the context of programming LEGO NXT Mindstorms™ Robots. *International Journal of Virtual and Personal Learning Environments* 1(1), 20–37.

Walker, J. (2010). How to identify the lifespan of a cell phone. Retrieved 22 October 2012, from www.ehow.com/how_7495298_identify-lifespan-cell-phone.html

Wei, K., Teo, H., Chan, H. and Tan, B. (2011). Conceptualizing and testing a social cognitive model of the digital divide. *Information Systems Research* 22, 170–187.

Winter, N. and Pemberton, L. (2011). Unearthing invisible buildings: device focus and device sharing in a collaborative mobile learning activity. *International Journal of Mobile and Blended Learning* 3(4), 1–18.

Epilogue
Looking to the future

The GCC region is one of the youngest societies in the world, with more than half of its population under the age of 25. The technology adoption rate is also one of the highest in the world. For example, according to the Saudi Ministry of Communications and Information Technology, the total number of mobile broadband subscriptions continue to increase and reached around 35.2 million by the end of Q2 2015, with a penetration rate of 113%. However, GCC countries, like many others, face the traditional challenges of an increased number of students in public and higher education systems, difficulty in recruiting highly qualified teachers, especially in the STEM fields (Science, Technology, Engineering and Mathematics), and the increasing level of dis-satisfaction rates among students and parents. The GCC region also has its unique challenges. For instance, education faculties and teacher education programmes are among the developing sectors in the region's universities. Lecture-based teaching methods are duplicated when using e-learning technologies in teaching.

Increasing numbers of faculty members in the region have been using technologies, albeit at different levels and for different purposes. Chapters in this book form good examples of the different purposes and levels of integrating technology in teaching. There is a need to focus on the content and how this is taught, in pedagogically sound approaches, rather than focus on the technology for its own sake. In other words, there is a requirement to understand the learning need(s) or 'problem' and decide the means that best address it.

Another unique challenge to GCC countries is the surrounding geopolitical instability that can interrupt schools and universities in the region. This poses challenges as well as opportunities for educators and institutions – they need to be creative and adopt innovative ways of teaching and learning, using e-learning technologies. The Saudi Ministry of Education, for instance, in collaboration with the National Center of eLearning and some universities' Deanships of eLearning, released a number of e-learning initiatives to educate its students in the bordering region during the upheaval in Yemen in 2015. E-learning provides the flexibility of delivering learning materials to anyone at any location and at any time.

Innovation in pedagogy and technology do not exist in a vacuum but rather depends a great deal on overall educational and administrative context in the region. For innovation to take place in teaching there has to be parallel support from administration and policy makers. Ministries of education, universities and industry need to join forces to harness knowledge and technology to develop the talent in the region. Young generations are increasingly becoming more digitally savvy and always connected, and educators in this day and age need to be aware of the new expectations these generations bring so that they can guide them to be life-long learners.

The GCC region is increasingly becoming interconnected both across the Middle East and with the rest of the world. This is partly due to the scholarship programmes in the region that send hundreds of thousands of young male and female students overseas to gain undergraduate and graduate degrees in a number of fields. Moreover, a number of GCC countries attracted and established global universities to educate their youth and increase the level of competitiveness amongst universities in the region.

For the GCC countries to develop and prosper in the twenty-first century, they must educate all their citizens to contribute to society. At the same time, there needs to be a shift in how education is designed and developed in this new era. Because of the availability of electronic learning materials, the new generation of students and emerging technologies, education should be learner-centred rather than teacher-centred. There needs to be sound pedagogical models to develop high-quality learning materials to deliver on emerging learning technologies. This book has contributions from leading experts to move education forwards in the current century.

There has to be a sense of urgency to transform education in the GCC countries. There are many external and internal forces demanding this transformation. The GCC countries have a large percentage of young students who are technology literate and they are comfortable using the emerging technologies, especially mobile technologies and social media. These young students will demand that education be delivered thus the need to use sound pedagogical models. Teachers must be trained on how to design and deliver quality learning materials using emerging technologies to meet the needs of this young generation of students. Another reason for using emerging technologies in education is that a large amount of learning materials is available in digital format, so students will need computing devices and skills to access them. Eventually, all learning materials will be available in digital format so that students can access them digitally. The challenge for teachers is how to design quality learner-centred materials to ensure deep learning occurs and that high-level learning outcomes are achieved.

Khalid Alshahrani, PhD
Mohamed Ally, PhD

Glossary

achievement A term used to measure the knowledge or proficiency of an individual in something that has been learned or taught
administration To make application of action or experiment
attitude The way a person views something or tends to behave towards it, often in an evaluative way
blend To mix (various sorts or grades) in order to obtain a particular kind or quality
blended learning Learning that combines traditional classroom lessons with lessons that use computer technology and may be given over the internet
Bloom's taxonomy Classification of levels of learning
brainstorming Method for suggesting many ideas for a future activity before considering some of them more carefully
case study Examination in detail of a particular process or situation over a period of time; a research method involving an up-close, in-depth and detailed examination of a subject of study (the case), as well as its related contextual conditions
cognitive load Cognitive load refers to the total amount of mental effort being used in the working memory. Cognitive load theory was developed from the study of problem solving by John Sweller in the late 1980s
cognitive skills Skills relating to or involving the processes of thinking and reasoning
collaborative learning Learning through working cooperatively with others to achieve identified purposes
computer-supported collaborative learning An instructional approach wherein students share knowledge using computers/internet communication.
critical thinking The mental process of actively and skilfully conceptualizing, applying, analysing, synthesizing and evaluating information to reach an answer or conclusion
culture The total of the inherited ideas, beliefs, values and knowledge that constitute the shared bases of social action
environment External factors and cultural forces that shape the life of a person or a population

experiment An act or operation for the purpose of discovering something unknown or of testing a principle, supposition, etc.
feedback Evaluative information derived from such a reaction or response
flip To turn; change orientation or direction
higher education Education beyond high school, specifically that provided by colleges and universities
hypothesis A tentative explanation that accounts for a set of facts and can be tested by further investigation
information literacy The ability to be able to identify, locate, evaluate and effectively use appropriate information for the issue or problem at hand
knowledge artefact An entity with both conceptual and material characteristics, such as a physical object (text, picture or graph, for instance), that is a carrier of ideas
learning The act or process of acquiring knowledge or skill
lecture capture Lecture capture refers to the technology and process of videoing a face-to-face or online lecture and making it available for students to watch
method A manner or mode of procedure, especially an orderly, logical or systematic way of instruction, inquiry, investigation, experiment, presentation, etc.
mind mapping A diagram used to organize information visually
model A systematic description to represent the construction or appearance of something
multimedia presentation A multimedia presentation is an audio-visual message designed to foster meaningful learning
paradigm A very clear or typical example used as a model
pedagogic models Approaches to the theory and practice of education
online ethnography Ethnographic study based on the digital methods and interactions of using Facebook, Twitter, blogs, websites and forums specifically within the educational online format
pillar A structure or part that provides support
preparatory Introductory or preliminary programme related to training that prepares for more advanced education
quasi-experimental A method based on or derived from experience; empirical, experimental evidence
reliability Repeatability or consistency. A measure is considered reliable if it would give us the same result over and over again (assuming that what we are measuring isn't changing)
rich tasks/learning Learning that engages students in exploring ideas and issues, solving complex problems and constructing knowledge rather than just memorizing it
scale An instrument with graduated spaces, as for measuring
screen recording Screen recording is a technique used to capture and save screen activities and sound in video format for the purpose of creating tutorials.

shared practice A learning or professional community develops a shared range of resources and experiences it can utilize to address problems

significant Having or expressing an indicative meaning

situated learning Learning situated within authentic activity, context and culture

social media Websites and computer-mediated communication applications that allow users to create and exchange ideas and content or multimedia in online communities and networks

sociocultural A term to describe the differences between groups of people relating to their social class and culture

statistics The mathematical study of the distribution of quantitative data on any subject

strategy A plan, method, or series of manoeuvers or stratagems for obtaining a specific goal or result

structured tasks Learning tasks that allow students to work independently of the teacher, guided by the elements of the tasks, which build complexity from simple to complex or from controlled to expansive

student reflection Reflection is a process of examining and interpreting experience to gain new understanding

technology The branch of knowledge that deals with the creation and use of technical means

theory A system of rules, procedures, and assumptions used to produce a result

treatment The act of administration or application

trend A general tendency or direction

transmission model Students are considered to be empty vessels into which educators must deposit knowledge. The model is characterized by a lack of critical thinking and knowledge ownership in students

validity The degree to which a tool measures what it claims to measure

variable Something that varies or that is prone to variation

Index

Academic Analytics Tool (AAT) 141
accessibility, mobile learning 84
acquisition of media, PresentationTube 103–5
ACRL *see* Association of College and Research Libraries
Activity Theory (AT) 171
adaptive learning toolkits 229
administration perspectives, technology integration 68, 73–5
affordability: mobile learning 84; technological resources 74
Akinyemi, A. 11
Al Aamri, K. 130–1
Alamir, A.H. 47
Al Aonizi, S. 54, 60
Al Fheed, M. 157
Al Hafez, M. 56
Al Hunayyan, A. 5
Ally, M. 54, 60
Al-Mukhaini, E. 133
Al Musawi, A. 129, 130, 132
Al-Otaibi, J. 132
Al-Qahtani, M. 131
Al-Sharhan, S. 5
Al Shaya, H. 129
Al-Shehri, S. 38–9, 131
Al-Shoiei, M. 131
Al Thukwaikh, N. 157
Altun, T. 74
Al-Zahrani, A. 158
Amasha, M. 129
Amenabar, N. 170
American University of Sharjah (AUS) 17–30
Amiri, A. 157

Ammar, M. 129, 130, 132
analysis approaches, social media 126–7
analytics dashboards 139–49
Anderson, J. 74, 75
anytime, anyplace learning 226
apps 231
Arab Open University (AOU) 52–66
Arduino microcontroller-based board 35
artificial intelligence 38
Association of College and Research Libraries (ACRL) 19
AT *see* Activity Theory
audio TEL projects 12–13
augmentation (SAMR) 22–3
AUS *see* American University of Sharjah
authenticity 47–8
Awadallha, A. 56
awareness: analytics dashboards 142, 143–4; smart classrooms and TEL 195; technology integration 68, 69, 71

Bahrain, mobile learning 92–3
Bandura's theory of self efficacy 69, 71–2
Bartlett-Bragg's five-stage educational blogging model 21–2
battery, mobile learning 85
behavioural competencies, smart classrooms and TEL 208
Bergmann, J. 153
best practice, mobile learning 230–1
blended course delivery 17–30; attainment 26–8; case study 18–19; course objectives 31; course of study 19–20; pedagogic models 17, 21–4; situated learning 17, 20–1; structured tasks 17, 24–6

Index 243

blended learning 52–66; advantages 54–5; assessments/evaluations 62; definition 52–6; ethical policy 60; external environment 63; fact-to-face tutorials 61–2; feedback 63; flipped classroom 150–66; inputs 58–9; learners' engagement 60; Merza's Open System 56–64; models 55–6; orientation/induction programmes 59; outputs 62; policy 58; process/interactive environment 59; resources 59–62; smart classrooms and TEL 189–90; tutors' engagement 60–1
blogging models 21–2, 27
Bloom's Taxonomy 22–3, 152, 158
Brady, - 53
Bransford, J. 153
Brew, L. 63
Brown, A. 153
Bryson, J. 54, 55–6, 62

Cakir, R. 37
CALL *see* Computer-Assisted Language Learning
Cameron, C. 54
capacity building, Qatar 114–15
capture/acquisition of media, PresentationTube 103–5
Chambers, A. 37, 38
change management, smart classrooms and TEL 203–5
Chapelle, C. 37, 39, 46, 47, 48
chemistry laboratories 158
Chickering, A. 56
class management systems, smart classrooms and TEL 201
Clayton Christensen Institute 53, 151
CMS *see* content management systems
Cocking, R. 153
co-constituality 6
Cohen, L. 7
collaborative activities 46, 84, 86, 129
collectivism 9–10
common heritage 9
communication: flipped learning 155; ICTs 113–14, 167–77
community 20, 55
comprehension 144–5
computational linguistics 38

Computer-Assisted Language Learning (CALL) 48–9
Computer Supported Collaborative Learning 129
content, website evaluations 34
content management systems (CMS), smart classrooms and TEL 202–3
correspondence and broadcast model 55
credentials, website evaluations 33
Culp, K.M. 75
cultural competencies, smart classrooms and TEL 207
culture, technology-enhanced learning 3–16
curriculum design 72–3

dashboards 139–49
data analysis approaches 126–8
data collection, analytics dashboards 143
Dawson, K. 69, 70
Deanship e-learning 170–5
Dede, C. 69, 70
design, website evaluations 33
De Silva, A. 62
development programmes 114–15
device characteristics, mobile learning 85
Dhanarajan, G. 169
dialogues, reflective 21–2, 25–6
Dickfos, J. 54
digital distractions/threats of mobile learning 232
digital portfolios 37
Disruptive Innovation Institute 151
distance learning 190, 227–8
D'Netto, B. 5
Dockstader, J. 69, 70
Drarka, A. 56
DSG (social media report series) 130–3
Dunbar, R. 5

e-content, smart classrooms and TEL 194, 202–3
EDU315 Emotional Intelligence 35
e-learning 167–77; change management 173–5; Deanship activity system 171; emerging challenges 171–3; future of 175–6; methodology 169; mobile learning 227; Saudi Arabia 167–8; SAU

evaluation 170–1; smart classrooms and TEL 189–90; transition phase 168–9
e-library components 195
Emotional Intelligence 35
entrenched digital divides, mobile learning 232
establishment 21–2
ethical policy, blended learning 60
ethnography approaches, social media 127

Fabry, D.L. 73, 74
Facebook 129–32
face-to-face tutorials 61–2
faculty perspectives 3–16
Fearon, C. 54
female–male interaction 47–8
Few, S. 140
Findlow, S. 4
five interactions model of blended learning 23–4
Fleck, J. 52–3, 55–6, 59, 61
flexibility, flipped learning 154
flipped learning 150–66; four pillars 153–4; Gulf region 157–64; higher education 155–6; technology and social media 155; theoretical basis 152–3
Flood, A. 6, 8
fragility, cultural 4
Franciszkowics, M. 155
full-fledged online learning, smart classrooms and TEL 190
future work 215–41

Gale, K. 69, 70
Gamson, Z. 56
Garrison, R. 53
GCC see Gulf Cooperation Council countries
Geçer, A. 60
Glenn, A. 75
globalization, technology-enhanced learning 4–5
global-local values conflict 4
Goodfellow, R. 5
Gower, J. 54
GPA calculator website 35
Graduate Student Research Award (GSRA) 115

green manifesto 232–3
GSRA see Graduate Student Research Award
Gulf Cooperation Council (GCC) countries: blended learning 52–66; mobile learning 83–97; social media 126–38
Gutierrez, K.D. 9

Hall, G.E. 71
Hannon, J. 5
Harris, W.T. 24
heritage 4–5, 9
Herlo, D. 54–5
Herrler, A. 54
Higgs, J.R. 73, 74
higher education (HE): blended learning 52–66; e-learning integration 167–77; flipped learning 155–6, 159–64; Qatar 117–20; technology integration 67–79; TEL 3–16
hijab 9
Hodgson, C. 54
Hofstede, G. 9–10
How People Learn 153
Human–Computer Interaction studies 38

ICTs see Information and Communication Technologies
identity 4–5, 20
induction programmes 59
informal learning activities, mobile learning 86
Information and Communication Technologies (ICTs) 113–14, 167–77
information overload 142
infrastructure component, smart classrooms and TEL 193–4
innovative learning: mobile learning 228–9; Qatar awards 114–15; smart classrooms and TEL 203
insight 144–5
institutional technological infrastructure 58–9
instructional competency models 207–8, 209
instructional technology and design 38
integrated e-learning 190–1, 192

intentional content, flipped learning 154
interactive multimedia based content 194
interactive smartboards 198, 200
internet: mobile learning 87–8; PresentationTube 98–109, *see also* online...
Internship website 35
introspection 21–2
investment, poor return 233–4
IP telephony 197

Jenkins, A. 54, 55–6, 62
Jhurree, V. 77
JSREP *see* Junior Scientists Research Experience Program
Jung, I. 169
Junior Scientists Research Experience Program (JSREP) 115
just-in-time learning 226

K-12 programmes 115
Kelley, P. 74
Kelso, M. 132
Khan, B. 56
Knewton (edited in Tolley) 53
knowledge artefacts 21–2, 25–6
knowledge competencies 207
Kruse, A. 141
Kuwait, mobile learning 89–90

Lamy, M.-N. 5
Lane-Kelso, M. 158
language: CALL 48–9; MOOC 183, 184; potential 46; SLA 47; technology-enhanced 36–50
Lareki, A. 170
Latchem, C. 169
Lave, J. 20
Lawless, K. 68
leadership: e-learning integration 168–9; technology integration 74–5
learner satisfaction, mobile learning 84
learners' engagement, blended learning 60
learning: analytics dashboards 139–49; community model 55; language/potential 46; learner's fit 47; management systems 194; mathematics 217–23; Qatar awards 114–15; social media 126–38; styles and speeds 84; support activities 86; technology-enhanced 3–16, *see also individual types of learning*
lecture recording tools 100–1
Lee, C.B. 71
Lenhart, A. 128
Lessen, E. 74
Levy, M. 37
libraries 195
lifelong learning activities 86
Lim, C.P. 37
LOCO-Analyst tool 141

McLaughlin, H. 54
Macpherson, M. 174
Mahesh, V. 55
management, e-learning integration 168–9
Mansour, E. 130, 132–3
Mapuva, J. 168
Martin, R. 129–30
Massive Open Online Courses (MOOCs) 178–87; access devices 184; benefits 180–2; computing devices 184; definition 179–80; enrolment pattern 185; language setting 183, 184; literature review 179–80; methodology 182; other countries/initiatives 181–2; participants/procedure 182; research questions 182; results/discussion 183–5; *Rwaq* 178–9; sessions/page views 184–5; study purpose 178; types 180
mathematics 158, 217–23
MATLAB Workshop 35
meaning focus 47
media and awareness campaigns 195
media capture/acquisition 103–5
Mehmood, S. 130, 132–3
Merza's Open System Model of Blended Learning 56–64
microcontroller-based boards 35
Middle School Science Challenge Program (MSSCP) 115
Middle States Association of Colleges and Schools (MSCHE) 19
Ministry of Higher Education (MoHE) 169

Ministry of Information and Communication Technology (ictQATAR) 113–14
mobile computing components, smart classrooms and TEL 194
mobile computing projects, smart classrooms and TEL 201
mobile learning 224–36; activity types 86; advantages/issues 84; Bahrain 92–3; definitions 83–4; development expectations 93; educational issues 85; educational predictions 93–4; future potentials 230–2; The Gulf 89–93; Gulf Cooperation Council countries 83–97; improvement 93; innovations 228–9; issues 84, 85–6; Kuwait 89–90; myths/misunderstandings 225–8; Oman 90–1; ownership 229–30; Qatar 90; risk 232–3; Saudi Arabia 86–9; social issues 85; technical hurdles 85; technological predictions 93; United Arab Emirates 91–2
mobile technology, mathematics 217–23
modification (SAMR) 22–3
monologues, reflective 21–2, 25–6
MOOCs *see* Massive Open Online Courses
Moodle 129
de Morentin, J.I.M. 170
MSCHE *see* Middle States Association of Colleges and Schools
MSSCP *see* Middle School Science Challenge Program
multimedia presentation applications, PresentationTube 98–109

National Centre for eLearning and Distance (NCeL) 167–9
national identity 4–5
navigation, website evaluations 34
networks *see* internet
Ng, E.M. 37
niqab 9
North Sea Piper Alpha oil rig disaster 26
Nunes, M. 174

ODL *see* open and distance learning
oil rig disaster 26

Oman, mobile learning 90–1
Omani basic education 129–32
Online Journal Project 35
online learning 10–13; meaning focus 47; PresentationTube 98–109; smart classrooms and TEL 190; social media 127, *see also* Massive Open Online Courses; social media
open and distance learning (ODL) 169
orientation/induction programmes 59
outcomes, uncontrolled/misleading effects of mobile learning 233
ownership of mobile learning 229–30

Paliktzoglou, V. 129
paper-based portfolios 37
Paris, S.G. 20–1
PBL *see* problem-based blended learning
PDRA *see* Postdoctoral Research Awards
pedagogy: blended learning 17, 21–4, 58, 158; flipped learning 158; social media 129–31; technology integration 68, 72–3
Peeraer, J. 73
perceived awareness 71
perceived concept 69–70
perceived self-efficacy 71–2
personal awareness *see* awareness
personalization, flipped learning 155
Petegem, P. Van 73
PGRTracker dashboards 144
Piper Alpha oil rig disaster 26
planning competencies, smart classrooms and TEL 208
policy: blended learning 58, 60; technology integration 74–5
Pongsajapan, R. 141
poor return on investment 233–4
Porcaro, D. 129
positive impact 48
Postdoctoral Research Awards (PDRA) 115
practical applications 81–214; analytics dashboards 139–49; e-learning integration 167–77; flipped learning 150–66; mobile learning 83–97, 231–2; MOOC 178–87; PresentationTube 98–109; Qatar education 110–25; smart classrooms

and TEL 188–214; social media/TEL 126–38
practical competencies, smart classrooms and TEL 208
practicality technology-enhanced language instruction 48
practitioner perspectives, technology integration 68–72
PresentationTube 98–109; design/development 102–3; discussion/recommendations 107–8; implementation 106–7; importance 102; lecture recording tools 100–1; media capture/acquisition 103–5; motivation/assumption 102–3; the need 101; online platform 105–6; producing/sharing video lectures 99–100
primary education, Qatar 115–17
problem-based blended learning (PBL) 54
problem statements, TEL 3–4
productivity, mobile learning 84
psychology 38
purpose-designed quality distance-education model 55

Qatar 110–25; capacity building 114–15; connected society 111–12; development programmes 114–15; development strategies 110–11; higher education 117–20; ictQATAR 113–14; institutional support 112–14; K-12 programmes 115; mobile learning 90; primary education 115–17; research 120–2; research/learning awards 114–15
quality assurance (QA) 205–7
quality distance-education model 55
quality indicators, website evaluations 33

recording tools 100–1
redefinition (SAMR) 22–3
reflective monologues/dialogues 21–2, 25–6
research: MOOC 182; Qatar 114, 120–2; social media 133; technology-enhanced learning 5–6
return on investment 233–4
Robertson, M. 75

Rogoff, B. 9
Ruben Puentedura's SAMR model 22–3
Rwaq 178–9

SAM *see* Software Asset Management
SAMR models 22–3
Sams, A. 153
satisfaction, mobile learning 84
Saudi Arabia: e-learning integration 167–77; mobile learning 86–9
Saudi e-University (SEU) 167–8
Saudi higher education: flipped learning 159–64; technology integration 67–79
SAU e-learning 170–5
Schleicher, A. 23
Schlenkrich, L. 128
schools, smart schools 194, 195–7
Science Challenge for Middle School Program (SCMSP) 115
SCMSP *see* Science Challenge for Middle School Program
Secondary School Research Experience Programme (SSREP) 115
second language acquisition (SLA) theories 47
second language instruction 37
self efficacy 69, 71–2
SEU *see* Saudi e-University
Sewry, D. 128
Shams, E. 158
shared learning resources 229
shayla 9
Shroff, R.H. 37
signal, mobile learning 85
Signal dashboards 145
Singleton, D. 52–3
situated activities, mobile learning 86
situated learning, blended course delivery 17, 20–1
SLA *see* second language acquisition theories
smart classrooms and TEL 188–214; behavioural competencies 208; blended learning 189–90; case studies 209–11; challenges/lessons learned 210–11; change management 203–5; class management systems 201; cultural competencies 207; e-content 194,

202–3; education quality assurance 205–7; e-learning 189–90; e-library components 195; innovation 203; instructional competency models 207–8, 209; instructional design competencies 208, 209; integrated e-learning 190–1, 192; integrated implementation frameworks 192–5; integrated QA models 205–7; interactive multimedia based content 194; interactive smartboard 198, 200; IP telephony 197; knowledge competencies 207; learning gateways 202; learning systems/platforms 202; LMS 194; mobile computing components 194; mobile computing projects 201; models 197–205; planning competencies 208; practical competencies 208; smart classrooms components 194; smart schools 194, 195–7; social competencies 208; supervision competencies 208; teachers' readiness components 195; teaching methods 208, 209; technical/technological competencies 207; video conferencing 197; wireless schools 197
Smith, D.W. 74
Smolin, L. 68
social competencies, smart classrooms and TEL 208
social issues, mobile learning 85
socially mediated learning 21
social media 10–11, 126–38; analysis approaches 126–7; data analysis approaches 126–8; education 128–33; flipped learning 155; GCC states 128–33; implications/best models 134–5; online ethnography approaches 127; pedagogical concerns 129–31; research concerns 133; socio-cultural concerns 132–3; technological concerns 132–3
socio-cultural concerns, social media 132–3
Software Asset Management (SAM) 144
Software Secure Inc. 62
Solak, E. 37
Sorensen, C. 74

Spitzer, K. 54
Spreckelsen, C. 54
Spring, J. 4
SQU *see* Sultan Qaboos University
Srivastava's Iterative Analysis framework 27
SSREP *see* Secondary School Research Experience Programme
standalone electronic courses, smart classrooms and TEL 190
Starr, S. 54
Stockwell, G. 37
structured tasks in blended delivery 17, 24–6
student-centred learning: analytics dashboards 139–49; flipped learning 154; language learning potential 46; teacher-centred dashboards 140–1; work matrices 143–5
substitution (SAMR) 22–3
Suhonen, J. 129
Sultan Qaboos University (SQU) 98–109
supervision competencies, smart classrooms and TEL 208
support, mobile learning 84, 86
Syam, M. 158

TAM *see* Technology Acceptance Model
Taswir, T. 130, 132–3
Te@ch Thought 52–3, 60–1
teacher-centred dashboards 140–1
teachers' readiness components, smart classrooms and TEL 195
teaching: flipped learning 154; mathematics 217–23; smart classrooms and TEL 208, 209; support activities/mobile learning 86
technical/technological competencies, smart classrooms and TEL 207
technology: flipped learning 155; infrastructure/blended learning 58–9; integration 67–79; language instruction 36–50; mathematics 217–23; mobile learning 93, 230–1; social media 132–3, *see also* technology-enhanced learning
Technology Acceptance Model (TAM) 36–7

technology-enhanced learning (TEL) 3–16, 126–38; activities/assignments 10–13; context 3; data analysis 8; data collection/participants 6–7; findings 8; further research 13–14; globalization 4–5; methodology/method 6; perception/assessment 9–10; problem statements 3–4; procedure 7; remarks/implications 13; research questions 5–6; smart classrooms 188–214; validity/reliability 7–8
Technology in Schools (2003) 69, 70
text, website evaluations 34
theoretical perspectives 1–79; blended course delivery 17–30; blended learning 52–66; technology-enhanced language instruction 36–50; technology-enhanced learning 3–16; technology integration 67–79
Tollefson, J.W. 4
Tolley, B. 53, 59, 60, 62, 63
training, mobile learning 224–36
transition phase, e-learning integration 168–9
Triandis, H.C. 9–10
Tripp, D. 7
Tsui, A.B.M. 4
tsunamis, cultural 4
tutors' engagement, blended learning 60–1

UAE *see* United Arab Emirates
Undergraduate Research Experience Program (UREP) 114–15

United Arab Emirates (UAE): blended course delivery 17–30; mobile learning 91–2; TEL 3–16
universities *see* higher education
UREP *see* Undergraduate Research Experience Program

Vannatta, R. 73
Vaughan, N. 53
video conferencing 197
video lectures, PresentationTube 98–109
video TEL projects 12–13
virtual information 228–9
Vygotsky, L. 21, 152

Ward, M. 62
websites: EDU315 Emotional Intelligence 35; ENG207 poster 35; evaluations 33–4, *see also* online learning
Weert, T. 74
Weil, S. 62
Wenger, E. 20
Winograd, P. 20–1
wireless schools 197
Woll, C. 55
Woltering, V. 54
work matrices 143–5

Yang, Y.F. 47–8
YouTube 12

Zaidieh, A. 128
Zone of Proximal Development (ZPD) 152

Taylor & Francis eBooks

Helping you to choose the right eBooks for your Library

Add Routledge titles to your library's digital collection today. Taylor and Francis ebooks contains over 50,000 titles in the Humanities, Social Sciences, Behavioural Sciences, Built Environment and Law.

Choose from a range of subject packages or create your own!

Benefits for you
- Free MARC records
- COUNTER-compliant usage statistics
- Flexible purchase and pricing options
- All titles DRM-free.

Benefits for your user
- Off-site, anytime access via Athens or referring URL
- Print or copy pages or chapters
- Full content search
- Bookmark, highlight and annotate text
- Access to thousands of pages of quality research at the click of a button.

Free Trials Available
We offer free trials to qualifying academic, corporate and government customers.

eCollections – Choose from over 30 subject eCollections, including:

Archaeology	Language Learning
Architecture	Law
Asian Studies	Literature
Business & Management	Media & Communication
Classical Studies	Middle East Studies
Construction	Music
Creative & Media Arts	Philosophy
Criminology & Criminal Justice	Planning
Economics	Politics
Education	Psychology & Mental Health
Energy	Religion
Engineering	Security
English Language & Linguistics	Social Work
Environment & Sustainability	Sociology
Geography	Sport
Health Studies	Theatre & Performance
History	Tourism, Hospitality & Events

For more information, pricing enquiries or to order a free trial, please contact your local sales team:
www.tandfebooks.com/page/sales

 The home of Routledge books

www.tandfebooks.com